Television and the Quality of Life: How Viewing Shapes Everyday Experience

COMMUNICATION

A series of volumes edited by:
Dolf Zillmann and **Jennings Bryant**

Television and the Quality of Life: How Viewing Shapes Everyday Experience

Robert Kubey
Rutgers University
Mihaly Csikszentmihalyi
University of Chicago

LEA

LAWRENCE ERLBAUM ASSOCIATES, PUBLISHERS
1990   Hillsdale, New Jersey   Hove and London

Lawrence Erlbaum Associates, Inc., Publishers
365 Broadway
Hillsdale, New Jersey 07642

Library of Congress Cataloging-in-Publication Data
Kubey, Robert William, 1952–
    Television and the quality of life: How viewing shapes
everyday experience / Robert Kubey, Mihaly Csikszentmihalyi.
        p.   cm.—(Communication)
    Includes bibliographical references.
    ISBN 0–8058–0552–4. —ISBN 0–8058–0708–X (pbk.)
    1. Television audiences.   2. Television—Social aspects.
I. Csikszentmihalyi, Mihaly.   II. Title.   III. Series:
Communication (Hillsdale, N.J.)
HE8700.65.K82   1990
302.23'45—dc20   89–38679
                                                            CIP

Printed in the United States of America
10   9   8   7   6   5   4   3   2

For Joan and Sid
—RK

and Isabella
—MC

Contents

Preface

By current estimates the first human beings emerged on Earth approximately 2 million years ago. In this vast stretch of time, approximately 100,000 human generations have lived and died, and yet ours are among the first to live in a world where much of daily experience is shaped by widely shared, instantaneous mass communication. Foremost among the mass media is television.

The A. C. Nielsen Company (1989) currently estimates that people in the United States view upwards of 4 hours of television each day. Given the likelihood that such estimates are inflated, let us assume a more conservative estimate of 2½ hours of television viewing per day over the period of a lifetime. Even at this more conservative rate, a typical American would spend more than 7 full years watching television out of the approximately 47 *waking* years each of us lives by age 70—this assuming an average of 8 hours of sleep per day.

Such a figure is even more striking when we consider that Americans have about 5½ hours a day of free time, or approximately 16 years available for leisure of the same 47-year span. From this point of view and based on a conservative estimate, Americans are spending nearly half of their available free time watching television.

Still, the number of hours spent viewing continues to creep upward by a few minutes each year, and people throughout the rest of the world seem every bit as attracted to the medium as do Americans. In fact, television is growing in popularity in almost every country on the globe. Programs such as "The Cosby Show" and "Dallas" are viewed by enormous audiences throughout the world—"Dallas" has aired in over 90 countries—and have caused the desertion of cafés and movie theaters, and forced public events to be rescheduled during broadcast hours. At a 1988 international meeting of television program buyers and sellers in Cannes, one estimate set U.S. television program sales to Europe at $2.7 billion for 1992, a 1,200% increase since 1983 (Miller, 1989). So great is the attraction of television that the East German city of Dresden experienced a crisis in labor supply when many residents moved closer to the western border to watch programs being broadcast by stations in West Germany (Cantor & Cantor, 1986).

Suffice it to say that television has become our species' preferred and most powerful means of mass communication. But although television continues to grow in popularity, there is much we still do not know about why people watch as much as they do or how the medium affects them. Nor are we at all certain about television's larger cultural impact.

Methodological and theoretical limitations make it difficult for social scientists to adequately assess the impact or value of any form of leisure or medium of communication. Some may prefer this state of affairs, seeing no purpose in understanding leisure and entertainment experiences that are often idiosyncratic, and which, one could argue, are best left hidden from the probing interests of the behavioral scientist. Certain moments of esthetic rapture, athletic excellence, or theatrical truth are transcendent; they defy analysis and are best understood in terms of personal meanings. Nonetheless, we still believe that there are important lessons yet to be learned about leisure, television viewing, and the conditions that promote optimal functioning and human growth.

It is also our belief that television viewing, like other cultural habits, would be ideally studied and evaluated in the widest possible context. Human activities are generally quite complicated and they often occur in complex social settings. Nor, in evaluating leisure and media activities, can one paint with a broad brush. Most things that people do are neither entirely good nor entirely bad. A simple comic strip may provide benefit to certain readers under certain circumstances, while not a few great esthetic works of art and religion have produced much conflict and resentment.

There is no longer enough information left to tell how much good, or how much harm was done to Byzantine society by the seemingly pathological fascination with chariot racing of the citizens of Constantinople. Similarly, we can only speculate about the positive or negative effects of the interminable erudite debates, favorite pastime of the Florentine upper classes of the 17th and 18th centuries. Did they sharpen a participant's faculties, were they largely a form of escape, or did those ritualized disputations prolong that society's survival? And what about the famous Mayan ballgames, or the Roman circuses? Did they strengthen the commonweal, or sap its energies?

It is unlikely that we shall ever be able to answer such questions. Some of the facts that might help are lost beyond recall, and even then to answer such questions would require the ability to measure and assess elusive cultural practices and their complicated interactions and consequences. Even when a living culture is still before us for study, there is no certainty that our interpretations will be correct.

We are hardly any less helpless when trying to understand a contemporary cultural phenomenon such as television viewing. But at least some of the pieces of the puzzle are at hand. With their help, we endeavor to assemble a meaningful picture. For despite the thousands of arti-

cles and books on the effects of television, we still do not fully understand how television is used and experienced in everyday life. And it is
certainly the case that we lack a broad enough perspective from which
such understandings can be reasonably and usefully evaluated.

To what realistic alternatives is television watching being compared?
What social and psychological costs do those alternatives have? Only an
integrated view of human activity that considers a broad range of alternatives and consequences will make an understanding of television viewing possible.

In writing this book, we were exposed to the ideological pressures,
pro and con, that the discussion of television inevitably engenders.
Nevertheless, there is one safeguard built into this volume. The research
method underlying our findings was not designed to test a particular
hypothesis about television. Rather, it was designed to provide a picture
of the way people feel as they move through everyday life, from leisure
to work, from eating meals to driving their cars—and of the way they
feel when they are watching television. The experience of television
viewing is studied in its natural context, embedded in its everydayness,
and much of what we say about the quality of that experience is in
comparison with the other daily activities that comprise the rest of life.

In addition to showing how television viewing fits into people's time
schedules, the method has permitted us to assess how people feel when
watching television in comparison with how they feel when they eat,
work, or converse with their friends. When are people most apt to report
that they are concentrating hard? That they are happy? That they want
to do what they are doing? By mapping out thousands of events against
each other on such dimensions, we can begin to assess in a comparative
manner the nature of the cultural practice we call television viewing.

But before we examine the findings, we first attempt to create a
conceptual and historical context in which they might be more meaningfully interpreted. This is our intent in the first two chapters.

Chapter 1 presents a theoretical model by which the information
value of any activity, including television viewing, can be assessed. In
chapter 2 we place television viewing in the context of other leisure
activities. Few would claim that television is good because it strengthens
the body, or because by watching it we will find eternal happiness. But
television viewing may be an excellent way to relax and recuperate and
may therefore be an optimal form of leisure. In fact, in a recent large-
scale national survey it was found that more Americans reported getting
pleasure from television than from sex, food, hobbies, religion, marriage, money, or sports. So far so good—But *what* is *leisure*?

Many of the great thinkers of the past, from Aristotle to Marx, have
set forth their opinions on what leisure and its role in human life should

be, and we believe it is important to address these ideas before assessing television's relationship to the quality of human experience. Are rest, relaxation, and pleasure what we want from our leisure activities? If not, why not? Is having more time available for leisure a wise goal either for the individual or for society?

These questions are not at all easy to answer, and involve assumptions that are inevitably value laden. Readers will have to decide whether the values we ultimately argue for are also theirs, or indeed whether they are appropriate to the questions at hand.

Chapter 3 turns directly to what is known and theorized about the use, experience, and functions of television viewing, setting the stage for chapter 4, in which the research methodology is presented.

In chapter 5 this method is used to provide a close look at when, where, with whom, and in what combination of other activities television is viewed, and how the experience of viewing television compares to experiences associated with other daily activities. We then examine whether the experience of television varies among demographic groups or among groups from outside the United States. We also look at how different television content is experienced and consider how the VCR has altered the use and experience of the medium. The chapter concludes with a discussion of some of the psychological properties of viewing.

Chapter 6 focuses on how television viewing is used and experienced in the family context. We examine whether television is a boon to family life, or whether viewing interferes with the quality of familial experiences.

The next chapter clarifies what occurs before and after people view, and what happens when television is viewed for longer periods of time. We examine some of the motives that underlie viewing and what viewing itself causes. We also consider whether viewing might help people adapt to daily life and under what circumstances it may interfere with optimal functioning. Chapter 7 concludes with a further discussion of what happens psychologically when people watch TV, and considers some of the possible biological underpinnings of the viewing experience. We also consider how the television industry creates programs that produce in people the kinds of experiences that have been described and which fit the model set forth in chapter 1. Finally, we present a model of optimal experience that helps explain some of the basic structural features of different activities, and why television and other activities tend to be associated with particular kinds of experiences.

Chapter 8 presents a behavioral and psychological portrait of the heavy viewer. In so doing, we describe how demographic characteristics interact with particular personality characteristics that drive heavy viewing. We also consider what the long-term consequences of heavy viewing might be, and whether viewing itself might help perpetuate these same personality characteristics.

Chapter 9 summarizes the major findings, and suggests why we think some of the theories that minimize the effects of television are problematic.

In the final chapter the findings and their implications are interpreted within the broad contexts of history and contemporary social formations. We consider how a society, and the forms of leisure it spawns, contribute to or detract from the development of human potential.

Although we have employed an unusual method that has proved extremely useful in studying human behavior, we nonetheless recognize that, as with any method and with any study, there are limitations to what can be done and the questions that can be asked and answered. We have not studied, for example, how people interpret what they see on television, or focused on the role of narrative in absorbing the viewer's interest, or its potential to inform and enrich experience. Nor have we spent a great deal of time analyzing television content.

No method will explain everything that there is to know about what happens when people watch television. And, although our measures were chosen for a reason, and fit a particular conceptual approach to understanding behavior and experience, they are quite simple. Still, they have proven quite useful, especially considering that the research presented here is one of the very first attempts to measure in a systematic way how people actually feel while watching television in their homes. No doubt other measures can and will be developed. But for now, we believe we have developed a revealing portrait of how and why people use and experience television in everyday life, one that we hope will inspire further research and debate. If it does that, we will be satisfied.

ACKNOWLEDGMENTS

In any long-term enterprise few people work alone and we are no exception. The research that made this book possible was supported by many people, institutions, and foundations.

Robert Kubey especially appreciates the support of the National Institute of Mental Health, the Richard D. Irwin Foundation, the Rutgers University Research Council, and the McGannon Communication Research Center for the Study of Issues in Policy and Ethics at Fordham University, which helped make possible many of his studies on television as well as the data analysis and much of the writing presented in the pages ahead. Mihaly Csikszentmihalyi gratefully acknowledges the aid of the U.S. Public Health Service and the Spencer Foundation, whose support for his studies on flow and optimal experience contributed to the development of the Experience Sampling Method (ESM).

Institutional assistance came from The Committee on Human Development at the University of Chicago, The Program in Social Ecology at the University of California at Irvine, and the School of Communication, Information, and Library Studies at Rutgers University.

We are also indebted to a great many friends and colleagues. We wish to express our appreciation to Norman Bradburn, Larry Chalip, Erika Fromm, Paul Hirsch, Bill Merrick, Tom Trabasso, and Marvin Zonis of the University of Chicago; Dick Budd, Stan Deetz, Vince Fitzgerald, Ed Hartman, Maureen McCreadie, Hartmut Mokros, Dennis Mumby, Brent Ruben, Jorge Schement and Lea Stewart of Rutgers University as well as the first fellows of Rutgers' Center for the Critical Analysis of Contemporary Culture. We are also indebted to Elizabeth Noelle-Neumann as well as to Ted Glasser and Horace Newcomb, each of whom commented on the manuscript at different stages.

Thanks also to Jennings Bryant and Dolf Zillmann, our series editors.

A great many colleagues have been of invaluable assistance either in making available or helping prepare ESM data for this book. Ron Graef was especially helpful with the database of American workers on whom most of this book is based and provided encouragement through the early stages of research. Reed Larson of the University of Illinois has long been an irreplaceable colleague to both of us, and we are indebted to him for his assistance in preparing the Canadian data that we examine in chapter 5 and for permitting us to analyze and discuss findings from other ESM databases that he has collected. We are also indebted to Roger Mannell and Jiri Zuzanek at the University of Waterloo, Ontario, for making the Canadian data available and to Fausto Massimini and Gianni Moneta of the Medical School at the University of Milan for providing and preparing the Italian adolescent data that we present in chapter 5. Judith LeFevre and Maria Wong helped prepare data for this same cross-national comparison. Thanks also to Stefan Hormuth and Marco Lalli of the University of Heidelberg for responding to our request for an analysis of ESM data from their German subjects. Sharafuddin Malik of the University of Riyadh in Saudi Arabia permitted us to analyze his ESM data collected from African and American graduate students, and Marten deVries of the University of Limburg in The Netherlands provided us with findings from his research.

Alan Barnett created the computer graphics for all of the figures and was a great pleasure to work with as was our extremely thorough editor, Robin Marks Weisberg. Gary Radford and Nancy Dimeo helped with the index. Tom Herzberg of Chicago provided the cover art. Enthusiasm from Larry Erlbaum and his associates, particularly Jack Burton and Joe Petrowski, helped fuel our final efforts.

We also owe a special debt of gratitude to the many research subjects who have permitted us to become involved in their lives. Without their cooperation this book would not have been possible.

Last, but certainly not least, our wives Barbara Lewert Kubey and Isabella Selega Csikszentmihalyi, deserve special recognition for their encouragement, patience, and daily support.

Robert Kubey
Mihaly Csikszentmihalyi

CHAPTER 1

A Way to Think About Information Reception

What we need to explain are not objects but experiences.

—Kohak (1978)

The people of the world spend upwards of 3.5 billion hours watching television every day. Some scholars explain this enormous expenditure of time and mental activity by stressing that viewing television involves a transfer of information that enriches the viewers' store of knowledge. Others emphasize that television provides viewers with much needed entertainment, relaxation, and escape. To what degree these and other things happen when people view television is the cause for much debate. Part of the uncertainty is due to the fact that we are still only in the early stages of developing theories and methods by which to measure or evaluate what people do with televised information, or what happens in the hours or days after reception. Nor have there been many attempts to study how viewers actually report experiencing television.

Theorists have developed models that help explain how information is received, coded, processed, stored, and retrieved. And there are models for describing how certain kinds of information effect people emotionally. To develop such a model involves stepping into the controversial area of making qualitative distinctions, and those who study information processes scientifically are often understandably reluctant to do so. Yet, taking human values and goals into account is necessary if we wish to assess the value of information, or television, for it is difficult to place the act of viewing in any kind of meaningful perspective without a model that explicitly recognizes qualitative distinctions in human experience. The aim of this chapter is to propose such a model.

A great number of theoretical and disciplinary approaches can be applied to understanding human activity. Television viewing is no exception. As the reader will soon see, we draw on a breadth of ideas from psychology, psychoanalysis, and psychobiology as well as from communication, sociology, anthropology, political science, history, and physics. But here at the beginning we present a relatively simple and general model. It by no means explains all communication and information phenomena, but we think it is a useful model to keep in mind, and we refer back to it from time to time—in the conceptualization of our measures, in the interpretation of the results, and in the final chapter where television's broader role in the development of the individual and society is discussed.

MENTAL ENERGY AND INFORMATION

We start with a few working principles that have informed our thinking.

Information can be thought of as anything that produces changes in consciousness—a perception, a sensation, an emotion, a memory, a thought. Odors, sounds, the slanting rays of the sun coming into a room, the words lined up on this page, all contribute bits of information to a person's consciousness.

For information to become meaningful, signs must pass through attention. If you stop paying attention to these words, they cease to have much information value. Attention, then, can be thought of as a general resource for cognitive processing (Hasher & Zacks, 1979) or the energy added to a structure that permits processing of information through that structure, the structures in question being links of previous information such as perceptual and semantic codes (LaBerge, 1975).[1]

The importance of attention can hardly be overestimated. As Zuckerman (1988) has written:

The most vital aspect of consciousness is attention, for without an adequate mechanism for focusing mental effort and an adequate program of priorities we cannot learn, communicate, or adapt to the changing contingencies of the environment. (p. 173)

As important as it may be, it is crucial to recognize that attention is also limited (Broadbent, 1958). Nobody knows how much information can be processed at any given moment,[2] but most everyone will agree that it is quite difficult if not impossible to do more than one thing well at the same time and that one's ability to attend is finite. Hence, "The limit on attentional capacity appears to be a general limit on resources . . . the total amount of attention which can be deployed at any time is limited" (Norman, 1976, p. 71).

Although 100 years ago William James (1890) clearly recognized how important attention was in human psychology, the implications of his insights have not been fully explored in the intervening years and "there has not been programmatic growth in research on attention" (Reeves, Thorson, & Schleuder, 1986, p. 251). Herbert Simon (1978), who has done much to keep the theoretical interest in attention alive, reached the following conclusion: "I am not aware that there has been any systematic development of a theory of information and communication that treats attention rather than information as a scarce resource" (p. 13).

Since Simon made that observation, Orrin Klapp (1986) has given considerable thought to how any individual's ability to construct meaning from information is limited relative to the speed of information creation and dissemination. He has concluded that "The weakest link in a vast chain of communication is often the human brain, because, for all its powers of abstraction, it is severely limited in channel capacity" (p. 100).

Because attention is needed to process information and to keep order in consciousness, and because attention is limited, we have found it useful to think of it as "mental" or "psychic energy."[3] And because attention is necessary to make conscious mental operations possible, how one invests attention over time will determine the content and will influence the quality of a person's life.

ORDER AND COMPLEXITY

To account for the qualitative dimensions of communication, we distinguish two broad characteristics of information: its order and its complexity.[4] It is important to stress that for our purposes these variables do not apply to objective characteristics of a message, but to the experience of the receiver. What counts most is not the structural order or complexity of the message, but how the message is processed. We believe in the utility of taking the subjective reality of the recipient as the starting point for our model.*

Order, then, refers to a subjective state in which a person experiences no substantial conflict among the elements of consciousness. Inner order is constituted by desires organized around a hierarchy of needs or goals. These hierarchies differ from person to person, but their main structural lines tend to be quite similar, at least within the same culture and historical period.[5]

When something appears to decrease the probability of achieving our goals, it will produce conflict, and therefore, disorder in consciousness. Depending on the nature of the goal that is impeded, the disorder will take the form of a unpleasant emotion such as anger, sadness, loneliness, guilt, or anxiety. But when we make progress in reaching a goal, or obtain the goal itself, order is restored in experience and so we feel joy, happiness, or a similar pleasant emotion.

When any new bit of information (a perception, sensation, memory, feeling, or idea) enters awareness, it potentially affects the dynamic balance in consciousness either by increasing order—if the information supports our goals—or by increasing disorder—if it implies a frustration of the goals in awareness. Of course quite often information has little or no bearing whatsoever on what we desire, in which case it leaves the balance of order unaffected, and our experience and mood unchanged.

Thus, each piece of information can be thought to possess a negative entropy, or *negentropy* quotient (NQ), depending on the amount of order it produces in consciousness. The concept of entropy as posited in the Second Law of Thermodynamics refers to the inability of a system to do work, or to the loss of energy. Entropy is also a measure of the degree of disorder in a system.

We are certainly not the first to use concepts from physics or the

---

*Klapp's (1986) example of "museum fatigue" well illustrates the importance that must be placed on the individual's subjective experience of information:

A person visits a museum with the best intentions of seeing it all with deep appreciation within an hour or so. But, to his surprise and embarrassment, for all his enthusiasm, his fatigue mounts, legs tire, and eyes glaze after seeing only a few halls full of treasures. . . He suffers from an overload of information, a boredom resulting from the amount and variety, not the quality, of the information he tried to assimilate in a limited time. (p. 123)

second law to understand human behavior.* In information theory, the concept of entropy has often been used to refer to the amount of randomness contained in a message (see for example Ashby, 1956; Beniger, 1986; Garner, 1962; Ritchie, 1986; Ruben, 1972; Shannon & Weaver, 1949; Wiener, 1961). Negentropy, on the other hand, describes the opposite state: the capacity of a physical system to do work, or for a message to convey information or reduce uncertainty.[7]

However, we are quite dubious about information theories of entropy such as Shannon's that focus on the message and neglect the state of the receiver, or that assume that attentional capacity is unlimited, or that message entropy and the entropy of the receiver are somehow identical (e.g., Watt & Krull, 1974).

In the model we are developing, *entropy* refers to states in which a person experiences conflict between goals, or between feelings, thoughts, and goals, and states that therefore reduce that person's capacity for sustained productive action. The order of one's experience is also very much dependent on internal physiological processes that themselves enter consciousness as information. This is because entropy, or the loss of energy, keeps breaking down the harmonious integration of mental processes. Every few hours the sensation of hunger intrudes into the thoughts of even the most exalted genius, and unless the person eats, he or she will not be able to marshal the mental energy required to think or maintain order.

Conversely, negentropy describes states in which the inner contents of experience are in relative harmony, and the person is in greater control of his or her mental energy; consequently he or she is generally in a positive mood and capable of productive action. The negentropy quotient of information, then, is its capacity to decrease conflict in consciousness.

To a girl struggling to do arithmetic homework, the rules for long

---

*Einstein's observation on the broad applicability of the classical laws of thermodynamics is of interest here:

A theory is more impressive the greater is the simplicity of its premises, the more different are the kinds of things it relates and the more extended its range of applicability. (see Miller, 1971, p. 46)

For Frederick Soddy, a Nobel laureate in chemistry, the laws of thermodynamics necessarily explain all activity, including human activity: the laws "control, in the last resort, the rise and fall of political systems, the freedom or bondage of Nations, the movements of commerce and industry, the origins of wealth and poverty, and the general physical welfare of the race" (Rifkin, 1980, p. 8). See also Wiener (1961) and Beniger (1986) in this regard.[6]

division potentially have a high NQ, because they will allow her to solve problems with much less effort and frustration. To a man who wants to bake a birthday cake, the recipe for a chocolate torte might have a high NQ. For someone who has suffered a series of personal tragedies and is at the end of his rope the "message" of the Gospels could have the highest NQ, because it allows him to re-order experience around new goals, thereby making mental energy available again.

The model implies that the quality of information is best evaluated in terms of individual goals. Because people have different and multiple goals and therefore different and multiple needs, the value of a message is necessarily relative.[8]

At the same time, the importance of some goals is shared widely enough to make messages relevant to them have a nearly universal and predictable NQ. This is true both for the kinds of extremely basic internal information our bodies generate (we all need to eat and sleep with some regularity in order to prevent disorder in experience) as well as for information that comes from outside. For example, the piece of information: "You have just won $1 million in a sweepstakes, tax free," if coming from a credible source, will make most people happy, because it offers a solution to many goals that previously could not be reached—buying a house, paying long overdue bills, or sending one's children to a better school. On the other hand, the message: "You have a terminal disease," if coming from a medical authority and if true, will obviously alter most any person's plans, and has a low NQ or a high entropy quotient.

Although few messages have either as high or as low a potential for negentropy as the two examples above, it can be useful to consider all acts of communication as lying on a continuum between these two extremes, depending on whether they produce harmony or conflict in consciousness.[9] And of course, there are other much more common forms of information that can either disrupt or help provide order to experience, forms of information that we normally take for granted and that we even help produce unconsciously as we make our way through life. The inventions of the "days of the week" and "the hours of the day," as just two examples, have enormous influence on structuring when we sleep, eat, work, play, or watch television, and thus help provide order and regularity to our existence.

People are also constantly taking in information about their environment and, if this information is suddenly quite different from what one normally expects, one experiences disorder in consciousness. In other words, without regular reassurance that the world is as we think it is, it would become impossible to pursue our goals. The penchant for order also helps explain why people talk so much about their environments, about themselves, and the people around them (Berger & Luckmann, 1967). People talk about these things, in part, to help maintain assurance in their world as they know it—they engage in "reality-maintenance" work. Indeed, the constructivist approach in communication theory (Delia, O'Keefe, & O'Keefe, 1982) and much psychological research provide numerous examples of how the human mind goes about seeking and providing order for itself.

So, although people are attracted by novelty and complexity, they also very much seek familiarity and order. And television is capable of providing information anywhere along the continuum that we have just described. Although it is certainly rare, there are people who first learned directly from television that they had won $1 million or that a loved one had died. And as with the rest of everyday life, most television information obviously falls somewhere between these two extremes in terms of its potential to create order or disorder in experience. Indeed, among its ordering functions may be the very kind of everyday reality-maintenance work that we have just described. One of our tasks in the chapters that follow is to consider where on the continuum most television viewing falls and why it falls where it does.

But to know the value of a bit of information or its ability to create order in experience, is not enough to know whether it makes a person happy here and now. It is also important to know whether the message has the potential of being used in a more complex fashion in helping the person become better able to cope with new situations that might arise in the future.

If consciousness processed only simple, redundant information it would be unequipped to handle difficult tasks. *Learning* means to process information that stretches one's present capacity to assimilate it. Thus, *complexity* defines another particularly relevant dimension of communication. Generally, a complex message is one that requires mental energy to encode and to decode. Therefore, each message has a certain *complexity* quotient, or CQ, depending on how much effort it will take to process it.[10]

Complexity without order typically leads to confusion and anxiety.[11] But when order is also present, complex messages are more likely to result in positive experiences that also lead to learning and growth. In fact, in chapter 7 we illustrate this relationship (see p. 143) between order and complexity and show why experience high in complexity and high in order often leads to personal growth.

But given the fact that both order and complexity depend on mental energy, or attention, which is a scarce resource, communication that will permit enjoyable, growth-promoting experiences is likely to occur less frequently than other forms of communication. Instead, much communication may be used simply to preserve the status quo and will be rather redundant and boring, or low on complexity.[12] Next in frequency might be the state of affairs in which CQ and NQ are both average.

Another implication of the model is that to turn a confusing message into one that will produce learning, attention must be invested into it until the information is integrated into an existing way of thinking (cognitive structure) or until a new way of thinking develops that can accommodate the message.[13] In fact, many learning experiences start in anxiety and confusion and have value or can be enjoyed only after enough attention has been invested in the information to decode the message. Indeed, because people tend to avoid information that increases entropy they will sometimes change information, deny it, or virtually not process it if it contradicts what they already believe. Instead, they may prefer to seek out information that confirms what they already know (Carter, Pyska, & Guerraro, 1969; Festinger, 1957; Freedman & Sears, 1965).[14]

Similarly, to transform a boring condition into an enjoyable one, the person must also invest attention to make the information more complex. Portions of a long car trip can be made enjoyable if the passengers attend closely to the scenery, or use surplus attention to make plans, play games, listen to music, or talk to each other.

Both these changes, from confusion to enjoyment or from boredom to enjoyment require the allocation of scarce mental energy to the information at hand. The same extra investment is needed to turn a *pleasurable* experience into an *enjoyable* one.

Pleasure, for our purposes, is different from enjoyment. *Pleasure* generally comes from processing "messages" that our genetic inheritance has made congruent with the biological goals of the body, such as the sensations we get from eating when hungry, from sex, from the relish we take in a healthy body. These messages may temporarily produce order in consciousness, but not psychological growth. *Enjoyment* requires a different form of active involvement to produce a positive inner state.

But although we have begun to develop a model that will help explain the reception of information, whether it be from scenery, from a book, or from television, it is clear that the attempt to find an unequivocal, absolutely objective standard must eventually be doomed to failure. We have suggested that televised information, like any other information, will be valuable to the extent that people can use it in the service of their goals. Whether an instance of television viewing creates order or disorder in consciousness depends on what the person wants and needs and what other options he or she has. As the patterns of goals vary, so does the potential value of television. Ideally, then, the value of the viewing experience would be assessed in terms of the total psychic economy of each viewer.

We cannot fulfill such an ideal. But because television viewing takes place in a real world full of other predictable activities and demands, we can begin by considering what people usually spend their time doing and thereby provide a context in which television viewing can be meaningfully evaluated. Because television viewing is an activity that almost invariably takes place during "free" time we must also give some thought to what leisure is, and how it is used.

ENDNOTES

[1]Of course there are other ways of thinking about attention. For example, although Kahneman (1973) would agree that attention is a capacity for arousal and the performance of mental work, he does not believe that it is a filtering mechanism.

[2]George Miller (1967) claimed that people have difficulty discriminating among sensory alternatives that exceed 7 in number.

[3]Our use of *psychic energy* is similar to Freud's (1900/1965) early use of the term to describe *mobile attention*. In later writings, Freud equated psychic energy with *libido* or *life force*.

[4]The importance of order and complexity as basic organizing principles has been recognized for some time. As early as 1920, Fry (cited in Berlyne, 1971) noted the importance of both order and "variety" in organizing and stimulating the senses. George Birkhoff (1933) also introduced complexity and order into his formula of "aesthetic measure," although like many, he considered complexity and order to be features of the object of perception rather than psychological phenomena linked to stimuli. Bennett and Landauer (1985) asked whether order and complexity are the same thing and came to the conclusion that they are not. These concepts are also discussed by Attneave (1954) and Berlyne (1958, 1960, 1971). Additional contributions on complexity have been made by Rosenbleuth, Wiener, and Bigelow (1943), Walker (1973), and by Heyduk (1975) who contends that the degree of preference for an event is inversely related to the distance between the event's psychological complexity and the individual's optimal or preferred psychological complexity level.

Rudolf Arnheim (1971) has also written on complexity and offered a critique of the information-theory approach to the concept of order. See Finn and Roberts (1984) for a review of the entropy concept in information and communication research, and Ritchie (1986) for an evaluation of Shannon and Weaver's (1949) model. See Arnheim (1971) and Schwartz (1969) for broad reviews of the entropy concept in human behavior.

Measuring order in television materials has received less attention than developing complexity indices (Rice, Huston, & Wright, 1982; Watt & Krull, 1974; Watt & Welch, 1983) that have been applied in studies by Rimmer (1986), Thorson, Reeves, and Schleuder (1985), Wartella and Ettema (1974), among others. Thorson et al. provided a useful review of the television complexity literature.

[5]For Maslow (1954), needs that are low in his seven-tier hierarchy need to be at least partially met before those above them can become important sources of motivation or themselves be met. The hierarchy starts with physiological needs (hunger, sleep, and thirst), then come safety needs, belongingness and love needs, esteem needs (to achieve, be competent, gain approval and recognition), cognitive needs (to acquire knowledge and understanding), aesthetic needs, and finally self-actualization needs (finding self-fulfillment and realizing one's potential).

[6]Although Freud apparently never referred directly to the Second Law, his notions about the "constancy principle" and tension reduction have led many to assume that his thinking was influenced by Newton and the prevailing mechanical principles of the day. David Riesman (1954) claimed that Freud "understood man's physical and psychic behavior in the light of the physics of entropy and the economics of scarcity" (p. 60). Carl Jung also conceived of the psyche as having the potential to combat entropy.

[7]A similar negentropy concept applied to information processing has been developed by Klapp (1986) who holds that entropy is the negative of information. Actually, Shannon showed how a system high in entropy potentially conveys *more* information than one low in entropy. In this view, a bit of data coming from a highly diverse and disorganized system may convey more information than a bit of data coming from a homogeneous and organized system. (See Wright, 1988, pp. 87–89, for a simple explanation of this.)

Depending on one's point of view, then, information can be equated with entropy *or* negentropy. We have chosen to use the more accepted understanding that order helps convey information. It should also be noted that in a closed system, disorder might necessarily be created at the same time that there is an improvement in order elsewhere. As we are thinking about it, the psyche is an open system.

[8]Many research findings support this view. See Zillmann and Bryant (1985) for a review of some of the relevant literature. In a study by Pearson (1971), for readers with low needs for arousal, stories on unimportant topics and those supporting the views of the respondents resulted in significantly more positive mood change and greater overall preference for continued exposure than those on important topics and those containing discrepant information. For those individuals with high needs for arousal, more important topics generated more positive mood change and greater preferences for continued exposure. But even for high need subjects, the need for arousal was exceeded when subjects were exposed to discrepant information, resulting in preferences for discontinuing exposure.

[9]The first two of Zillmann and Bryant's (1985) six propositions for a "theory of affect-dependent stimulus arrangement" are relevant here:

1. It is proposed that individuals are motivated to terminate noxious, aversive stimuli of any kind and to reduce the intensity of such stimulation at any time. It is further proposed that individuals are motivated to perpetuate and increase the intensity of gratifying, pleasurable experiential states. . .

2. Based on this hedonistic premise, it is proposed that individuals are inclined to arrange—to the extent they are capable—internal and external stimulus conditions so as to minimize aversion and maximize gratification. (p. 158)

[10]We recognize that this is a simple way to conceptualize complexity. However, our thinking is similar to some of the conceptualizations of "cognitive complexity," a concept that dates in name at least to Bieri (1955) and Crockett (1965). See Streufert and Streufert (1978) for a comprehensive review.

According to Walker (1973), people generally prefer moderate complexity to extreme complexity or simplicity. Note, however, that as with order, complexity need not be "in" the message itself. In this regard, Reeves and Thorson (1986) have shown that some televised messages that were rated as "complex" in pictorial information or verbal content were *easier* to process than less complex material. In explanation, they make a distinction between global and local complexity. For them, local complexity involves the intake of messages. Here, more complex messages did require more effort by viewers. Global complexity, on the other hand, is related to meaning and it is here, for them, where greater complexity may be more easily processed.

[11]Klapp (1986) drew a similar distinction between "good" and "bad complexity," where-

in bad complexity is experienced as "boring and frustrating" and "contains maximum disorder" (p. 90).

[12]Redundancy is critical to animals generally. E. O. Wilson (1975) concluded that *redundancy* "characterizes animal communication systems" better than any other single word (p. 200).

[13]The Piagetian (1975/1977) terms of *assimilation, accommodation,* and *equilibration* in cognitive structures are relevant here.

[14]In this regard, Zillmann and Bryant (1985) have concluded that "exposure to information may be sought not so much because of expectations regarding particular excitatory and hedonic reactions but primarily because they contain soothing, comforting information" (p. 182). We would note, however, that the word "soothing" would seem to connote a hedonic reaction.

CHAPTER 2

The Problem of Leisure

This time, like all times, is a very good one if we but know what to do with it.
—Emerson (1837)

To be able to fill leisure intelligently is the last product of civilization.
—Russell

What do people do with the time and mental energy at their disposal? Some work as much as possible, some as little as they can; some sleep 10 hours each night, some only 5. But most people tend to spend roughly similar amounts of time attending to the same broad categories of activity, day in, day out. Moreover, the broad pattern of time allocation in daily life differs relatively little around the world.

In most large societies, people who have jobs spend roughly one third of their waking hours at work or traveling to work; about 40% of their time is spent in maintenance activities such as eating, cooking, shopping, cleaning the house, personal care, and childcare; and approximately 30% is devoted to leisure activities (Szalai, 1972).[1]

Of this one third of waking time that is free, the single activity that clearly absorbs the most time in modern societies is watching television.[2] To understand better what happens during this time it is important that we also give consideration to the other things we do during an average day, especially the category of leisure activities, of which television viewing is the primary component.

We have seen that work, maintenance, and leisure each take up about one third of adult waking life. Work accomplishes many things, but perhaps most basically for most people, it generates the necessities of survival: food, clothing, shelter; as well as the exchange value needed to obtain many of the other material goods and goals people desire.

Maintenance activities keep restoring the body and its environment to their desired states, compensating for the constant erosion of entropy— the tendency for things to become disordered. Cleaning and housework, for instance, can be a necessity for health reasons but also because we have certain expectations about how things should look and how things in a house should be ordered (clean dishes in the cupboard, dirty dishes in the sink, clean socks in a bedroom drawer, books on shelves, rugs even and smooth on the floor, and so on ad infinitum). However, as soon as we specify one place in which a thing should be (e.g., socks in the bedroom dresser drawer), we automatically define an almost infinite number of places where that thing should *not* be (Bateson, 1972). And because in the ordinary course of events things tend to return to a uniform state of randomness, the socks with time will almost certainly *not* be found in the drawer where they are supposed to belong, unless someone expends psychic energy counteracting the inevitable. The same holds for our appearance: each morning—and for some people several times during the day—we invest attention in restoring our looks to some approximation of the ideal. If a gust of wind disturbs our hair, nothing will make it look more ordered, except the time we take to comb it back in place.

Productive and maintenance activities are necessary to compensate for wear and tear, and every animal must spend a certain amount of its life energy simply to continue living. Among mammals, the shrew's peculiar metabolism forces it to spend practically all its waking time hunting and eating; male lions, on the other hand, sleep as many as 20 hours a day. Baboons, whose social organization is in several respects similar to our own spend about 70% of their time foraging and grooming and 30% in "leisure," that is resting, playing, and socializing (Altmann, 1980).

Work and maintenance are necessary, but humans long ago decided that they are not sufficient to make life worth living. Nowadays, without some "free time" or leisure, life seems nearly intolerable. We do not know precisely when this expectation became a crucial issue in human and cultural evolution. Most likely it rose in importance once work and maintenance began to be perceived as being imposed by outside forces.

Leisure as a concept arises out of a dialectical opposition to obligatory work (Dumazedier, 1974; Gunter & Gunter, 1980). In simple subsistence societies there is no "free time" because work is not seen to be obligatory. The hunter goes after game when he is hungry, when ritual demands, or when the season is propitious, and he does not feel that he "has to do it." Cultural anthropologists generally agree that in such societies there is not the kind of distinction felt between work, religion, play, and social interaction as in our own society; all of these activities are thought to blend into one another (Firth, 1929; Sahlins, 1972).

The need for separate leisure time becomes most pressing when people are forced to work at someone else's bidding, a situation first made widely possible by the agricultural revolution approximately 10,000 years ago. Farming led to the division and private ownership of land. When crops can be overproduced and a surplus stored away, some families and groups will be able to achieve control of a larger share of resources, and eventually will own more land and consequently control the lives of those less fortunate (Marx, 1844/1972; Parsons, 1951; Wittfogel, 1957). Hunter–gatherers seem to live by more egalitarian arrangements; given their economic base, social inequality is less feasible, and therefore less pronounced among them.

For hundreds of thousands of years, it is generally thought that human beings did not exploit each others' labor in an organized or systematic manner. But that changed with the advent of farming, in the last few seconds of relative evolutionary time. Now a person was able to benefit from having another work, because the product of labor could be exchanged for more than it took to buy the worker's time. This situation helped make possible the split between obligatory activities— those a worker does for someone else—and leisure, which is what he or she does freely.

By the time of the Greeks, this distinction was firmly entrenched. The philosophers who helped shape Western values were agreed that a person who had no leisure could not be fully human. The work people did to keep themselves alive, the effort necessary for production and maintenance, was now seen to be a burden shared with lower animals. Only in free time, pursuing voluntary leisure activities, did people develop their uniquely human potentialities. Slaves were not quite human because all their potentialities were wasted, caught in the endless cycles of production and maintenance (Arendt, 1958).

Of course nobody believed that just having free time on hand magically transformed an animal into a person. The thinkers of Greece, themselves men of leisure, placed precise responsibilities on those who had the good fortune of not having to work for a living. A man's free time was to be used to achieve immortality either in the political arena, or in the realms of thought and truth. The Greek word for leisure, *schole*, is where the word "school" and its derivations originate, because for the aristocracy of that time learning and leisure were synonymous. Plato in Book 2 of the *Republic* and Aristotle in the first book of *Politics* argue that the leaders of society need leisure to acquire those qualities that make them fit to rule. Free time was necessary to cultivate the *bios theoretikos,* or contemplative life, which together with heroic deeds was the only way to give purpose to existence.

It is well known that the refined values the Greek philosophers upheld applied only to a tiny fraction of the population. The realization of human potential was an option open only to men, and generally only to those men who owned enough land or goods to afford slaves to provide for their living, and thus to free their mental energies from more mundane pursuits.

This is not the place to review all the changes that the concept of leisure has undergone in the centuries between the great days of Athens and our own. There are several excellent reviews that reveal the history of leisure.[3] Still, it is instructive to survey very briefly what many people in Western cultures did in their free time, and the value they placed on it.

The Romans called leisure *otium,* and for the first centuries of the Republic they viewed it as an opportunity for transcending the limitations of nature as did the Greeks. Rather than contemplation, however, the early Romans followed the peculiar genius of their culture and used leisure more as an opportunity to perfect the active life, the Greek *bios praktikos,* involving physical fitness and useful knowledge.

But after a long habit of wealth and privilege had dulled their ambition, free time became for many citizens of Rome a burden to be filled with pleasure and amusements. Keeping the populace occupied with amusing stimulation became one of the main priorities of the government in the centuries of decline, and the excesses to which the Romans abandoned themselves in their free time have become legendary: gladiator combat to death, animals goaded to tear each other to pieces, Christians covered with pitch and fired as human torches. At one time Rome had over 800 public baths, each provided with impressive halls where citizens could congregate to relax, talk, eat, gamble, and exercise. The Circus Maximus, the main arena for chariot racing, accommodated over 300,000 spectators (Kelly, 1982).

As Christianity became established in Europe, the meaning of free time underwent redefinition and became a spiritual opportunity, a chance to get to know the purpose of the Lord and learn to abide by it. In the fifth century, for example, Augustine wrote in his *Confessions* (Howie, 1969) that, "the attraction of a life of leisure ought not to be the prospect of lazy inactivity, but the chance for the investigation and discovery of truth"—a very Aristotelian sentiment, except that it was assumed that only through God could truth be discovered. With time, this kind of spiritual contemplation came to be a prerogative of the clergy and leisure became a serious sin (Le Goff, 1980); or, as later Italians said, *"l'ozio e il padre dei vizi,"* leisure is father of all vices.

Actually, quite a few of the concerns of the Greek and Roman philosophers about the functions of entertainment seem remarkably contemporary. For example, in a controversy still unresolved after 2,300 years, Aristotle held that drama could serve a cathartic function, disagreeing with Plato who condemned theater for arousing passions and undermining the state (Wimsatt & Brooks, 1957). In the *Republic* Plato wrote, "Then shall we simply allow our children to listen to any story anyone happens to make up, and so receive into their minds ideas often the very opposite of those we shall think they ought to have when they are grown up?" Cicero was similarly critical of the excesses of the Roman theater and sounded as if he might be writing contemporary television criticism: "If we are forced, at every hour, to watch or listen to horrible events, this constant stream of ghastly impressions will deprive even the most delicate among us of all respect for humanity." In fact, by the 5th century, the Church abolished the Roman theater as an art form so debased by commercial exploitation as to have lost any relevance to the good of society.

In practice, people in the late middle ages seem to have had widely different opportunities to experience leisure. For the French shepherds of the 14th century described by Le Roy Ladurie (1979), for instance, the distinction between work and free time may have been nearly as meaningless as for prehistoric hunters. They roamed mountain meadows alone with their flocks for months at a time, adapting to the natural rhythms of the weather and the requirements of the sheep, doing everything that needed to be done—from baking to sewing and singing, from healing the animals to fighting wolves. Now and then they would take off to visit friends in a neighboring village, to refresh themselves or to discuss fine points of religious dogma. What part of their life was work, what part leisure?

On the other hand, hired workers, especially in the cities, had already learned the distinction between free and obligatory time. The May 12, 1395 ordinance of the Provost of Paris addressed to weavers, fullers, washers, masons, carpenters, and other such wage laborers specified that "the working day is fixed from the hour of sunrise to the hour of sunset, with meals to be taken at reasonable times" (Le Goff, 1980, p. 47). Except on holidays, for these workers, leisure was driven from the light of day.

When a measure of political stability and affluence returned to Europe during the Renaissance, free time again became an opportunity for humanistic pursuits, at least among the opinion makers who gained their living from rents and investments. And it was during this period that Montaigne (1927) developed the "modern" conception of entertainment as an acceptable means for the relief of daily discontent and stress.[4] For Montaigne, even transitory merriment during entertainment could be beneficial.

Then once more after the Reformation, leisure acquired a negative value. The early Puritans were merchants and craftsmen who had to devote nearly all their mental and physical energy to their vocation if they wished to contest the power and privilege controlled by the entrenched nobility. To this and other ends they devised what we now call the Protestant Ethic, a code that made productive work the only worthwhile activity (Weber, 1904/1958). When not working, a person was supposed to prepare his soul to join his maker. Everything else was sloth, and therefore sinful. The Puritans' impact on the conduct of everyday life was seen to be so dangerous by the secular authorities that King James I in 1618 was moved to promulgate from all the pulpits of England his *Book of Sports,* the intent of which was to reassure his people that it was all right to have fun on holidays, especially if it included the practice of archery, running, wrestling, and other strenuous activities useful to the monarch's warlike ambitions (Kelly, 1982).

It was the new literate bourgeoisie in this same period who demanded, and for the first time could sponsor, a "popular culture"—a culture that departed from the interests and standards long established by the clergy, nobility, and aristocracy. Popular theater offerings of the period began to pay less attention to the activities of bishops and kings and increasingly featured stories about the lives and experiences of the bourgeoisie.

It is from the clash of values inherent in such shifts in power that many of the current disagreements about what constitutes appropriate entertainment originate (Lowenthal & Fiske, 1957; Mendelsohn & Spetnagel, 1980). As we have seen, "proper" leisure and entertainment activity have often been defined by ruling elites in ways designed to benefit their own interests and thus, much criticism of certain forms of leisure, and especially of a popular art such as television, has its roots in class antagonisms that are fueled by economic inequalities and differences in political power.[5]

The great upheavals in production and lifestyle brought about by the industrial revolution had their own impact on leisure. The early factory gobbled up the energies of many of its operatives 14 hours or more a day, 6 days a week (Kelly, 1982; Thompson, 1967). Physical exhaustion and subsistence wages left little leeway for enjoying the few free hours they had. It was typical for men in the mining, metallurgical, and textile industries to start their working careers at 6 or 7 years of age, so that they lacked any education in skills of reading, writing, and mathematics, or any of the social graces that might have allowed them to gain control over the course of their future lives. Not surprisingly, many workers spent what little money they had drugging themselves with drink (Le Play, 1879). More surprising is that even in the worst factory conditions there were workers who used the available shreds of free time to write poetry, participate in the activities of learned societies, work for the church, or to organize politically (Wallace, 1978).

The condition in which most workers lived in the great industrial centers of Europe in the mid-19th century convinced Karl Marx, and many others, that the capitalist organization of property and labor prevented the majority of people from becoming fully human. Marx concluded that although animals expressed their "nature" from birth—a fish was a fish as soon as it hatched, a kitten didn't have to do anything to become a cat—human beings were born more or less as clean slates, and their "nature" was built up slowly through their lifetime, as a result of their everyday "life activity," which essentially consisted of what they did for a living. One's relationship to the modes of production as well as one's own mode of production defined one's consciousness. Thus, work became the most important part of one's nature. A potter invests her mental energy in making utensils of clay, and thereby she is a different person from the fisherman whose energy is invested in the craft of fishing; their essential nature is shaped by the status of their work but also by the patterns of information to which they attend in their occupations.

In the clumsy early stages of industrial capitalism, Marx thought that the potential development of the worker as a human being was frustrated by the wage relations that bound him to the factory owners. The factory estranged the worker from his product, which resulted eventually in the estrangement of the worker from his or her own nature, and often the estrangement of the worker from the rest of the working class (Marx, 1844/1972).

It is interesting to note that the Marxist view of human nature is in many ways similar to the Aristotelian view. Both see human nature as indeterminate, a bundle of potentialities that must be realized through a lifetime of action. The difference is that Aristotle believed that the fulfillment of potentialities could best be accomplished in leisure, while Marx believed that it was necessary to accomplish it in work.

This seemingly substantive divergence between the two viewpoints is more apparent than real. It can be accounted for largely in terms of the organization of the societies in which they lived and the technological development separating the two philosophers, rather than a basically different understanding of the dynamics of human development. In ancient Greece, much work was done by slaves and consisted of traditional farming and housekeeping chores that presented few opportunities for a person to grow in complexity. Hence, it made sense to say that only in leisure was it possible to learn new skills and to develop the mind.

By the 19th century, the situation had become more complicated. On the one hand, the industrial division of labor had created more jobs that required new knowledge and were intellectually challenging. On the other hand, the requirements of industrial production forced a great many of the workers to perform increasingly simple and repetitive tasks. Already a century earlier, Adam Smith (1776/1980), one of the greatest advocates of industrial productivity, had to admit this paradox when he recognized that the industrial division of labor enriched the commonwealth, but turned many workers into helpless idiots. Or as Braverman (1974) observed much more recently, concentrated power in the hands of management permits an increased opportunity to develop skills for managers but results in a "deskilling of labor" for most workers.

Despite the redundant simplicity of most industrial jobs, it was clear to Marx, as it was not to Aristotle living in agrarian Greece, that work had the potential to spur people to become more complete and integrated human beings. His way out of the dilemma was essentially to suggest rotating work roles, so that no individual would get stuck doing the same job forever. By farming in the morning, writing theater reviews at noon, weaving in the afternoon, and playing music in the evening, and without having to become a farmer, critic, weaver, or musician, one might benefit from the complexity of technological production without being rigidly molded by its limitations.

Of course, if such an utopian arrangement were ever to be implemented, the distinction between work and leisure might again disappear. People might work only when they felt like it, doing what they felt like doing at the moment. Even if what they did was productive "work," in terms of subjective experience it would not be alienating work. It would be similar to the situation of the hunter–gatherers who "work" when it is natural to do so, and who, it is believed, therefore view their "work" as something spontaneous, like breathing.

What Marx suggested has never been implemented on a large scale although many "utopian" communities attempt to arrange the division of labor along these lines. The kibbutzim in Israel are one example as are realizations of B. F. Skinner's *Walden Two*. But how feasible it would be to run an entire industrial or post-industrial society in this manner remains very much in doubt.

Indeed, as we suggest in the final chapter, there is much to criticize about the current nature of work and leisure in both capitalist and socialist economies. But to complete our very brief review of how leisure has been conceived in different historical periods, let us turn to the present day by focusing on the academic study of leisure.

In the 20th century, as more free time has become available, both new and old questions about what happens during leisure and how it might be best used have emerged as problems worthy of scholarly consideration.

There is even a psychiatric literature on the subject. In recent years, the chief psychiatrist of a hospital in Florence has described the "Stendhal" syndrome, instances of tourists fainting or experiencing a range of symptoms, from rapid heart beat to stomach pains, while looking at great works of art. Other observers have suggested that such "patients" merely suffer from the common strains of modern travel (Haberman, 1989).

More rigorous attention by psychoanalysts to symptoms occurring in leisure time date back at least to 1919 when Sandor Ferenczi (1919/1950) observed that leisure could present problems in the form of what he called the "Sunday neurosis," which he characterized as an increase in physical symptomatology and anxiety in psychiatric patients on their day off. In the middle 1950s, other psychoanalysts described "Christmas neurosis" (Boyer, 1955) and the "vacation" and "holiday syndromes" (Cattell, 1955; Grinstein, 1955). These studies ultimately led Gussen (1967) to conclude that some people were incapable of enjoying free time that did not involve "highly structured, external stimuli because of anxiety from the threat of regression and the closeness to repressed impulses" (p. 61).

Well before the advent of television, early 20th-century intellectuals worried about the impact of increased leisure time and the public's predilection for film and periodical fiction. Charles Cooley (1902), for example, thought that the new media caused "an over excitation [of impulses] which weakens or breaks down character" (p. 145). Robert Park (1927) similarly concluded that such media were demoralizing and disrupted social control. He concluded, "It is in the improvident use of our leisure, I suspect, that the greatest wastes of American life occur" (p. 675).

With the wide public adoption and popularity of television in the 1950s, modern intellectuals began to regularly express concern about how people used free time and many took the position that people had obtained more leisure time than they knew what to do with. Arthur Schlesinger, Jr., for example, made the observation that "The most dangerous threat hanging over American society is the threat of leisure . . . and those who have the least preparation for leisure will have

the most of it." In 1954, Robert Hutchins (cited in International Thesaurus of Quotations, 1970) left little doubt as to his view of leisure,
television, or the working man when he wrote: "More free time means
more time to waste. The worker who used to have only a little free time
in which to get drunk and beat his wife now has time to get drunk, beat
his wife—and watch TV" (p. 349). In this same period, The Group for
the Advancement of Psychiatry (1958) expressed formal concern that
leisure actually posed a "significant danger" to many Americans.

These concerns went unabated throughout the 1960s. For Charlesworth (1964), for example, "The salient fact about leisure is that it is
growing much faster than is our capacity to use it wisely." Or as Gussen
(1967) wrote:

> Free time is not necessarily acquired by choice but may be forced upon vast
> groups of people ill prepared to use it constructively or even to adapt to it
> without psychological ill effects for themselves as individuals and for soci-
> ety as a whole. (p. 52)

For a good many modern critics, then, leisure is "beyond the capacity of
most people," particularly in societies where there are few strong traditions to guide people in the productive use of free time (de Grazia,
1962).

Although all of these concerns have alerted us to potential problems,
the fact remains that we still know very little about leisure or its benefits.
Bennett Berger, for example, has lamented that the study of leisure is
"little else than a reporting of survey data on what selected samples of
individuals do with the time in which they are not working and the
correlation of these data with conventional demographic variables" (see
Meyersohn, 1969, p. 53). Or as Gussen wrote, "we are as yet pitifully
ignorant of how free time and the uses made of it affect the individual,
his immediate environment, and the community" (p. 54). In our view, the
current state of affairs is due in large part to the fact that behavioral
research on the subjective meaning, value, and experience of leisure is
only infrequently attempted.[6] In fact, some researchers seem reluctant
to evaluate leisure phenomena or even to ask the most basic of questions.

What actually happens when we are involved in leisure? What *is* the
subjective experience like? Are there short- and long-term consequences
that can be forecast? These are not idle questions, when we consider that
they involve one third of life, and the third that by some accounts is
supposed to provide the greatest meaning to the rest of existence.

To answer these questions in the abstract is impossible, because leisure
is so variegated. But at least we can begin by studying how a number of
specific leisure activities are experienced and by focusing on television

viewing, the activity that by far takes up the largest segment of people's leisure time.

ENDNOTES

[1]Studies of U.S. adults from the middle 1970s and middle 1980s are in general agreement with these figures, although they report slightly less time spent working and more in leisure: 28% of waking time spent working, 37% spent in maintenance, and 35% in free time (Robinson, 1977, 1989). With more households now sending two adults to work each day, a recent Harris poll indicates that some Americans may be spending less time in leisure than they did in the recent past but this poll should be considered less valid than Robinson's considerably more intensive studies of time use.

[2]According to Samuelson (1989), John Robinson estimated that 40%, or 2.2 hours of the 5.5 hours of daily free time of Americans is devoted to television viewing. As is seen later, we arrive at the same proportional estimate. Adults who do not work full time, children, and the elderly watch more on average, with the majority falling somewhere between 2 and 4 hours of daily viewing. Of course, even 2 hours a day adds up to an enormous slice of one's waking free time.

[3]See for example, de Grazia (1962), Dumazedier (1967), Kelly (1982), and Neulinger (1974).

[4]It is Mendelsohn (1966) who credits Montaigne with this development although as early as the 13th century even St. Thomas Aquinas wrote that "intermittent suspension of the rational faculties is obligatory." Montaigne's emphasis on the recreational value of entertainment foreshadowed Freud's approach that saw people as suffering from the repression of numerous impulses that could be partly gratified via entertainment and particularly through identification with someone else who was being gratified.

[5]It is easy to understand why entertainment that addresses the direct concerns of an audience will be popular with that audience. Contemporary popular entertainment typically tells stories about the audience to the audience, even if the story is set in the future or the past. We see this phenomenon operating as directly as ever in the recent rash of television programs and movies about the adult lives of baby boomers. With over 70 million baby boomers now in young and middle adulthood and with much disposable income, the commercial television networks have successfully launched new programs such as "thirtysomething," and "The Wonder Years." For a more complete treatment of the baby boom's impact on changes in contemporary media see Kubey (1988). For excellent analysis of the popular themes in many modern television shows see Gitlin (1986), Marc (1984, 1989), and Newcomb (1974, 1979), among others.

[6]See Csikszentmihalyi (1979) for a more detailed discussion of this point.

CHAPTER 3

The Limits of Television Research

TV is going to be the test of the modern world. . . . We shall stand or fall by TV—of that I am quite sure.

—E. B. White (1938)

From the first cave paintings through the written word and the printing press, to broadcast and satellite transmissions, the history of mankind has been intimately linked to the development of communication.[1] Charles Cooley (1897) saw in the history of communication a way to organize the whole of human history and moral progress. Communication, for him, was the primary engine of social change:

Society is a matter of the incidence of men on one another; and since this incidence is a matter of communication, the history of the latter is the foundation of all history. The mechanisms of communication include . . . all the ways through which thought and feeling can pass from man to man. (p. 77)

Nor was the centrality of communication to human experience lost on John Dewey (1915) in this passage from *Democracy and Education:*

23

Society not only continues to exist *by* transmission, *by* communication, but it may fairly be said to exist *in* transmission, *in* communication. There is more than a verbal tie between the words common, community, and communication. Men live in a community by virtue of the things they have in common; and communication is the way in which they come to possess things in common. (p. 4)

Today, the thing hundreds of millions of humans most have in common with one another, aside from their humanity, is television. It has become our culture's dominant form of leisure and its most powerful means of mass communication. In four short decades it has become the primary channel for the information that we share as a nation and as a world.

More Americans now have television sets than have refrigerators or indoor plumbing, and the medium has clearly become an American institution, substantially altering and influencing every other institution and ranking with the family, the school, and the church as contemporary culture's prime forces of socialization. Television's style of presentation is even substantially changing the style of modern fiction (Tichi, 1989).

The reach and pervasiveness of television is phenomenal. Recently, while camping in the Grand Tetons, one of us ambled through a wooded campsite populated by recreational vehicles. As we walked past each camper we were initially perplexed to hear what seemed to be the same serious strained argument between a man and a woman. By the third RV we realized that here, high in the mountains, our fellow campers were devoting a portion of the morning to the latest plot developments of the same soap opera.

Back in the city, on any evening of the year, one can make much the same observation relying instead on sight. Through the windows of home after home comes the same distorted bluish flickering rectangle of television. In fact, at any given moment on any given evening, well over one third of the people in the United States are watching television. On weekday evenings in the winter, half the population is sitting in front of a TV (Nielsen, 1982). Comparatively, the only activities absorbing more time than TV are sleep and work.

Such facts have caused the National Institute of Mental Health (1982) to conclude that "for many people, leisure time means just about the same thing as television time; their off duty hours are spent mainly in front of the television set" (p. 8). In the more critical opinion of Peter Conrad (1982) "the original technological revolution was about saving time, shortcutting labor; the consumerism which is the latest installment of that revolution is about wasting the time we've saved, and the institution it deputes to serve that purpose is television" (p. 108).

THE TELEVISION LITERATURE
AND THE NEED FOR EXPERIENTIAL RESEARCH

The facts and figures on television research are no less astounding than the figures on the medium's pervasiveness and denote an exponential explosion in research and scholarship. Of the 2,800 articles, reports, and books on television published between 1946 and 1980, 2,500 (90%) were written in the 1970s—two thirds of these since 1975 (Murray, 1980). At current rates, new titles appear every day. And yet, with thousands of published research studies, we still know relatively little about how television is actually experienced in the home. Nor do we know much about how other leisure activities are experienced, even though many leading theorists define leisure experientially and hold that it would be most accessible to scientific study using experiential accounts or subjective self-reports of internal states (Kaplan, 1975; Neulinger, 1974, 1981).

A massive review of the television research literature conducted by Comstock, Chaffee, Katzman, McCombs, and Roberts (1978) that drew heavily on the first National Institute of Mental Health (NIMH) report on television and behavior, listed the full description of the viewing experience as among the first priorities for future research. The second and more recent NIMH report similarly notes that there remains very little research on emotional and experiential responses to television. It concludes that increased research attention to this area is "highly desirable" (p. 89) and should be given "top priority" (NIMH, 1982, p. 6).

We, too, believe that understanding the viewing experience is important and that it may well be a goal "logically prior" to studying television's other effects.[2] Understanding the nature of the subjective experience of viewing, whether it be active or passive, for example, and under what conditions it varies, is crucial to grasping how the medium affects learning and behavior. Indeed, many critics often claim that it is the *activity* of television viewing (not its content) that contributes to alleged problems ranging from poor language and reading skills in children and declining SAT scores in adolescents to apathy and marital difficulty in adults.[3] It has been suggested that viewing may induce a unique cognitive–affective state that accounts for some such phenomena (Lindlof, 1982; Singer, 1980).

Whether the cognitive–affective televiewing state is truly distinct is a question that we attempt to at least partly answer in the following chapters. But the experience of television may also be altered by whom people view with and by activities that occur simultaneously with viewing.

Once again, many researchers have noted a dearth of research relating media effects and experiences to their social and ecological context.[4]

Bramson (1961), for example, called for "a rejection of the image of the isolated, anonymous, detached individual-in-the-mass, in favor of an individual who receives the messages of the mass media within a social context" (pp. 152–153). Ann Nietzke (1978) has similarly argued that television "is a very potent, intimate presence in many homes . . . scientific studies and tests fall short of capturing this reality of how individual human beings live with television" (p. 66).

Researchers have begun to heed such suggestions and are studying television viewing in the home with increasing frequency. Allen (1965); Bechtel, Achelpohl, and Akers (1972); and Collett (1986) have all filmed or videotaped people watching television in their homes with their families. At the same time, Bryce (1987), Lemish (1987), and Palmer (1986), among others, have brought ethnographic observational techniques into the home to study viewing.

But although others have observed viewing behavior in the home they have not employed techniques to assess the viewer's subjective experience. In the following chapters we describe this experience as it occurs in different social contexts and in conjunction with other behaviors as well as compare it to other typical life activities. We also try to understand how the use and experience of television fit into the daily cycle of work, sleep, and family life.

TRADITIONS AND TRENDS IN MASS COMMUNICATION RESEARCH

For those who are not students of mass communication, we have chosen to briefly outline some of the traditions that have helped shape the research directions we have taken, and indicate how our work may depart from those traditions. Much of the discussion to follow centers on the power of media effects and on the related question of whether the audience is an active or a passive participant in the mass communication process,[5] as well as on what psychological states are associated with viewing. We also comment on the general perspective known as the "uses and gratifications" approach, as well as point to some of its limitations. We also consider how television may be used for escape and provide a brief introduction to some of the issues at stake in this debate as well.

The Magic Bullet

The early theories of mass communication that developed in the first half of this century reflected the then contemporary influence of stimulus–response and mechanistic models in psychology, wherein direct links between medium and behavior were posited ("the magic bullet" and "hypodermic needle" models). As early as the 19th century it was already thought that the great masses of urbanized and industrialized peoples were disconnected (or atomized) from one another and free from strong social ties and a sense of community (Le Bon, 1896). Following this line of thinking, Harold Lasswell (1927), writing shortly after World War I, called mass propaganda the "new hammer and anvil of social solidarity" (p. 221). In these years, it was thought by some that mass communication tended to influence all members of the audience in much the same way and that audience members were essentially passive and malleable recipients.

It was the study of media effects during the 1940 presidential election as reported in *The People's Choice* (Lazarsfeld, Berelson, & Gaudet, 1944) and a wide variety of other cultural processes in *Personal Influence* (Katz & Lazarsfeld, 1955) that suggested that the "magic bullet" might be a dud.[6] These studies concluded that media effects were not all-powerful. Instead, effects were newly conceived as limited and tied to individual factors and demographic characteristics.* A "two-step flow" process was delineated wherein public opinion effects were found to be largest when media messages were transmitted from one person to another rather than directly by the media. Further evidence of the importance of existing social organization to the potential power of the media came from Shils and Janowitz (1948) who showed that the effectiveness of Allied propaganda against the German Army in World War II depended upon the breakdown of social cohesion in the German combat units.

---

*Although it is rarely mentioned, some of the demise of the "magic bullet" approach to media effects might be attributed to actual changes in just how directly powerful any particular media message is today versus how powerful it might have been earlier in the century. When the public was less experienced with the electronic media and there were simultaneously many fewer media outlets available, a single medium, such as radio, or a single message, might be both more novel and potentially more powerful. Indeed it has been posited that attentiveness to each new medium declines as the number of available media increases (Neuman & de Sola Pool, 1986). Today, the public's attention is spread across hundreds of television and radio outlets and people have been able to take increasing control over what they view or listen to by virtue of the VCR and various audio playback technologies. It was much more common in the 1950s, for example, for a great percentage of the public to have watched the same television program on a particular evening. In the late 1980s, television producers complain that it is much more difficult for a new program to "break through."

A BRIEF OUTLINE AND CRITIQUE
OF THE USES AND GRATIFICATIONS APPROACH

Personal Influence and *The People's Choice* were highly influential and served as catalysts for the development of the uses and gratifications approach that has itself had considerable influence over the past 30 years.[7] Grounded in the functionalist paradigms of sociology and psychology, uses and gratifications research focuses on the social and psychological origins of people's needs, the resulting "need expectations" associated with mass media, and ultimately, the differential patterns of exposure that result in "need gratifications."

Uses and gratifications researchers rejected the "mass audience" thinking of the Frankfurt School and held, instead, that "people bend the media to their needs more readily than the media overpower them" (Katz & Gurevitch, 1976, p. 215). Individuals' particular personality characteristics, backgrounds, social roles, and the differential needs that spring from these factors influence how people use and respond to the media. Over the years, uses and gratifications researchers have delineated a great array of uses to which media can be put. McQuail, Blumler, and Brown (1972), for example, formulated a typology in which they emphasized the following uses of television: escape and emotional release, companionship and social utility, personal reference and value reinforcement, and reality exploration and information surveillance.

But the uses and gratifications approach has been criticized on many grounds, some of which we discuss here and also in chapter 9. Among other things, the approach has been criticized for being "atheoretical" or, at best, "theoretically ambiguous" (McQuail, 1985). Even some of the approach's founders have been highly critical in observing that there is no general theory linking gratifications to their social origins (Blumler, Gurevitch, & Katz, 1985; Katz, Blumler, & Gurevitch, 1974). Such self-criticism has helped encourage a lively debate.

But in the following quote, Elihu Katz (1987) accepts enough criticism to make one wonder what might be left of the approach that is worth salvaging:

> Gratifications research has been through a long period of soul-searching and self-criticism. Too mentalistic, too empiricistic, too functionalistic, too psychologic in its disconnection from social structure—say the critical theorists . . . and they are largely correct. Early gratifications research has leaned too heavily on self-reports, was unsophisticated about the social origin of the needs that audiences bring to the media, too uncritical of the possible dysfunctions both for self and society of certain kinds of audience satisfaction, and too captivated by the inventive diversity of audience uses to pay much attention to the constraints of the text. (pp. 37–38)

But even though Katz and others have abandoned the one-sidedness of their earlier positions and even though the approach has begun to take both the text and social structure more seriously, one wonders what uses and gratifications now stands for and whether contemporary critical studies of how audiences decode, "negotiate," and enter into oppositional readings of texts deservedly falls under the uses and gratifications rubric as Katz wishes to claim (1987, p. 38).

There are other problems as well. The assumption in uses and gratifications thinking that audience members *voluntarily* use the media to satisfy particular needs is itself problematic, because it neglects to consider that media users do not *always* choose with complete freedom what they are exposed to. Members of a family will often watch programs because a sibling, parent, or spouse is watching. Likewise, some boys expose themselves to extremely graphic violent material in film or on video in modern rites of passage into some distorted sense of what manhood consists of (Kubey, 1987b).

Uses and gratifications researchers also give inadequate consideration to the fact that most any television viewer has many different simultaneous needs that might be gratified by a wide variety of television content available on the screen at any given time. For example, an individual may simultaneously have a general latent need for the release of sexual tension; for escape from the family; for intellectual stimulation; for relaxation; and for information about the stock market, about an illness that was recently diagnosed, and about any number of other topics of vital concern to that person. Hence, any number of media messages may help gratify one or more of the person's concurrent needs and, although the person may have initially turned on the television in order simply to relax or to see a specific program, from that point onward—and particularly if the viewer switches about the dial "to see what's on"—television messages will then interact with the person's needs in ways that the viewer—and the social scientist—would have difficulty predicting.

In a similar criticism, Rosengren and Windahl (1972) pointed out a good many years ago that the utility of the approach may have been outlived by the "growing consensus that almost any type of content (or media) may serve practically any type of function."

But of particular concern to us is that uses and gratifications thinking conceives of "gratifications" and "effects" as being separate phenomena. To the contrary, gratifications, or entertainment experiences, *are* effects. As Zillmann and Bryant (1986) argue, the entertainment experience is "*the* effect of entertainment consumption. It is the primary effect that is sought out and pursued for the benefits that it entails" (p. 320).

Furthermore, uses and gratifications thinkers frequently write about "gratifications obtained" but, at best, they are almost always measured by having respondents report retrospectively on whether a particular medium or kind of program does or does not gratify a particular need (i.e., they are rarely measured as they occur). Zillmann (1985) and Zillmann and Bryant (1985) have pointed to an additional weakness in this particular aspect of the approach in claiming that most people are not particularly cognizant of why they choose what they choose nor are people generally able to fully explain what they derive from their media experiences. According to Zillmann, retrospective explanations may often be ones that people have heard elsewhere and/or that they believe are acceptable. Indeed, these are just a few of the accuracy problems inherent in retrospective reports (Bernard, Killworth, Kronenfeld, & Sailer, 1984; Yarmey, 1979).

It has also been suggested that there is a reluctance to consider that media activities may be engaged in for their own sake—for what Dewey (1934) called their "consummatory value" and thus, it has been argued that uses and gratifications thinking often fails to capture the dynamics of the immediate mass media experience.[8] Jay Blumler (1979), a uses and gratifications exponent, has himself expressed concern that although uses and gratifications theorists talk about getting a grip on the nature of the audience experience it is "in danger of being ignored." As a result of such limitations, Carey and Kreiling (1974) proposed that the study of mass media would be illuminated by "a model of action and motivation more appropriate to aesthetic types of experience than the purposive model" (p. 245).

> In functional analysis one never finds serious attention being paid to the content of experience. . . . Popular art is, first of all, an experience, in Warshow's (1964) terms an "immediate experience," that must be apprehended in something like its own terms. (pp. 239, 244)

In other words, uses and gratifications—as well as some behaviorist and classical psychoanalytic approaches—often explain behavior in ways that only give minor consideration to how behavior might be rewarding in and of itself. To respond to this limitation, Rolf Meyersohn (1978) has suggested that the study of intrinsic motivation might well provide "the most promising lead" in understanding the experiential rewards of entertainment and media.

In the research to be presented in the chapters ahead, a model of intrinsic motivation and a method for studying it are employed. People's experiences during media involvement are studied *as* they occur and these experiences are then linked to experiences and needs coinciding with other activities. For one of the first times, then, uses and gratifications are recorded by respondents in a naturalistic setting and studied in a direct, quantifiable manner. Our effort also attempts to accomplish what others have claimed uses and gratifications does not do, namely: discern the relationship between the "functions of mass media consumption [and] . . . the actual experience of consuming them" (Carey & Kreiling, 1974, p. 232).

CULTURAL STUDIES, CRITICAL STUDIES, AND USES AND GRATIFICATIONS

We would be remiss if we did not at least touch on a few of the developments in cultural and "critical" approaches to mass communication. We also wish to consider that some aspects of these approaches are comparable to developments in the uses and gratifications approach even though some critical researchers might be inclined to reject such a comparison.[9]

Let us first introduce the most general outline of what has been occurring in this area. In brief, the rise of cultural and critical studies in anthropology, communication, literary studies, and other fields has brought about a new emphasis on the *text* as the focus of study (Fiske & Hartley, 1978; Hall, 1980; Newcomb, 1984; Schudson, 1987). A text, whether it be a novel, a television program, or a cultural practice is something that is *read* (i.e., interpreted), or *deconstructed* in terms of its underlying ideological meaning formation. There are many variants in these developing traditions but there is also an increasing concern among some cultural and critical studies scholars to understand how and why audiences use and interpret texts as they do. Indeed, there is a growing number of critical studies of audiences, especially of disempowered groups.

Janice Radway (1984), for one example, has shown how the romance novel resonates with and embodies the particular concerns and needs of a group of married, middle-class mothers who are regular readers of the genre. Robert Allen (1983), as another example, has argued that the soap opera is among the most "open" (Eco, 1979) of television texts and that, depending on the length of experience with the program, different viewers will read the soap opera in different ways and derive more or less from these readings.

This interest in how audiences use and interpret texts is similar in some ways to the uses and gratifications approach wherein people are conceived of as using and experiencing the media in line with their idiosyncratic backgrounds and needs. In fact, current uses and gratifications thinking is now in line with the idea in critical theory that the text delimits the production of meaning (Blumler, Gurevitch, & Katz, 1985).

In this regard, John Fiske (1986) has emphasized that although open television texts permit different people and different subcultures to generate meanings, these meanings meet the needs of specific subcultural identities and that the range of multiple meanings is itself constrained by a culture's dominant ideology that structures both the text and the audience's perspective and needs. In this sense, because a text is a physical entity with definable characteristics, it necessarily acts as a reservoir for a particular predetermined meaning or range of meanings. Put another way, because the mass media are themselves part of a cultural system, they present information within interpretive structures (e.g., metaphors) that "frame" news events as well as fictional treatments in line with the dominant political culture (Gamson, 1988; Gitlin, 1980; Tuchman, 1978). And just as some textual analysts study the power of social structure to shape both texts *and* audience or reader responses, so too have uses and gratifications scholars proposed a uses and *dependency* model of mass communication wherein a more deterministic view informs traditional conceptualizations (Rubin, 1984; Rubin & Windahl, 1986; see also Ball-Rokeach, 1985, on media system dependency).

We have no doubt that the nature of people's responses to and uses of television programs as well as the programs themselves are linked to a culture's social and economic structure and existing constructions of meaning. But we also believe that more enduring features of the human condition and human biology are critical to understanding why television content and form have developed as they have and why people use and experience the medium as they do.

While we are discussing such questions, we wish to remind the reader that we do not analyze audience interpretations in this volume. Suffice it to say that in line with the aims of our research, we have tried to understand audience experiences with television *as they occur* in a fairly direct and uncomplicated way that differs from how those interested in audience interpretation or the psychological functions of narrative would themselves choose to think about television.

Furthermore, although we are in agreement with much of what cultural and critical studies scholars propose, there remains much controversy here as well. With regard to the issue of studying audience interpretations, let us briefly note a few potential problems that have been raised by others and in so doing, indicate a few advantages our approach may offer in the study of audience behavior.

Ang (1985) has argued, for example, that a viewer's immediate experience of a program may deviate significantly from the more cerebral and logical explanations often offered. Audience members who are interviewed about a television program may tend "to construct a more critical reading than they might do otherwise" (Wren-Lewis, 1983, p. 196). Fry, Fry, and Alexander (1988) similarly claim that elaborated meaning may largely be produced when viewers account for and reconstruct their experiences. Zillmann (1985) is particularly concerned about attempts on the part of the respondent to impress the investigator. Certainly, it is not hard to imagine evaluation apprehension and other method reaction effects coloring the responses of an individual asked by an academic interviewer to unpack the meaning of what he or she watches on TV. In contrast, we believe the method we employ is much less prone to these kinds of potential distortions because we ask respondents to report on their experiences immediately after they occur, and in a relatively simple manner that is straightforward and unthreatening.

TELEVISION VIEWING AS ESCAPE:
INDIVIDUAL AND SOCIETAL PERSPECTIVES

We have already discussed how uses and gratifications researchers generally assume that people use television to accomplish a goal, receive a reward, or modulate a psychological state. But not a few scholars and critics assume that many such modulations constitute *escape* and for some, escapist viewing is ultimately thought to be of negative value to the psyche and the social fabric.

Indeed, an argument of nearly 40 years' duration persists between those who believe that television viewing is a significant cause of alienation, family disharmony, hostility, and tension and those who claim that viewing is more properly understood as an *escape* from, and a reasonable and functional solution to, these same undesirable phenomena.[10] Particularly in the popular literature, but in research studies, too, television-viewing functions have often been compared to the functions of drugs and alcohol.[11]

At a macrosocial level, some scholars argue that leisure and television serve to perpetuate the basic patterns of industrial life by providing escape from the monotony of work "without making the return to work too unbearable" (Howe, 1957, p. 497). From this critical perspective, the corporate sector finances and produces television programs that are used by viewers to temporarily release themselves from the pressures of the workplace while simultaneously fostering acceptance of industry's materialistic values via advertising, and thereby helping motivate viewers to return to the workplace the next day in order to earn the money necessary to buy the things advertised on television the night before. In such thinking, television provides viewers with an illusion of involvement, but viewing is thought to be ultimately passive, thereby diminishing active involvement in society. Theodor Adorno (1957), for example, wrote:

> The suspicion widely shared, though hard to corroborate by exact data, [is] that the majority of television shows today aim at producing, or at least reproducing, the very smugness, intellectual passivity, and gullibility that seem to fit in with totalitarian creeds even if the explicit surface message of the shows may be antitotalitarian. (p. 479)

In this view, television may help provide psychological order but ultimately it is a false order or a "false consciousness."

But as previously suggested, there are many who view the order that television provides as being harmless and/or healthful.[12] Uses and gratifications proponents like Katz and Foulkes (1962) conclude, for example, that television viewing provides an adaptive retreat from ordinary responsibilities that helps restore and maintain normal activity: "that the media transport one to the world outside of one's immediate environment is the very essence of their function" (p. 384). Zillmann and Bryant (1986) draw similar conclusions from their many experimental studies:

> Consumption . . . can be highly adaptive. This is the case when consumption serves to improve on prevailing moods, affects, and emotions, shifting them from bad to good or good to better. . . What should an individual who comes home from a long day's work in a steel mill, or, for that matter, in an executive office do about this undesirable situation? . . . mass media can provide highly beneficial emotional experiences that are truly recreational and may be uplifting. These effects of entertainment, presumably because of the ready condemnation of entertainment as cheap escapism, have received very little attention from researchers. (pp. 320–321)

Critics of such a point of view would claim that it ignores macrosocial issues and that consumption of escapist media helps perpetuate the conditions that made escape necessary in the first place. Or as Douglas and Isherwood have written ". . . consumption decisions become the vital source of the culture of the moment. . . . Consumption is the very arena in which culture is fought over and licked into shape" (1980, p. 57).

Television viewing is also frequently mentioned as a mechanism for coping with everyday stress (Greenberg, 1974; Murray & Kippax, 1979), and is thought by Jerome Singer (1980) among others to reduce negative affect by presenting novel stimuli in a safe context.

Actually, we find merit in all of these views and to our mind, none need necessarily contradict any of the others (i.e., more than one process

can be going on simultaneously, especially at different levels or in different units of analysis).

We do wish to emphasize, however, that the escapist functions served
by television, whatever they may be, need to be considered within the
broader contexts of history and the nature of the human condition.
Some scholars and critics place much emphasis on *television* (or other
mass media) being important means of escape, without considering that
people have sought ways to escape everyday consciousness and boredom, to prevent thinking about themselves, to seek diversion and be
nearer the dream state long before television was invented.[13] Pascal
(1900/1941), for example, made a most persuasive case that it is characteristic of humans to be bored and unhappy and to seek amusement.*

Aware of humankind's long history of such behavior, Jean Cazeneuve
(1974) and Gregor Goethals (1981) have each argued that the psychological functions of television viewing are highly similar to those served by
ancient myth, ritual, and religious ceremony: each appeals to the human
conditions of boredom and the need to be released from it via the trans-
formation of reality into spectacle.†

Of course, it is extremely difficult to answer what long-term personal
and societal functions are associated with escape via television. Even
understanding what actually happens during viewing, which we attempt
to do in the chapters that follow, although perhaps not quite as complicated, is by no means simple. And even here, there is no consensus about
the viewing state—in part, it seems, because there is little empirical

---

*In the *Pensees*, Pascal (1900/1941) captured humankind's peculiar need for escape as
well as anyone:

> Man is so unfortunate, that he would be bored even without cause for boredom, by
> the very nature of his character; and so frivolous, that having within him a thousand
> essential causes of ennui, the least trifle, such as a billiard table and a ball to drive,
> suffices to distract him . . . if man, however, full of sadness he be, can be prevailed
> upon to enter on some diversion, he will be happy for the time being; and if man,
> however, happy he be, is not diverted and occupied by some passion or amusement,
> which prevents ennui from asserting itself, he will soon be discontented and unhap-
> py. (*Pensees*, No. 139)

†Probably the earliest recorded notion that entertainment (or more accurately—tragedy) could perform a restorative function was Aristotle's concept of "catharsis" wherein the
emotions and spirit are purified and purged by pity and terror aroused in the drama. This
functional similarity is particularly interesting insofar as the origins of theater and, hence,
much television fare, can be traced to primitive religious ceremony and ritual display.
Furthermore, it is claimed that Greek tragedy originated in harvest and fertility feasts and
associated ideas of the death and renewal of life.

evidence from the field but also because of serious paradigmatic and political differences in various approaches to the study of television.

CONCEPTUALIZATIONS OF THE VIEWING STATE

Activity and Reactivity

Although many observers have described TV viewing as "passive," "relaxing," or a medium of "low involvement"[14] there are others who hold that viewing is active. Actually, much of the disagreement is related to how these terms are defined and conceptualized. Low-involvement conceptualizations range from conclusions about the level of cortical activity during viewing to more sociological grounded approaches that consider variables such as work and sleep hours and that operationalize television use in exogeneous terms. Activity–passivity conceptualizations range from viewers being deemed active because they choose what they view and interpret what they view, to how much attention people pay to the screen when viewing or the audience's state of consciousness vis-á-vis economics and politics.

Frankfurt School theorists have argued that the mass media render the audience passive and one-dimensional (Horkheimer & Adorno, 1972; Marcuse, 1964). Via the induction of passivity, viewers become bound to television and therefore, to the economic system as a whole. Gitlin (1972) has argued, for example, that television is an essential instrument by which power elites and corporations encourage passivity in the masses. For him, television "flattens consciousness," "the habitual watcher seems literally *entranced,* hypnotized" (p. 351). Like Gitlin, Schiller (1973) points to the "dimunition of mental activity" associated with viewing as well as "the pacifying effect on critical consciousness" (p. 30):

> The content and form of American communications—the myths and the means of transmitting them—are devoted to manipulation. When successfully employed, as they invariably are, the result is individual passivity, a state of inertia that precludes action. This, indeed, is the condition for which the media and the system-at-large energetically strive, because passivity assures the maintenance of the *status quo.* (p. 29)

These issues remain very much on the cutting edge of mass communications studies as scholars consider how state power is acquired and maintained, how mass consciousness is formed, as well as which facets of audience attention are under the viewer's voluntary control and which might be deemed involuntary, or under the control of the medium.

Answers to these questions are of particular import because they are directly relevant to how people, especially children, comprehend, learn from, and may be persuaded by, what they view on television.[15]

As we discuss in chapter 7, there are also researchers who are interested in the "automaticity of viewing" and how "formal features" in television program design and syntax (zooms, pans, rapid cutting, movement, loud sudden noise, close-ups, and so on) may cause attention to be drawn to the screen.[16] In some of these studies, the viewer is conceptualized as "reactive" in response to the formal features of television (Calvert & Gersh, 1985) and it has been argued that this reactivity may be largely a biological process (Singer, 1980). There is now EEG evidence to suggest that some formal features *command* involuntary responses and that they may "derive their attentional value through the evolutionary significance of detecting movement" (Reeves, Thorson, & Schleuder, 1986, p. 271; Reeves, Thorson, Rothschild, McDonald, Hirsch, & Goldstein, 1986).

However, there are others who claim that the viewer is still active even under these circumstances because the ability to comprehend such program elements is what actually permits attention to be elicited (Anderson & Lorch, 1983).* Others claim that even if such responses are involuntary they may still have a positive benefit in helping viewers learn (Zillmann & Bryant, 1981).

Television as a Magnet for Attention

Given the familiarity of popular references such as "boob tube," "idiot box," and "couch potato," it should come as little surprise that many assessments of the viewing state are highly negative, although many of the most critical attacks come from those who have not methodically studied television viewing. Theodore Roszak (1968), for one, concluded that the major psychic effect of TV is "narcotic disintegration of the sensibilities" and "malaise: the fixed stare, the mindless drift" (pp. 266–267).

Another highly critical observer, a former advertising executive, Jerry Mander (1978), kept an informal record of what he deemed were the most frequent terms used in ordinary conversation and correspondence to describe how people felt about television viewing. His list reveals a prevalent set of beliefs about what happens to people when they watch TV:

---

*Actually, a similar observation was made by Hugo Munsterberg (1916) over 70 years ago in *The Photoplay*, an early study in the psychology of film. Munsterberg wrote, "To be sure, the perceptions which force themselves on our involuntary attention may get their motive power from our own reactions" (p. 75).

"I feel hypnotized when I watch television." "Television sucks my energy." "I feel like it is brainwashing me." "Television spaces me out." "Television is an addiction and I'm an addict." "My kids look like zombies when they're watching." "TV is destroying my mind." "TV makes my kids walk around like they're in a dream." "Television is turning my mind to mush." (p. 158)

Not a few research subjects have reported that the television set is a dominating presence whose power they can not easily resist (Bower, 1973; Edgar, 1977; NIMH, 1982; Steiner, 1963). Smith (1986), in an analysis of the popular literature on television addiction found that so-called addicts reportedly felt that they had little control over their viewing.

Some of the most compelling evidence of this phenomenon is anecdotal. Take, for example, these remarks from Mander's collection: "If a television is on, I just can't keep my eyes off it" and "I don't want to watch as much as I do but I can't help it. It makes me watch" (p. 158).

During a radio talk program, social psychologist Milton Rosenberg (1978) recounted his experience with television in this way:

When I've got television on in my home and I have to get up for one of the conventional reasons . . . . I feel temporarily unfulfilled even if I don't really want to see what's on the set. Some part of the total sensory experience has suddenly been subtracted and I'm left in some slight state of tension until I can turn my gaze back to the screen.

And psychologist and survey researcher Percy Tannenbaum (1980) has written:

Among life's more embarrassing moments have been countless occasions when I am engaged in conversation in a room while a TV set is on, and I cannot for the life of me stop from periodically glancing over to the screen. This occurs not only during dull conversations but during reasonably interesting ones just as well. Judging from the behavior of the people with whom I was talking at the time and from reports of friends and colleagues, I am far from alone in this behavior and its accompanying chagrin. (p. 112)

These representations of the power of television to attract attention and of the viewing state and its effects compel us to ask what it is about the interaction of people with television that causes such phenomena. In reaching our own understanding, we have drawn from many sources and from many different fields as well as from findings gained in laboratory experiments.[17]

But although we ask some of the same questions as our colleagues who study viewing in the lab, we are most concerned—at least at the outset—in what happens when people view in real life and how they use television in their own homes, the place where it is most frequently viewed. To understand normative viewing, experimental studies are not sufficient in and of themselves. What is needed is evidence taken in the real conditions in which people watch television, in the complex context of their daily life with all its attendant vicissitudes.

A host of researchers has lamented this lack of naturalistic research on the viewing experience.[18] Paul Hirsch (1980b), for example, has suggested that "indirect and unobtrusive measures (short of spying in the living room) should not be that difficult to develop" (p. 99). Webster and Wakshlag (1985) similarly concluded a review of methods designed to measure amount of exposure to television by writing that "the ideal measurement, then, would be one that is completely unobtrusive, records behavior as it occurs, and requires no particular effort on the part of the respondent" (p. 55). Although we have not been able to satisfy all of these criteria, we think we have come close with the method described in the next chapter.

ENDNOTES

[1]According to Innis (1964, 1972), communication technologies have played crucial roles in breaking old power monopolies. The medieval church held a monopoly on religious information until the printing press allowed the widespread printing of bibles and other religious material that bypassed church scribes and significantly altered the relationship of the church to parishioners. In the case of Rome, Innis shows how a society's dominant medium of communication directly affects the culture's stability and its ability to govern or acquire territory.

[2]Among those who concur in this view are Gans (1980); Hirsch (1980a); Katz, Blumler, and Gurevitch (1974); and Wiebe (1969).

[3]An additional gap that we wish to address in our research is the dearth of television viewing studies using adult subjects. Adults between the ages of 18 and 65 comprise 65% of the U.S. population but represent the age group most neglected by social scientists who study television (Dimmick, McCain, & Bolton, 1979). Television research has concentrated almost exclusively on children and adolescents. A small but growing literature of over 100 titles has spotlighted the elderly's use of television (see Kubey, 1980, for a review of this literature).

[4]See for example: Bechtel, Achelpohl, and Akers (1972); Cooley (1926); Frank and Greenberg (1980); Friedson (1953); Gans (1980); Klapper (1960); Kline (1971); LoScuito (1972); Robinson (1972a).

[5]The discussion that follows on the history of mass communication research and on uses and gratifications is adapted from a critique of uses and gratifications by Kubey (1989e). He is responsible for the claims in the pages ahead.

For reviews, research, and discussion on audience activity see Levy and Windahl (1984, 1985), Hawkins and Pingree (1986), and Rubin and Perse (1987).

[6]For overviews of *Personal Influence* and *The People's Choice* and many other key media studies, see Lowery and De Fleur's (1988) *Milestones in Mass Communication Research*.

Although the two books have been influential they continue to be controversial. They have been criticized perhaps most recently by Ferrarotti (1988) who, in *The End of Conversation*, made the argument that the mass media *have* reduced people's contact with one another (pp. 30–33).

[7]For developments in uses and gratifications research, see Rosengren, Wenner, and Palmgreen (1985), Rubin (1986), and Rubin and Windahl (1986).

[8]The significance of immediate mass media experience has been discussed by Booth (1982), Lindlof (1982), McLuhan (1964), Schwartz (1973), and Stephenson (1967), among many others.

[9]See McQuail (1985) and Blumler, Gurevitch, and Katz (1985) for conceptual comparisons between uses and gratifications and critical and cultural studies and attempts toward accommodation.

[10]Among those whose writings support the proposition that television is a disruptive force are: Adorno (1957); Conrad (1982); Gerbner and Gross (1976); Gerbner, Gross, Morgan, and Signorielli (1980); Gitlin (1972); Horkheimer (1974); Maccoby (1951, 1954); Mander (1978); Marcuse (1964); Postman (1984); Roszak (1968); Singer (1980); and Winn (1977). Some of those who hold that television often performs a positive functional role are: Brody, Stoneman, and Sanders (1980); Faber, Brown, and McLeod (1979); Foley (1968); Fowles (1982); Friedson (1953); Glick and Levy (1962); Hazard (1967); Johnstone (1974); Katz and Gurevitch (1976); Klapper (1960); Nordlund (1978); Pearlin (1959); Rosenblatt and Cunningham (1976); Singer (1980); Tannenbaum (1980); Zillmann (1979); and Zillmann and Bryant (1986).

[11]See, for example, Katz and Foulkes (1962), Pearlin (1959), Schramm (1973), and Winn (1977).

[12]Media messages for Gerhardt Wiebe (1969), whose analysis is reminiscent of Freud's (1929/1961) in *Civilization and Its Discontents,* typically play a "restorative" role:

> *Restorative* media messages feature crime, violence, disrespect for authority, sudden and unearned wealth, sexual indiscretion, freedom from social restraints. The themes of these most popular media messages seem to make up a composite reciprocal of the values stressed in adult socialization.... The *restorative* mechanism hypothesized here has as perhaps its chief merit the characteristic of releasing hostility in small amounts.... Perhaps one measure of a society's health is the degree to which it can tolerate the restorative mechanism without risking escalation into action that threatens some segment of the social structure. (pp. 532–533)

[13]Klapp (1986), for example, has listed 30 major writers, ranging from Voltaire and Balzac to Kafka, Beckett, and Camus, for whom ennui is a major theme. Benjamin Franklin described the problem in *Poor Richard's Almanac* (1733) as follows: "After three days men grow weary of a wench, a guest, and rainy weather."

[14]Some of those who contend that television is a medium of low involvement include Bogart (1965); Gans (1980); Goodhardt, Ehrenberg, and Collins (1975); Krugman (1971); Lindlof (1982); LoScuito (1972); McLeod and Reeves (1980); Robinson (1969, 1977); Rochberg-Halton (1979); Tannenbaum (1985); and Webster and Wakshlag (1983).

[15]For reviews of many of the relevant studies on how children understand and comprehend television, see Anderson and Collins (1988), Bryant and Anderson (1983), Bryant, Zillmann, and Brown (1983), Condry (1989), Kelly and Gardner (1981), Krull and Husson (1979), Lyle and Hoffman (1972), Palmer (1986), Wartella (1979), Dorr (1986), and Greenfield (1984).

[16]Anderson, Alwitt, Lorch, and Levin (1979), for example, have referred to television's ability to induce "attentional inertia"—the longer people look at the television screen, the

greater is the probability that they will continue to look. See also Hawkins and Pingree (1986) on the "automaticity" of viewing. Audio cues also help determine attention to the screen (Anderson, Lorch, Field & Sanders, 1981; Krull & Husson, 1979).

[17]Various experimental studies have provided background on baseline viewing as well as shown that specific televised messages can elicit from viewers a variety of responses, ranging from hostility to relaxation. Lab studies also show that experimentally induced emotional and excitatory states can lead some viewers to gravitate to more or less specific kinds of content.

Representative publications or reviews by some of those most active in experimental research on television and film are Bryant and Zillmann (1984); Hawkins and Pingree (1986); Linz, Donnerstein, and Penrod (1984); Reeves, Thorson & Schleuder (1986); Wakshlag, Tims, Fitzmaurice, Hancock, and McCarthy (1986); Zillmann (1985); and Zillmann and Bryant (1985), to name a few.

Zillmann and Bryant's (1985) review of the experimental literature on arousal concludes that nature films generally rank lowest on arousal; followed by action drama, comedy, and game shows, which tend to be moderately arousing; with highly violent and fear-evoking drama toward the top of the continuum. Not surprisingly, highly violent and fear-evoking materials of a nonfictional variety (sports contests, newscasts) are even more arousing. They reported that sexual content is "among the strongest arousers available" (p. 164).

EEG studies, discussed in chapter 7, represent the other main trend in laboratory research aimed at assessing the viewing experience as it actually occurs (see, e.g., Appel, Weinstein, & Weinstein, 1979; Krugman, 1971; Mulholland, 1974; Walker, 1980; Weinstein, Appel, & Weinstein, 1980). For a review of EEG research and television viewing, see Rothschild, Thorson, Reeves, Hirsch, and Goldstein (1986).

[18]See, for example, Comstock, Chaffee, Katzman, McCombs, and Roberts (1978); Himmelweit, Swift, and Jaeger (1980); Hirsch (1977a); Lindlof (1987); LoScuito (1972); Lull (1987); McGaan (1983); NIMH (1982); and Robinson (1972a).

CHAPTER 4

Charting a New Course:
The Experience Sampling
Method

Behavior doesn't take place in a vacuum, it takes place in a world.
—Altmann (1984)

Considerable evidence suggests that . . . direct information from the person is the best source of data.
—Mischel (1973)

It is in the self commentary that the way to a scientific psychology must lie.
—Harré & Secord (1972)

It might be useful to consider for a moment how empirical research on the effects of television viewing is sometimes conducted. A university researcher persuades 40 undergraduate students from class to volunteer as research subjects. On a day and at a time predetermined by the researcher and anticipated for 2 weeks by the students, each subject travels to the research facility housed in an eight-story university building. The subjects get off the elevator and enter a room, 20 by 30 feet. The room is tiled in linoleum and illuminated by fluorescent lights. Arranged in the room are 40 stackable plastic chairs and a 23-inch color TV sitting atop a large mobile stand.

Before viewing, the subjects are asked to answer nearly 100 survey questions about their backgrounds, their normal viewing habits, and their attitudes on a variety of issues. After completing the survey, they sit and watch a preselected TV program for 15 minutes. Once they have finished viewing they are asked to answer a new set of questions about how they felt while viewing as well as some of the same attitude questions a second time. A second TV program is shown and the same questions are asked again. Data collection is now complete and each subject receives a few points of course credit and is thanked for their participation.

To be fair, researchers who study viewing in the lab do occasionally obtain research subjects from outside the university and some let respondents choose what they will view. Some try to make the laboratory setting more like a living room, with a couch, carpeting, a few plants, and snacks to eat. But even the best of attempts can only be an approximation of how people actually watch television in their own homes or wherever else they happen to view.[1]

For example, consider how one particular person actually views television on one particular evening.

Ms. Hankins arrives home one Thursday evening around 7:30 after an unusually taxing day teaching math to junior high school students. Her monthly late afternoon faculty meeting ran later than usual and then she got caught in traffic.

Her husband fixed dinner and fed the kids. He greets her at the door with a kiss and later with a reheated serving of spaghetti. Before putting her daughters to bed, Ms. Hankins debriefs her husband on the faculty meeting and how new policies will affect her life.

Her husband flicks on the living room TV searching through the channels three times with the remote control before discovering that one of their favorite movies from the 1940s has just begun on Channel 9. He sits in his recliner. Ms. Hankins props herself up on the couch, plate of spaghetti balanced between her chest and stomach, fork in one hand and a glass of wine within arm's reach.

At different moments over the next hour and 45 minutes, Ms. Hankins watches the movie, finishes her dinner and drink, glances at the mail, and occasionally converses with her husband about work, the kids, the movie, and her parents who are due for a weekend visit. She leaves the room three times—once for the bathroom, once for an apple in the kitchen, and once to answer the phone—the third wrong number that week.

On the couch she changes position a number of times. At different moments the movie makes her laugh and nearly cry in virtually the same places as the last time she viewed it. A few of her husband's remarks make her laugh, too, but he also makes her angry when discussing her parents' plans. She falls asleep on the couch just as the movie is winding up.

This is how one person might view television during one evening. The method we have employed and that we will describe shortly does not permit us to track a subject in this much detail, but across many respondents we *are* able to capture the multifaceted nature of viewing behavior as it occurs in real places and in real time. And in preference to the frequent subjects of much television research, the undergraduate psychology or communication major, we have examined data from a wide variety of people of varying ages and from different countries.

THE SAMPLES

The research in this book is based on findings from nine different Experience Sampling Method (ESM) studies conducted over the past 13 years. With the help of colleagues, more than 45,000 self-report observations collected from nearly 1,200 subjects have been analyzed. The samples include 92 older Canadian adults studied in 1982–1983, 105 Germans studied in 1986, 20 African and 20 U.S. graduate students living in the United States in 1980, and four separate samples totaling 837 Italian and United States adolescents who participated in studies in the years 1980, 1985, 1985–1988, and 1986–1988. We report findings from all of these groups but focus most of our analyses on 107 U.S. adults, aged 18–63 years, whose activities and experiences were sampled, one week at a time, over the period of 1 year from 1976 to 1977. Because most of our attention is focused on this sample, we describe the group in greater detail in the following pages. More information on the other samples is provided in the chapters that follow.

Selection of the Main Adult Sample

These 107 working adults volunteered to participate, without compensation, from five companies in the Chicago area. The companies were initially contacted for a study of work and daily life.[2] To study normal adults who worked, we initiated contacts with employers in order that respondents might be permitted to collect experience sampling data during work hours. Confidentiality was strictly maintained and each company was prohibited from access to any of the subjects' personal reports.

Various divisions and departments from each company participated and were selected by joint agreement between company executives and the research team. Subjects were free to choose whether they wished to participate and just over 50% volunteered. A small number were necessarily excluded due to illiteracy. Slightly over one third of the volunteers were then randomly selected to participate, leaving us with 133 respondents. Ultimately, 80%, or 107 subjects, completed the week of self-reporting.

The five companies and their respective participating employees included a manufacturer of office equipment (secretaries), a catalog sales company (secretaries and managers), a manufacturer of railway equipment (assembly line workers), an airline food preparation division (assembly line workers and managers), and a manufacturer of audio-visual equipment (assemblers, secretaries, and managers).

Sample Composition

Subject composition can be reviewed in Table 1. To summarize, 63% of the respondents were female, 37% were male. Twenty-nine percent were single and never married, 54% married, and 16% divorced or separated. There was one widowed, female subject. Just under 75% of the sample were White, 17% were Black, and 6.5% Hispanic.

Subjects ranged in age from 18 to 63 with a mean age of 36.6 years. Forty-three percent were over 35. The average annual earned income was about $28,000 (1989 dollars),[3] with incomes ranging from $14,000 to just under $60,000. Of the subjects, 25% worked at assembly line jobs;

TABLE 1
Sample Demographics

Variable	n	%	Variable	n	%
Sex			**Education**		
Male	40	37.4	Some high school	13	12.1
Female	67	62.6	Completed high school	34	31.8
			Some college	46	43.0
Marital Status			Completed college	11	10.3
Single	31	29.0	Some grad. school	2	1.9
Married	58	54.2	Completed grad. school	1	.9
Separated	5	4.7			
Divorced	12	11.2	**Occupation**		
Widowed	1	.9	Managers	38	35.5
			Clericals	41	39.3
Race			Assemblers	27	25.2
Amer. Indian ..	1	.9			
Black	18	16.8	**Age**		
Hispanic	7	6.5	19–24	20	18.7
White	79	73.8	25–34	28	26.2
Other	2	1.9	35–39	22	20.6
			40–47	18	16.8
Income[a]			48–63	19	17.7
Under $16,000	12	11.3			
16–24,000	57	53.7			
24–32,000	23	21.7			
32–40,000	8	7.5			
40–60,000	6	5.7			

[a]1989 dollars

39% were clerical workers or secretaries; and 36% were supervisors, buyers, and engineers; hereafter referred to as *managers*.

Of the group, 88% had completed high school, 43% had attended college, 13% had completed college.

Table 2 breaks the sample demographics down by occupation. As in the total population, there is not an equal distribution across different kinds of jobs. In this sample, 81% of the managers were male, whereas 93% of the clerical workers and 78% of the assemblers were female. There were few Black managers or clericals, but the assemblers were evenly divided between Blacks and Whites. Managers tended to be married and less frequently divorced than the clericals and assemblers who were much more likely to be single or divorced or separated.

Most managers had graduated from college or had attended at one time. Half of the clericals had gone beyond high school, but only 25% of the assemblers had ventured past secondary school. Table 2 shows that the chi-square tests run for each of these six demographic variables were

TABLE 2
Demographic Breakdown Percentages by Occupational Category

Category	Sex		Race		Marital Status		
	Male	*Female*	*White*	*Black*	*Single*	*Married*	*Div/Sep*
Managers	81	19	84	5	14	78	8
Clericals	7	93	84	10	36	43	19
Assemblers	22	78	44	44	41	37	22
X^2	49.5		26.8		15.3		
df	2		2		4		
p	.0000		.0008		.0180		

Category	Education[a]		Income[b]		Age		
	Low Ed.	*High Ed.*	*Under $24,000*	*Above $24,000*	*18–30*	*31–45*	*46–63*
Managers	14	86	19	81	22	43	35
Clericals	50	50	93	7	48	33	19
Assemblers	74	26	89	11	37	52	11
X^2	24.5		55.6		9.5		
df	2		2		4		
p	.0000		.0000		.0498		

[a]Educational level is broken down as follows: "low" education refers to those with a high school diploma or less education; "high" education includes those with some college or graduate education or college or graduate degrees.
[b]1989 dollars

all significant beyond the $p = .05$ level—most were beyond the $p = .001$ level.*

The sample was not meant to represent a cross-section of all adult TV viewers. Even with the many other samples from which data were collected, we do not represent all viewers. Chapter 5 presents a few findings from a sample of elderly respondents, but for all the other analyses that follow, unemployed and retired persons and housewives are not represented (see Frank & Greenberg, 1980; and Kubey, 1980 for analyses of these groups' viewing habits).

But although not perfectly representative of all groups that watch television, we believe the data are generally applicable to the research questions posed and that the findings characterize, in the main, general trends in viewing. This is because across the many different ESM studies examined, subjects of different ages and backgrounds and from different countries reported using and experiencing television in very similar ways. This is not to minimize differences, they do exist, and we point them out as well.

---

*For the reader unfamiliar with statistical terms or for those who may need a quick refresher, a brief review is presented.

The p value indicates the probability that a certain relationship or difference between measures occurred by chance. The smaller the p, the more *significant* the finding and the less likely the result was due simply to chance. For example, if $p < .01$ is reported this means that there is less than 1 chance in 100 that the result reported is due to chance. When we do not report a p value, the statistic in question was *not* significant (i.e., the probability due to chance was greater than $p < .05$—the generally accepted level of significance in the behavioral sciences). Occasionally we report p values that are nearly significant when we wish to bring a particular result to the reader's attention.

The symbol χ^2 above, or chi-square, simply tests whether the frequencies observed in a table are significantly different from the even distribution one would expect if there was no relation between the variables tabled.

A statistic that we report more frequently is the t test. It simply tells us whether the difference between two means is significant.

The statistic r, which we also frequently report, measures the strength of correlation between two measures or variables. R can range from a value of -1.0 to $+1.0$. The higher the number, the more closely related are the two variables. A correlation of shoe sizes, for example, with actual lengths of people's feet would be very high, probably around $r = .90$. Grade-point average (GPA) and IQ in a class of students might produce an r of .60. Negative correlations occur between measures that are inversely related (e.g., size of car engine and miles per gallon of gas). A correlation of 0 means that there is no relationship.

By squaring the correlation, we find the proportion of variation in one variable that is accounted for by variation in the other variable. In the example just given, 36% of the variation in GPA could be explained by knowing IQ.

Finally, the term n stands for the number of subjects or observations under study. The symbol, df, which we occasionally report stands for degrees of freedom, and also basically refers to the number of people or observations measured.

THE EXPERIENCE SAMPLING METHOD

On the Rationale for Naturalistic Approaches and the Limitations of the Lab

We are not alone in our preference for naturalistic methods over laboratory studies of television viewing, particularly to answer the kinds of questions that are being asked. Criticism of television researchers' dependence on the laboratory comes from many sources.[4] Take for example what James Anderson (1980) has written,

> The emphasis on experimentalism in communication studies has resulted in a fundamental imbalance in our discipline—nowhere more apparent (than) in . . . mass communication. . . . We have attempted to describe causes and consequences of televiewing without an adequate understanding of what it is and how it gets done. This imbalance has littered our field with hypotheses of little utility. (p. 2)

Or as Ulric Neisser (1976) suggested, researchers should make an effort to understand behavior "as it occurs in the ordinary environment and in the context of natural purposeful activity." Sarbin (1977) has similarly argued for "the study of the individual in his or her natural surroundings, in context, in the culture, and in the historical time" (p. 71).

Besides obviously lacking what Neisser called "ecological validity," findings from laboratory studies of television viewing are also criticized because they have often not matched findings from the field.[5] Two major field studies on television and aggression in adults conducted by Milgram and Shotland (1973) and by Loye, Gorney, and Steele (1977) offer little support for, or in the case of Feshbach and Singer (1971), actually contradict laboratory results.

Among the most serious problems in experimental studies of television viewing is the way in which the laboratory method interacts directly with the measurement of cognitive and emotional involvement, audience activity versus passivity, alertness, and concentration during viewing. It is not at all hard to imagine that research subjects will be much less relaxed and that they may view with greater concentration, alertness, and purpose when being observed in a lab, especially if they think that they will be asked questions about what they viewed afterward. Being wired up with electrodes for EEG measures would also obviously alter some, if not all, subjects' viewing experiences and very possibly distort the very phenomena of cortical arousal, attention, and concentration that lab researchers often study.

In many instances, laboratory research subjects' choices of what to view are extremely limited, if offered at all, and subjects often view with a group of people and/or people who are complete strangers to them. As mentioned earlier, all too often, the research subjects are undergraduate social science majors of very narrow age ranges, who receive partial academic credit for volunteering. Furthermore, experimental observations of viewing behavior also often track subjects for only a few minutes or for less than a hour rather than over the few hours in which viewing often takes place and in which viewing may become more passive.

Any of these factors may help explain why some of the findings to be reported have led to the conclusion that viewers are less alert and more passive when viewing at home and in their natural surroundings than some experimentalists have concluded from laboratory research.

Researchers have also been advised with increasing rapidity to examine the nature of media experiences. Denis McQuail and Michael Gurevitch (1974) have argued for the development of techniques that would permit researchers to study media experiences using subjective accounts. To this end, it is their view that "descriptive, qualitative, and exploratory procedures are more appropriate than controlled experiments and representative sample surveys." Studies that fulfill their ideal "are likely to be small but detailed and intensive" (pp. 295–296).

The present application of the Experience Sampling Method (ESM) to the study of television very much fits this description. The method permits the intensive examination of a wide range of reportable human feelings, thoughts, and behaviors as they occur in the normal course of daily life.

How Experience Sampling Method Data Are Collected

ESM data consist of self-reports made at random times during the waking hours of a normal week. The scheduling of self-reports is controlled by one-way radio communication. Each subject carries a pocket-sized electronic paging device (a "pager" or "beeper") for a period of 1 week as well as a booklet of self-report forms. Radio signals with a 50-mile transmission radius are emitted from a radio transmitting tower according to a predetermined random schedule. The signals cause the beepers to make a series of audible "beeps" that serve as the stimulus for subjects to complete a self-report form.* Although the form asks approximately

---

*For further information on ESM procedures and on how to resolve some of the methodological and statistical problems that crop up, see Csikszentmihalyi and Larson (1987); Kubey (1984); Kubey (1987a); Larson and Csikszentmihalyi (1983); and Larson and Delespaul (in press).

40 questions, the great majority of subjects are able, after a bit of experience, to complete it in less than 2 minutes.[6]

The schedule in this particular study called for seven to nine signals per day at random times between the hours of 8 a.m. and 10 p.m. Signals were not allowed to come closer together than 15 minutes or further apart than 3½ hours.[7] At least one signal was sent in every 2-hour block of time, but respondents were not made aware of this scheduling nor, as we have noted, did they have any idea that television viewing would be singled out for study (see Appendix A for the random signalling schedule used). For example, this set of ESM respondents was not asked which television programs they were viewing when signalled. Television content data has been collected in other ESM studies and findings from these data are reported in the next chapter.

As mentioned earlier, 80% of the initial sample successfully completed the week's scheduled sampling. Those who dropped out usually decided to do so on the first or second day. The most typical reasons for quitting were forgetting the pager or self-report booklet or being "too busy" to fill them out.

On average, each subject responded to 85.3% (or 47.8) of the 55 to 60 signals sent.[8] The difference between signals sent and reports completed by each respondent was due to occasional signal failure (three to four per week), to the respondent's forgetfulness, to unsuitable circumstances, or because respondents were temporarily out of the transmitter's range. Fortunately, none of the respondents took a weekend or business trip out of town and beyond the 50-mile transmission radius.

It was assumed that the first few reports might be most subject to method reaction effects stemming from the novelty of carrying the pager. For this reason it was decided to eliminate the first three reports for each subject from the database, but subjects were not made aware of this procedure. This elimination resulted in 4,791 records for the purposes of analysis. Actually, intensive examination of possible novelty effects studied with respondents carrying pagers over many weeks has demonstrated few problems (Hormuth, in press).

In order to familiarize respondents with what they were to do with the pagers and self-report forms, each subject participated in a 45-minute introductory session immediately prior to the onset of signalling at which time they learned more about the study and filled out a sample self-report form (an Experience Sampling Form or ESF) under supervision (see Appendix B for the instructions given to research assistants and respondents).

Subjects were requested to respond to as many signals as possible during the week, but it was understood that there could be circumstances in which it would be difficult or impossible to respond or have the pager turned on. A beeping sound might be too distracting, for example, at a concert, under pressure at work, or in church. Driving a car proved to be the most inconvenient situation for immediate response, but in most such instances people were able to respond within a few minutes of the signal.

After being signalled, each respondent entered the day's date, the time, and the time the ESF was actually completed. It was decided prior to data collection to exclude reports for any sheet filled out more than 20 minutes after a signal. Such delayed reporting occurred in less than 1% of cases and the vast majority of sheets were filled out immediately and within 1 minute of the signal.

Other Procedures

Two to 4 weeks before experience sampling began, a lengthy questionnaire was administered (see Appendix C) which included standard demographic items, a large number of work attitude questions and statements, questions about the person's most preferred activities, a modified version of the Maddi Alienation Index (Maddi, Kobasa, & Hoover, 1979), as well as 20 sentence-completion items. Within the first week after the completion of experience sampling, research assistants conducted extended (2- to 4-hour) personal interviews and debriefing sessions.

Using the ESM to Measure the External Dimensions of Experience

Any experience, from watching television to brushing one's teeth, has both an internal and an external dimension. The *internal dimension* is concerned with the nature and quality of consciousness: how people think and feel. *External dimensions* focus on situations that interact with and alter how people think and feel.

In this study, we have defined three external dimensions with regard to where people were, what they were doing, and whom they were with as they were signalled. The first variable, then, is *location,* and is based on what our respondents said in response to the open-ended question, "As you were beeped, where were you?" Responses were coded into 36 environments and four major groupings: work, home, public, and transportation (see Appendix D). Agreement among our coders for the 36 environments was 97%.

The second external variable refers to the person's *activity.* On the pager sheet respondents are asked, "As you were beeped, what was the

MAIN thing you were doing?" We also asked people "What other things were you doing?" In this way, we obtained reports of *primary* and *secondary* activities. These were coded into 154 categories that were later collapsed into a variety of more inclusive classifications such as eating, grooming, working, housework, and so on (see Appendix E).

The third external dimension is *companionship*. Here, our respondents completed the statement: "Were you: alone, with friends, with co-workers, with supervisor, with family, with strangers, other?"

Once data on the three external dimensions were collected, they could be used in varying combinations in subsequent analyses. For some questions, self-reports of location and activity were employed simultaneously to create *activity contexts* such as working at home or home leisure. For others, the companionship coordinate allowed even greater specificity. It was possible, for example, to analyze data in terms of *social* activity contexts such as watching television alone at home or eating with friends in public. As is seen later, the social and environmental dimensions of an activity can substantially alter how that activity is experienced.

Because respondents were asked to denote what day and time of day they were signalled, it was possible to subdivide the data even more precisely. In this way we could examine whether people grew more tired as a day drew on or, for example, how people felt while working alone on weekday afternoons before a heavy night of television viewing.

Measuring the Internal Features of Experience

The purpose of gathering information about the respondents' subjective experience is to ascertain how internal states vary in the natural course of daily activity. Under what circumstances and at what times is experience most satisfying, most ordered, or most complex?

For these purposes, experience may be thought of as that information that we find in consciousness when we turn our attention inward. Although experiential states and processes are extremely varied, they have been divided by psychologists into three main types: emotion; cognition; and conation, or will (Hilgard, 1980).

Emotion (or affect) can be thought to refer to the internal condition of experience as a whole—whether it is basically positive or negative. At a very basic level, negative emotional states generally denote the conveyance of internal information that the person's goals are not being met in some way, thereby creating disorder in experience. Positive emotions such as happiness or joy, for example, quite reliably indicate that at least one or more of a person's short- or long-term goals is being met.

This model of emotion is intentionally simple. It does not explain in detail the various nuances among states such as love, elation, grief, anger, boredom, fear, and so on. Still, if one wishes to describe at a fundamental level what underlies most emotional states, the entropy-negentropy continuum is both useful and encompassing.

Cognition here refers to how attention interacts with the environment, and transforms otherwise meaningless stimuli into useful information. As suggested in chapter 1, high concentration is indicative of involvement in cognitively complex processes. Finally, *conation* (will or motivation) denotes processes by which people direct their mental and physical energies and manage to sustain and focus them on goals.

Having described what we mean by internal and external features of experience, we can now explain how the ESM is used to assess entropy, negentropy, and complexity in consciousness and how these phenomena were operationalized in our study.

Affect and Activation.   The assessment of affect and emotion is critical to understanding human behavior. As Wessman and Ricks (1966) have written:

> It is becoming increasingly clear that affect plays a critical part in initiating, maintaining, and regulating man's environmental encounters. . . . It instigates, accompanies, facilitates, and sustains active engagement by human beings oriented toward complex worlds that they in part create. (p. 3)

The emotional dimension of experience has been studied frequently and thus there are traditions in how it is conceptualized and measured. We were concerned with affect but also with the closely related dimension of emotional state that we call *activation*. To measure these, items with opposite terms at opposing ends of a 7-point scale were employed, following Osgood, Suci, and Tannenbaum (1957). One end of the scale represents the *negentropic state* (happy, strong, free), whereas the other end represents the *entropic state* (sad, weak, constrained). Each time they were signalled, respondents marked how they felt on these scales or whether they felt neither way. The completed self-report form in Figure 1 is offered as an example.

In previous ESM research, the two factors of affect and activation have been shown to be related but also to consist of relatively discrete variables derived via varimax rotated factor analysis.[9] For the purposes of this study, the affect cluster consists of the highly intercorrelated variables of sad–happy, irritable–cheerful, hostile–friendly, and lonely–sociable. The activation cluster consists of the variables passive–active, drowsy–alert, weak–strong, and bored–excited.

Date: **8/09**   Time Beeped: **9:30**   am/**pm**   Time Filled Out: **9:30**

AS YOU WERE BEEPED

Where were you? *Livingroom*

What was the MAIN thing you were doing? *watching TV*

Why were you doing this? (circle answers)   I had to do it................yes
I wanted to do it...........(yes)
I had nothing else to do.....yes

What other things were you doing? *nothing*

What were you thinking about when you were beeped? *getting up and going to bed*

	no	some	quite	very
How well were you concentrating?		(4)		
Was it hard to concentrate?			(7)	
How self-conscious were you?	(0)			
Were you in control of your actions?				(9)

0   1   2   3   4   5   6   7   8   9

Describe your mood and physical states as you were beeped:

	very much	quite much	some what	do not feel either	some what	quite much	very much	
hostile	0	o	.	(-)	.	o	0	friendly
alert	0	o	.	-	.	o	(0)	drowsy
happy	0	o	.	(-)	.	o	0	sad
tense	0	o	.	-	.	o	(0)	relaxed
suspicious	0	o	.	(-)	.	o	0	trusting
irritable	0	o	.	(-)	.	o	0	cheerful
strong	0	o	.	-	(.)	o	0	weak
active	0	o	.	-	.	(o)	0	passive
lonely	0	o	.	(-)	.	o	0	sociable
creative	0	o	.	(-)	.	o	0	dull
resentful	0	o	.	(-)	.	o	0	satisfied
free	0	o	.	(-)	.	o	0	constrained
excited	0	o	.	(-)	.	o	0	bored

	none	slight	bothersome	severe
headache	(+)			
body aches	(+)			
other physical symptoms	(+)			

0   1   2   3   4   5   6   7   8   9

FIGURE 1.   A sample experience sampling form.

Were you: (✓) alone ( ) with friends ( ) with co-workers ( ) with supervisor

( ) with family ( ) with strangers ( ) other _____

CIRCLE THE NUMBERS BELOW THAT BEST DESCRIBE HOW YOU FELT ABOUT WHAT YOU WERE DOING WHEN YOU WERE BEEPED. For example, if you felt that the activity was very challenging for you, you might circle a number toward the right hand side of the scale.

```
                                    0   1   2   3   4   5   6   7   8   9
Challenges of the activity          +--(1)--+---+---+---+---+---+---+---+
                                    low                             high

Your skills in the activity         +---+---+---+---+--(5)--+---+---+---+
                                    low                             high

Do you wish you had been doing      (0)--+---+---+---+---+---+---+---+---+
   something else?                  not at all                very much

Was anything at stake for you in    (0)--+---+---+---+---+---+---+---+---+
   the activity?                    nothing                   very much
```

List all the things you remember doing since you were last beeped (or in the last hour or so). CHECK YOUR ANSWERS--WRITE DOWN HOW OFTEN IF MORE THAN ONCE.

_____ day dreaming
_____ talking or whistling or singing to yourself
_____ watching people or things or just staring into space
  ✓   watching TV or going to a movie
_____ listening to the radio or a record
_____ listening to a presentation or lecture
  ✓   reading a book or magazine or newspaper
_____ reading something related to work or school
  ✓   snacking, smoking, or chewing on things
_____ chewing on objects (pencil, paperclip, finger . . .)
_____ walking, pacing, or running
_____ small muscle movements (tapping your finger, swinging your leg)
_____ rubbing, grooming, or scratching yourself
_____ typing or working some other office machine
_____ doing something different on your job
                    (specify _____)
_____ driving a car or motorcycle
_____ riding a bicycle
_____ playing a game or sport alone
_____ shopping or browsing
_____ doing art work, playing a musical instrument or other hobby
                    (specify _____)
_____ cleaning, cooking or other work at home
_____ talking or joking with friends or relatives
_____ talking with coworkers or fellow students
_____ talking with supervisor or teacher
_____ talking on the telephone related to job or school
_____ talking on the phone to a friend or relative
_____ parties or games with others
_____ touching or holding a child or adult

FILL OUT ONCE EVERY 24 HOUR PERIOD

Time you went to bed last night: _____

Approximately how long did it take you to fall asleep (in minutes): _____

Time you woke up this morning: _____

How would you describe the quality of your sleep last night?

```
            0       1       2       3       4       5       6       7       8       9
            +-------+-------+-------+-------+-------+-------+-------+-------+-------+
         very poor          moderately          moderately          very good
                             poor                  good
```

Cognitive Efficiency. As cognition has been studied increasingly in recent years, it has become abundantly clear that individuals vary dramatically in their ability to process information (Carver & Scheier, 1981). Cognitive efficiency also obviously varies for the same person across time. Drawing on current research, everyday language, and our particular research concerns, the following three questions were adopted: "How well were you concentrating?," "Was it hard to concentrate?," and "How self-conscious were you?" The respondents rated themselves on each of these items on 10-point scales from "no" or "not at all" to "very." As we have suggested, concentration is indicative of involvement in cognitively complex mental operations. These measures can also be compared to Salomon's (1981, 1983) measure of "Amount of Invested Mental Effort."

These items reflect the application of mental energy. A person may concentrate attention with ease as when driving a car on the open road or with difficulty when studying complex and unfamiliar material. Self-consciousness is of particular interest because it generally interferes with focused information processing by withdrawing mental energy to monitor the self and internal processes.

Intrinsic Motivation. In comparison to emotion and cognition there is much less precedent for studying will or conation. Of particular interest is how much people actually want to do whatever it is that they are doing—in other words, the extent of intrinsic motivation. ESM studies have consistently shown that among the most central determinants of the quality of experience is whether people want to do what they are doing, and whether they feel free or constrained in their actions.

Responses to a number of questions have proven to be powerful descriptors of intrinsically motivated experience. The first of these questions is: "Do you wish you had been doing something else?" Responses are made on a 10-point scale, once again graded between "not at all" and "very much." Additional measures include respondents' ratings of their sense of being in control of their actions and reports of freedom versus constraint as well as responses to the question, "Why were you doing this?" Possible responses included "I wanted to do it," "I had to do it," and "I had nothing else to do." All of these variables tap facets of what a person who is intrinsically motivated theoretically should think and feel (De Charms & Muir, 1978; Lepper & Greene, 1978).

Other Items. Respondents were also asked to jot down what they were thinking about at the time of the signal. Additional items measured other subjective variables and involved the rating of the *stakes, skills,* and *challenges* the person perceived relative to their main activity.* (See Side 2 of the ESF in Figure 1.) The ratings of perceived challenges and skills are of particular interest in the conclusion of chapter 7 when television viewing experience is examined with respect to a model of optimal experience.

Respondents were also asked to check if they had engaged in any of 28 activities in the previous hour or since the previous signal. Finally, once each day, in the morning, respondents reported on the length and quality of the previous night's sleep.

CAN WE TRUST SELF-REPORTS?

By necessity, internal states have always been studied by more or less indirect means such as self-reports, inferences from facial expressions, and physiological measures that include the electroencephalograph, galvanic skin response, and heart rate. Although there has long been concern about self-reports (Nisbett & Wilson, 1977), psychologists have demonstrated that they are often quite valid and that they reflect a stable attribution process.†

Depending on what one is studying, the best way to learn what people are thinking and feeling is often simply to ask them. As Gordon Allport (1953) and others have shown, people are capable of describing and differentiating their feelings with considerable facility. Most adults and children as young as 8 years old can make sensitive assessments of their emotions (Carver & Scheier, 1981; Ellingwood, 1969; Kotsch, Gerbing, & Schwartz, 1982; Wolman, Lewis, & King, 1971).

When it comes to studying the quality of experience there is no better single source of information than what a person says about how he or she feels.[10] In contrast, even the best trained observer has no direct access to the content of another person's experience. In fact, inferences about internal states made by outsiders are generally less reliable than

---

A Note to the Reader: It should be kept in mind throughout this research that higher numerical scores and means denote higher reports of challenge, skill, stakes, concentration, difficulty of concentration, control, self-consciousness, and wish to be doing something else. Responses were later recoded so that positive emotional states were always on the high end of the scale (5,6,7) and negative moods on the low end (1,2,3). A response of "4" meant that the person did not feel either mood. Higher scores also generally refer to more positive states except in the case of self-consciousness, difficulty of concentration, and wish to be doing something else.

†In using terms derived from everyday language (i.e., native categories such as "happy," "excited," and "bored") we have followed Mandler (1975) and Ryle's (1949) advice that mental and emotional states are best studied using the very linguistic forms that people give them.

reports made by research subjects (Lazarus, 1966; Mischel, 1981) and acceptable validity coefficients have long been reported between "expert" ratings and self-ratings of happiness and well-being (Goldings, 1954; Jasper, 1930; Washburne, 1941; Wessman & Ricks, 1966).

Harré and Secord (1972) claimed that it is the uniquely human ability of one's own self-monitoring that makes experiential and self-report information both possible and dependable.

> The things people say about themselves and other people should be taken seriously as reports of data relevant to phenomena that "really exist" and which are relevant to the explanation of behavior. Traditional arguments against taking self-reports seriously overlook the fact that at least some statements are not a "sign" of a state of mind, but themselves constitute that state of mind (e.g., to complain is to be discontented). It is through reports of feelings, plans, intentions, beliefs, reasons, and so on that the meaning of social behavior and rules underlying social acts can be discovered. (p. 7)

It is also worth noting that in everyday life we accept what people tell us about their internal states. When a person tells us she is bored, we assume that she *is* bored. Ryle (1949) pointed out that it would be odd to ask: "Are you sure?"

A different problem of validating self-reports, however, is akin to one of the child's earliest epistemological and phenomenological questions, namely: "How do I know that my experience of the color I call 'blue' is the same experience as what you call 'blue'?" But just as most everyone agrees on what we mean by blue or red, so too do people agree on what it is like to feel bored, happy, or tense—the very mood adjectives that appear on the pager sheets.

In summary, valid and rich data about people's inner experiences and their level of mental activity can be collected by simply asking people to report their immediate experiences using a checklist or other self-report form. For many mass communication research purposes, this approach is preferable to ignoring people's ability to report on their own experience, and instead trying to surmise or reconstruct it by measuring whether they are looking at a TV set, or by taking measures of the electrical activity in the brain.

Assessing Reliability

It should also be kept in mind that psychologists normally attempt to assess a stable dimension of the person, whereas the ESM measures variability over time within persons. ESF items, therefore, should reflect personal consistency *and* variability across time in response to external events. Indeed, ESM studies have demonstrated both strong personal consistency as well as variation.

For the sample of U.S. adults, for example, the average correlation coefficient for individual affect and activation means between the first and second halves of the week was .72 ($p < .001$) for both cluster variables, and for the variables of concentration, skill, and challenge it was .61 ($p < .001$).[11] The overall correlation for amount of variability between the first and second halves was .56 ($p < .001$). Furthermore, the interrelationships between items are strong and stable from the first to the second half of the week (Graef, 1979) and data from a 2-year ESM follow-up study with adolescent subjects demonstrated remarkable stability of individual response characteristics over that period (Freeman, 1982).[12]

It is also noteworthy that in the debriefing interview, except for two minor exceptions, people described their week as being "typical" or "average." In the estimation of over 90% of respondents, the signalling caught them in typical weekly activities.

Validity

Let us take a relatively verifiable measure, such as the amount of time spent in activities, as a starting point in the examination of validity. Allocations of time estimated in this study are quite similar to those obtained with the diary method of sampling used by Robinson and Converse (1967) and Szalai (1972) for a representative U.S. sample. Over comparable activities, the two methods produced a high Spearman rank-order correlation of .92 (Csikszentmihalyi & Graef, 1980). Robinson and Converse's subjects watched approximately 20% more television and more frequently engaged in sexual intercourse, but these discrepancies are due to differences in methodology and, in particular, the fact that our subjects were not signalled past 10 p.m. when a fair percentage of adult television viewing and sexual activity takes place. Furthermore, the frequency of television viewing for our subjects is also somewhat lower because they are all full-time employees and the vast majority of their viewing is limited, at least on weekdays, to the evening.

Many contingency checks increase confidence in the veracity of self-reports. For example, subjects—as they should, if honest—almost invariably indicate being with others when they report talking as their activity. In those instances where subjects report being alone *and* talking, further checking has shown that they were invariably talking on the phone. Subjects likewise never report watching television at work or working the assembly line at home. Furthermore, television watching rarely occurs between 8 a.m. and 4 p.m. on weekdays, but occurs with much greater frequency during these same hours on Saturday and Sunday—just as common sense would suggest and has been demonstrated with diary methods and A. C. Nielsen and Arbitron ratings.

Such basic consistencies and similarities to diary results demonstrate that at least as far as social contexts, time of day, and open-ended environmental and activity reports go, subjects were honest and reports are valid. To then check on the validity of mood state reports, it is instructive to study them with regard to these same validated social context and activity reports. In examining the sociable–lonely item, for example, people almost invariably report feeling more sociable when in the company of others as opposed to when they are alone. Moreover, people consistently report feeling most sociable at parties, playing games, or eating, and less sociable while working or traveling on public transportation even though they may still be in the vicinity of other people.

Internal or construct validity can be extended by examining the relationship between the sociable–lonely item and other mood reports. Feeling sociable is correlated .55 with friendly–hostile, .32 with alert–drowsy, and .08 with concentration. With the number of observations ranging above 4,700, all of these correlations were significant beyond the $p = .001$ level.

The magnitude and order of these correlations make logical sense. As Bradburn (1969) wrote, "The fact that self-reports confirm our everyday expectations in so many cases gives us confidence in their validity in those cases where they do not support common belief. . . . Direct reports of individual happiness have considerable validity" (pp. 39, 52).

Such "bootstrap" approaches to construct validation are recommended by Cronbach and Meehl (1955) and have proved legitimate and useful in our research as well as that of others. As the relationships just outlined demonstrate, the method is taken seriously by respondents. There is little reason to believe that they are doing anything but reporting their internal states as best they can.

Moreover, an individual's self-reports for the whole week of sampling tell a coherent story for that person. For persons who have experienced a disappointment in midweek, there is an immediate drop in affect and, then, a gradual return to baseline. When more serious disruptions have occurred, the week's affect ratings swing from medium or high to low.

Other ESM studies have afforded additional evidence of reliability and validity (see Csikszentmihalyi & Larson, 1987, for a review). Marlin Hoover (1983) has shown that heart rate is significantly and positively related to ESM self-reports of activation and significantly but somewhat less positively related to self-reports of anxiety.[13] Patrick Mayers (1978) demonstrated that students' ESM self-reports of concentration and involvement in class correlated with teachers' ratings of student involvement in class as well as with final grades.[14] Furthermore, remarkable similarities have been observed between Italian and U.S. teenagers' moods across a wide range of typical daily activities (Carli, Fave, & Massimini, 1988).

A WEEK IN THE LIFE OF TWO WOMEN

The ESM has now been described and the rationale for its application presented. But before launching into the findings it may prove interesting to illustrate two subjects' week of experiential reports. The following figures also provide a taste of what the ESM, in conjunction with other data, can tell about the nature of individual lives. We conclude the chapter, then, with the presentation of two subjects' records for a week of sampling.

The subjects worked for two different companies but carried pagers during the same week.[15] As a result, most of the signals occurred at the same time for both women. (They were both watching "Planet of the Apes" at the 8:55 p.m. signal Wednesday evening.) We present illustrations of Subject A's week of reports on the happy–sad and active–passive variables (Figures 2 and 3), whereas for Subject B, we present the happy–sad responses only (Figure 4). Note that the subjects' thoughts are presented inside parentheses and quotation marks. Features of each subject's identity have been changed to preserve anonymity.

Subject A

Subject A is a 56-year-old widowed White female, who lives alone and approximately 30 minutes from her job as a senior administrative assistant in a major national company. She spends part of her time teaching company procedures to new employees and executives and has worked for the company for over 20 years. She rates her job as "moderately satisfying" and is most disappointed by the lack of opportunity for further advancement. Her major complaint about her job is having to answer the same questions repeatedly and constant interruptions by telephone calls. She most enjoys baking, knitting, swimming, playing the piano, and spending time with her grandchildren.

By most indications, the subject is a fairly happy and well-adjusted person. She scored positively on every subscale of the Maddi Alienation Index. Her most serious concerns are with financing her retirement and

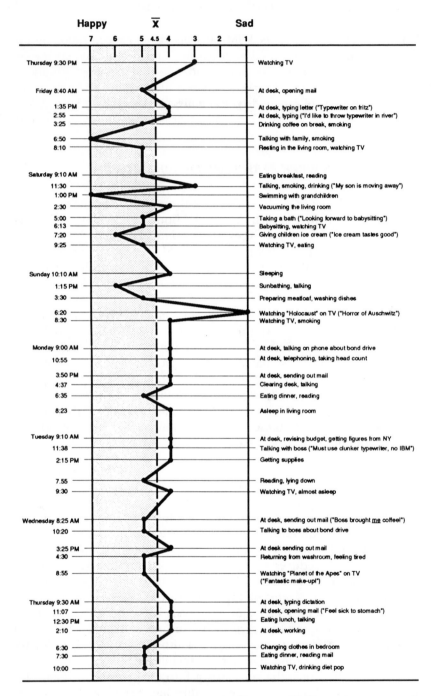

FIGURE 2. Subject A's week of happy–sad self-reports.

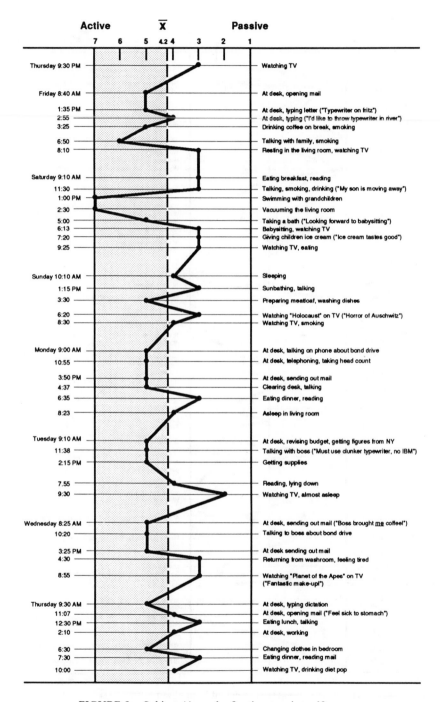

FIGURE 3. Subject A's week of active–passive self-reports.

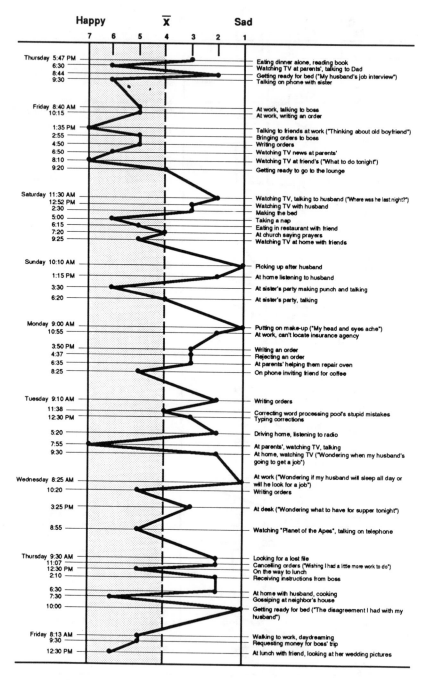

FIGURE 4. Subject B's week of happy–sad self-reports.

with the future welfare of her children and grandchildren. Among her regrets is having had to work when her children were growing. She reports occasional loneliness but good health and deep, effortless sleep. Her sentence completions are upbeat.

The subject watched somewhat more television than the rest of the group. Except for one occasion of viewing at her son's house while babysitting, all of her viewing took place when she was alone at home. As is seen in the chapters ahead, for adults who live alone, television is often used as a social substitute to ward off loneliness.

During the debriefing interview, the subject volunteered that a few times each week she becomes so engrossed in a television program that she forgets her problems and feels like she's in "another world." Her low moment for the entire week, one of high tension, sadness, and hostility occurred while watching a rerun of "Holocaust," among the very few extreme and negative affective reports of television viewing from the entire sample.

Except for watching "Holocaust," her weekend moods tend to be better and more labile than during the week at work when she usually reports feeling neither happy or sad. On weekends, her activity, and therefore her experience, is much more under her control than during the week at work. Her moods also tend to be better on weekday evenings once she is home from work or with her grandchildren. Television is occasionally associated with a good mood but just as frequently with a negative one. On the active–passive variable, it can be seen that television viewing, as for most people, is usually reported as a passive experience.

Reports such as these, and their accompanying mood and cognitive state ratings provide the daily experiential data for ESM studies. The record represents a fairly typical range of work and leisure activities over the course of a 7-day period. The respondent confirmed that the pager had caught her doing the things she usually does in an average week: "I got a kick out of it, answering the questions and all. . . . A couple of times I just couldn't stop work to fill out the form. It didn't catch me eating out on one evening, but mostly caught me doing the usual things."

Subject B

Subject B is a married 34-year-old White female. She also works as an administrative assistant and spends most of her time at work answering phones, and taking sales orders or resolving problems with them. She reports that her job is monotonous and feels that she functions too often as a telephone operator. Like Subject A, she dislikes the constant interruption of the telephone and having her concentration disrupted so frequently.

She reports that her greatest pleasures in life are reading, talking to people, and going to a play or dancing at a nearby lounge. Each of these activities provide "escape" and entry into a "different world." She feels best when dancing because "I am at ease with myself because I'm not me." If she couldn't go dancing, there would "be nothing for me, just existing."

The Maddi Alienation Index revealed that the subject scored high on the need for fantasy. She strongly agreed with the statements that "it would be exciting to have a secret life" and that "the most exciting times in my day are those when I am daydreaming or fantasizing." The Index also indicated that she is "alienated from self." Here she agreed with the statement that "I rarely understand why I think and feel as I do." Also striking is her comment that when she is "at ease" she is not herself.

A disturbing sense of unhappiness, failure, and need for escape comes across in her sentence completions. Some examples:

I can't	"sleep at night without pills"
I failed	"myself"
The future	"holds nothing for me"
Marriage	"is a failure"
Sometimes	"I want to kill myself"
What pains me	"is my failure in life"
I hate	"myself"
I am very	"unhappy"
I secretly	"wish I could run away and start a new life"

Her self-reports on the happy–sad variable as seen in Figure 4 fluctuate much more than do Subject A's and are lower on average (mean of 4.0 vs. 4.5). These reports help clarify the sources of enjoyment and unhappiness in her life. Work is repetitive and unrewarding and while at work she often reports daydreaming, her thoughts go to "an old boyfriend," "what I'll do for entertainment tonight," and "maybe there'll be a party" (not shown).

There is a good deal of evidence that Subject B's relationship with her husband is conflicted and disintegrating. Whenever she reports being with him or thinking about him she reports being sad (scores of 1, 2, or 3). Her best reports on the happy–sad variable are at her friend's house (6.5), at her parents' or sister's (5.3), or at home on the phone with her friend or sister (5.3). Relative to being with her husband, even being alone at home is not bad.

It is interesting to note how important the telephone can be to a person experiencing frequent unhappiness and disappointment. The phone links her to positive relationships and it is only at these times that she feels happy at home. Time at home with her husband is unpleasant and her concern about his not working seems to be wreaking havoc with many of the experiences that occur apart from him. This may well be why she spends a fair amount of time at her parents' or at the neighbors'. (Not surprisingly, the couple divorced about a year after the data were collected.)

It is possible that experience at home with her husband might be even more unpleasant were they not watching television. It may be that the subject uses television as a distraction, for escape and company, and as a support and atmospheric barrier in a home situation that has become conflicted. But we cannot begin to disentangle whether her use of television (or her frequent visits at others' homes) is merely symptomatic of problems, causative, or neither of these.

Just as it is difficult to disentangle cause from effect in one person, it is also difficult when we aggregate self-reports across many people. But that is one of the things that will be attempted in the chapters that follow. But before we tackle more complex analyses, let us first describe in detail when, where, and how people use and experience television.

ENDNOTES

[1]For some, measures of viewing need to be taken "in situ, not in the laboratory" (Bechtel et al., 1972, p. 274; Robinson, 1972a, 1972b). Experimentalists *have* studied emotional and behavioral induction in laboratory conditions, sometimes with manipulations or deceptions, and often with little or no regard to baseline TV viewing. Diary methods have proved valuable but their use has generally been limited to the study of program choices and time devoted to television. Furthermore, according to Bechtel et al. (1972), for every 4 hours of reported viewing in diaries, only 3 hours are actually spent viewing the TV set. The EEG has not been applied to the study of television viewing outside the laboratory, nor is it reasonably unobtrusive. In summary, diaries, behavior logs, the electroencephalograph, laboratory experiments, surveys, and stimulated recall methods each fail to measure viewing in the flow of a person's daily experience and within its typical environmental and behavioral context. See Webster and Wakshlag (1985) for a review and critique of many of the most popular television exposure research methods.

[2]Carrying out analysis on any database originally designed for other purposes presents a variety of special problems, but in this instance there is at least one distinct advantage: confidence that none of the 107 subjects who completed the week of sampling was influenced by the specific research concerns of the present study.

Previous studies of television utilizing the diary method have been biased by evaluation apprehension and other method reaction effects that caused respondents to view somewhat less, more selectively, and to miss fewer minutes of any particular show (LoScuito, 1972). These ESM self-reports of television viewing are less likely to have been similarly tainted by subject or experimenter expectancies, as television only became a topic for research after the collection of the data had been completed.

[3]The consumer price index was used to convert all references to income to 1989 dollars. This involved a simple doubling of all income figures from 1976 to 1977.

[4]See for example, Brodbeck and Jones (1963); Hirsch (1977a); Liebert and Schwartzberg (1977); LoScuito (1972); McGhee (1980); Singer (1980); and Withey (1980).

[5]See Bechtel et al. (1972); Comstock et al. (1978); Hovland (1959); Lindlof (1982); Salomon (1979).

[6]People who envision assembly line workers with a conveyor belt moving before them may wonder how such persons could fill out self-reports while on the job. All of the assembly line workers in this study worked on nonmoving materials and were able to stop for the few moments it takes to complete a self-report form.

[7]The signals were transmitted according to a different pattern for each day of the week, and the same pattern for the same day of the week. Thus, the week's sequence varied according to which day of the week a subject began carrying the pager.

[8]The range of completed forms ran from 30 to 56 sheets or from 54% to 100%.

[9]Details of factor analysis with ESM variables can be found elsewhere (Csikszentmihalyi & Larson, 1984; Graef, 1979; Kubey, 1984; Mayers, 1978).

[10]Walter Mischel (1973) has written: "Considerable evidence suggests that . . . direct information from the person is the best source of data. . ."

[11]In a similar ESM study of 75 adolescents, the correlations between individual mean scores in the first half and second half of the week was .75 for "free-constrained," .59 for "wish to be doing something else," and .83 for skills (Larson, 1979).

In Salomon's (1984) studies of Amount of Invested Mental Effort (AIME) for general television viewing, reliability of self-reports of AIME over a 2-week period were measured at .67. Number of inferences about a television show correlated .72 with AIME for a television show just watched.

[12]In the follow-up study of 27 adolescents, the average correlation between individual means after a 2-year interval was .77 for affect and .62 for activation (see also Csikszentmihalyi & Larson, 1984). Norman Bradburn (1969) has similarly shown that an individual's global report of happiness is highly stable over time (mean gamma coefficients of over .70 for both sexes).

[13]Edward Donner, in an experimental adaptation of the ESF induced stress in business executives by presenting them with a difficult, timed intelligence test. The executives indicated significantly greater stress and tension on the ESF immediately upon completing the test.

[14]Larson (1979) has reported that many of these same high school students reported re-experiencing the feelings reported in pager booklets during debriefing sessions.

[15]There is imperfect correspondence across the two women's records due to one or the other occasionally missing signals or not being able to report.

CHAPTER 5

The Use and Experience of Television in Everyday Life

Many critics and scholars blithely assume that television viewers sit before the tube passive and prostrate, attention totally transfixed by the screen.
—Hirsch and Panelas (1980)

Television is a very potent, intimate presence in many homes . . . scientific studies and tests fall short of capturing this reality of how individual human beings live with television.
—Nietzke (1978)

Assumptions about the nature of television viewing often lead to particular kinds of conclusions about the medium's ultimate impact. But at least as far as some critics are concerned, social scientists have not yet sufficiently answered many questions about how television viewing is used and experienced.

The first portion of this chapter focuses on the most basic questions about viewing: where does it take place, with whom, and at what time of day? Does all other behavior cease once the television is turned on or do people continue to engage in other activities while they watch? By placing television viewing in its behavioral, social, temporal, and environmental contexts we hope to provide answers to these questions.

In addition to finding out whom people view with and what other activities engage their attention while they view, a more important question concerns how television is experienced. Do people feel passive when they view? Does viewing make them feel tense or relaxed? How does viewing differ from other experiences and how uniform is the experience (i.e., do people feel much the same way when viewing or do different groups of people report different experiences)?

The answers to these questions will begin to help explain why people use the medium and how viewing affects them. To begin at the beginning, we wish to first estimate the proportion of time the respondents in this study spent in various activities during the week, including TV viewing.

HOW OFTEN DO PEOPLE VIEW TELEVISION?

Table 3 lists the percentages of time spent at home, at work, and in public, and in 17 major activities. As can be seen, over the 7-day week, nearly equal proportions of waking life between 8 a.m. and 10 p.m. are

TABLE 3
Adults' Use of Time

Activity by Environment	% of Signals
Work	
Working	27.5
Socializing, eating, other	14.8
Total	42.3
Home	
Watching television	6.6
Cooking	2.4
Cleaning	3.4
Eating	2.3
Snacking, drinking, smoking ..	.9
Reading	2.7
Talking	2.2
Grooming	3.1
Hobbies, repairing, sewing, gardening	3.7
Other chores	3.0
Idling, resting	4.0
Other, miscellaneous	5.8
Total	40.1
Public, others' homes	
Leisure and other activities ...	8.8
Shopping	3.1
Transportation	5.7
Total	17.6

spent at home (40.1% of time) and at work (42.3%). Note that only about 65% of the time at work is actually spent working.

Viewing television, which accounts for 6.6% of primary activity reports at home, is by far the single most time-consuming home activity. It is also the dominant leisure activity, absorbing roughly 40% of all leisure time.

In total, subjects reported watching television as a main activity 7.2% of the time (344 signals) and as a secondary activity 2.8% of the time (136 signals), for exactly 10% of all the times they were signalled. From this figure we can roughly estimate that respondents watched television for about 1.4 hours each day between the hours of 8 a.m. and 10 p.m.[1]

DO SOME DEMOGRAPHIC GROUPS VIEW MORE THAN OTHERS?

Not surprisingly, some people never reported viewing during the week, whereas others reported watching television quite often.[2] Similarly, some demographic groups watched more than other groups although one-way analyses of variance showed that only for race was there a significant difference among groups (Table 4).*

The ANOVA for race resulted in an F of 2.7 ($p < .05$), but the extremely heavy viewing of the one American Indian respondent accounts for much of this variance. Still, Black respondents did report watching more television on average than did the White or Hispanic subjects.

Women reported watching slightly less than men, largely because they spent more time in food preparation, cleaning, laundry, and child care. This helps also explain why the clerical workers, who are almost exclusively female, viewed less on average than the managers and assemblers, who are largely male.

Amount of education was negatively correlated with the proportion of viewing ($r = -.17, p = .09$)† while income was positively correlated ($r = .15, p = .13$). Single and married subjects reported watching television the same proportion of time during the week, whereas the divorced

---

*Proportion of time spent viewing was measured by adding the number of primary and secondary TV responses for each subject to the total number of "TV checks" from side two of the ESF. This sum was then divided by the total number of reports made by each subject over the week's sampling in order to arrive at a percentage score. Because a subject could report an instance of primary or secondary viewing *and* a check indicating having viewed since the previous signal for the same observation, the amount of viewing measure should be viewed simply as a ratio scale (ranging from .00 to .75 with a standard deviation of .17) but not one than can be translated into exactly how much TV any individual watched.

†Throughout the book, p values denote two-tailed tests unless otherwise noted.

TABLE 4
Amount of Television Viewing by Demographic Group

Group	n	Mean[a] Amount of TV Viewing	TV Viewing s.d.	Group	n	Mean[a] Amount of TV Viewing	TV Viewing s.d.
All Subjects	107	.33	.17	Education			
				Some high school	13	.36	.16
Sex				Completed high school	34	.34	.19
Male	40	.35	.16	Some college	46	.32	.16
Female	67	.31	.18	Completed college	11	.27	.18
				Some grad. school	2	.42	.20
Marital Status				Completed grad. school	1	.45	.00
Single	31	.34	.17				
Married	58	.34	.17	Occupation			
Separated	5	.41	.23	Managers	38	.33	.15
Divorced	12	.22	.14	Clericals	41	.29	.19
Widowed	1	.27	.00	Assemblers	27	.36	.16
Race				Age			
Amer. Indian	1	.75	.00	19–24	20	.26	.17
Black	18	.39	.17	25–34	28	.36	.17
Hispanic	7	.31	.15	35–39	22	.37	.20
White	79	.30	.17	40–47	18	.33	.16
Other	2	.36	.04	48–63	19	.30	.15
Income[b]							
Under $16,000	12	.23	.16				
16–24,000	57	.34	.17				
24–32,000	23	.35	.16				
32–40,000	8	.35	.21				
40–60,000	6	.35	.11				

One-Way Analysis of Variance of Amount of Viewing	F	p	Correlation with Amount of Viewing	r	p two-tails
Sex	1.2	.29	Income[c]	.15	.13
Marital status	1.6	.18	Education[d]	−.17	.09
Race	2.7	.03	Age[e]	−.08	.45
Income	1.3	.29	Length of time w/ company[f]	.18	.07
Education	.7	.64	No. of dependents	.15	.26
Occupation	1.7	.18			
Age	1.4	.22			

[a]The amount of viewing score is a ratio scale ranging from .00 to .75
[b]1989 dollars
[c]Controlling for age, sex, education
[d]Controlling for age, sex, income
[e]Controlling for sex, income, education
[f]Controlling for age, sex, income, education

respondents and single widowed subject reported less. Of all the groups, the five separated subjects and the three with the most education appear to have watched the most television.

Generally, these findings follow trends in large-scale survey research studies with working adults, except that income and viewing are usually negatively correlated.[3]

The viewing estimates vary a good deal less than they would for a nonworking sample. Because all the respondents work full time, spending roughly 40 hours a week at work, time left free to view television is necessarily limited and limited in a fairly uniform way. This helps explain why the differences among the groups are relatively small. Indeed, Bower (1985), among others, has confirmed that the opportunity to view strongly predicts how much people actually view. Bower controlled for opportunity to view in a survey of over 2,000 Americans and concluded that "A person's age, sex, race, education, income make little difference—everyone views television about the same amount except when prevented from doing so by external factors, like work" (pp. 40–41).

The strongest correlation between amount of viewing and any demographic variable was with the length of time respondents had worked for their companies ($r = .18$, $p = .07$). Viewing was also slightly higher for those with more dependents ($r = .15$, $p = .26$). The explanation is quite simple: Viewing increases somewhat as a function of being more settled in both work and family life. People with children stay home significantly more and consequently watch more television. Indeed, the correlation between the number of dependents and the percentage of total time spent with the family at home was .32 ($p = .01$). Furthermore, a home and family-centered orientation is also compatible with work stability. In support, the correlation between length of time spent with the company and percentage of time spent with friends was $-.32$ ($p = .001$).

WHERE, WHEN, AND WITH WHOM DO PEOPLE WATCH TELEVISION?

Nearly all television watching occurred in the respondents' home (92.7%) or at a friend or relative's home (6.1%). In total, 25% of all time spent at home was spent watching TV.

Seventy-five percent of viewing occurred in a living or dining room, 12.7% in a bedroom, 4.3% in a kitchen, and 5.6% in "other" rooms.

Insofar as television is generally viewed at home, it is not surprising to learn that people tend to view with people they know well. Only 1% of the time is television viewed with co-workers or strangers. People viewed with other members of the family 60% of the time and 6% of the time with friends. Thirty-one percent of viewing was done alone.

Not surprisingly, the incidence of viewing with the family varies substantially for single and married subjects. When married subjects watched television, they were with other family members 71% of the time, whereas the corresponding percentage for single subjects was only 38%. Considered another way, single respondents were more than twice as likely to view television alone.

Although subjects may gravitate to television when they are alone, viewing is not something that people can do whenever they choose. Rather, it is very much dependent on the timing of productive and maintenance activities such as working, cooking, eating, and sleeping (Figure 5). And, of course, the television industry long ago learned to schedule its programs with these factors in mind.

Very little weekday viewing occurs in the hours before 5 p.m. On weekends, by comparison, the amount of viewing is slightly higher in the morning and much higher in the afternoon.

The home activities that television competes with in the evening hours are presented in Figure 6. Primary television viewing absorbs less than 15% of time at home between 5 and 7 p.m., whereas eating and cooking together consume almost twice as much early evening time. During these same hours, television is often used as a background to dinner. For this reason, reports of secondary viewing double at the dinner hour. By 9 to 10 p.m., however, television has become the dominant activity with 37% of time devoted to viewing.[4]

WHAT DO PEOPLE DO WHILE WATCHING TELEVISION?

As discussed in the previous chapter, an enduring question about television concerns whether or not it is a low-involvement medium. For McLuhan (1964), for example, viewing was "highly participatory" and would "not work as background." One way of assessing involvement is to consider how often viewing is accompanied by other activities. If typical television viewing is as involving as McLuhan or as dominating as Bronfenbrenner (1973) suggested, it should be relegated to the background of other activities only infrequently.

The ESM permits us to distinguish between those occasions when respondents defined viewing as the primary activity versus those occasions when viewing was secondary to another activity. Television viewing was reported as a background activity (i.e., secondary to some other activity) during 28.3% of all viewing occasions. Thus, out of 480 reports of viewing, 71.7% were reported as primary (Table 5). There were only 175 occasions (36.5%) when no other activity whatever was reported

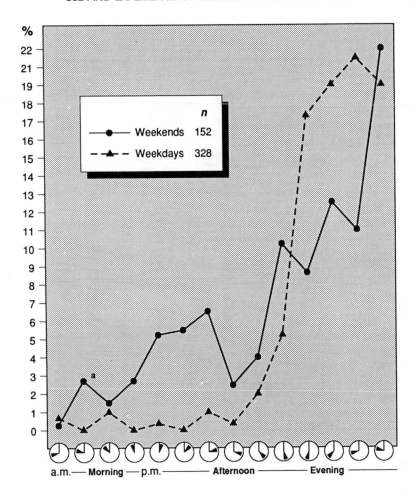

aFor example, 2.6% of all weekend TV signals were reported between 9 and 10 in the morning.

FIGURE 5.   The relative distribution of primary and secondary reports of television viewing by each hour of the day.

accompanying viewing. Thus, 63.5% of the time television was being viewed, people reported doing something else as well.[5]

Of course, activities such as eating, talking, or smoking may not preclude sustained involvement with the screen. Reading, in contrast, is much more difficult to carry out as a secondary activity to television and thus, it is almost three times as likely to be reported as primary versus secondary to viewing. If like reading, many of the things that went on while people watched television seriously interfered with viewing, respondents would have more frequently denoted TV as a secondary ac-

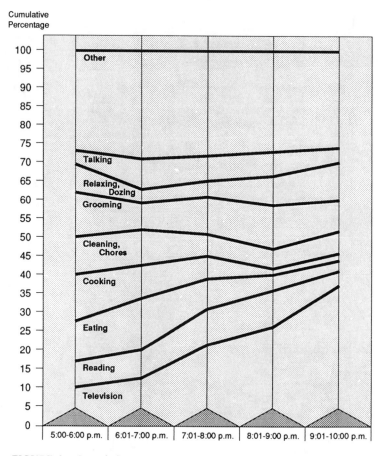

FIGURE 6.　Cumulative percentages of time spent in evening activities at home.

tivity. Still, the vast majority of respondents report that their viewing is accompanied by other activities and it is our conclusion that contrary to the views of others, very few people consistently watch television to the total exclusion of other activities.

The Predominance of Oral Activities Accompanying Viewing

When people are doing something else as they watch television, chances are they are eating or talking. For nearly 25% of the time that television was described as a secondary activity, meals were marked as primary.

However, a subject's marital status is likely to influence how often one

TABLE 5
Television as a Primary and Secondary Activity

Activities Reported in Conjunction with TV Viewing	Secondary Activity Percentages when TV Is the Main Activity		Main Activity Percentages when TV Is Secondary	
	n of Signals	% of Signals	n of Signals	% of Signals
Talking	62	18.0	19	14.0
Meals	40	11.6	32	23.5
Smoking	19	5.5	8	5.9
Grooming	10	2.9	7	5.1
Chores	8	2.3	6	4.4
Reading	6	1.7	17	12.5
Cleaning	5	1.5	11	8.1
Child care	5	1.5	5	3.7
Other	14	4.1	31	22.8
No secondary activity ..	175	50.8	—	—
Total	344	100.0	136	100.0

views while eating. Single subjects ate 37.5% of their meals at home while watching television. For married respondents, the figure was 22.7%. In other words, television is used by some singles in lieu of company when dining.

In total, 34.9% of all secondary activities accompanying television viewing were eating or smoking. This incidence of "oral consumption" while watching television was extremely high compared to its less frequent occurrence in conjunction with other activities. Adding talk (36.7%) as another secondary oral pursuit raises the "oral percentage" still further to 71.6%.[6]

Time Deepening Across Cultures

It must be noted that just because our American respondents often watch television while doing other things does not mean that this is how television is viewed everywhere. In industrialized societies such as our own, people are generally more likely to engage in "time deepening" (Scheuch, 1972), that is, engaging in a number of activities simultaneously.[7]

Indeed, in an examination of another ESM database composed of 40 graduate students, evenly divided between Black Africans studying in the United States and White U.S. students of the same age, it was discovered that the Africans, who were much less familiar with TV generally, reported considerably fewer secondary activities accompanying television and greater concentration while viewing than their White counterparts.[8]

In other words, the Africans appeared to view television more intently—as Americans may also have in the early 1950s when TV was still a novelty. Of course these findings could be confounded by the fact that the African students were viewing the television products of a foreign country. In other words, the offerings were more novel and therefore of potentially greater interest than indigenous television materials might be.

Such differences in concentration with television are important because the effects of viewing are modified by how intently one views. Gavriel Salomon (1979) has found that Israeli children invested more mental effort during viewing and retained more of what they saw than American children who, he suggested, take television for granted because it is so ubiquitous and because they define the TV task as "mentally undemanding."

For both Israeli children and for African students abroad, then, television represents a more salient and novel stimulus. In other words, the way television is used and experienced is related to the amount of experience a person has had with the medium and thus, the television experience may vary from one culture to the next. Still, as we show later in this chapter, for Italians and Canadians as well as among people of widely different ages, television is often experienced in much the same way as has been found in the sample of U.S. adult workers.

HOW OFTEN DO PEOPLE THINK ABOUT TELEVISION IN DAILY LIFE?

We also checked how often respondents reported thinking about television. Not surprisingly, almost 90% of all reported thoughts about television occur while viewing. Virtually all of the other thoughts about television occur at home and potentially within earshot of a TV set (e.g., while washing dishes in the kitchen). Perhaps more surprising is that there were only five occasions out of nearly 3,000 when subjects reported thinking about television when they were not at home.

Although television does not seem to be directly on the minds of viewers when they are apart from the set, this does not mean that the medium influences thinking and behavior only during viewing. Studies focusing on what people learn from television suggest that viewing influences thoughts and behavior that occur away from the set in ways that are often subtle and out of conscious awareness.

THE MOTIVATION TO VIEW

If people generally report wanting to view television, it is a fair assumption that some, or many, of the features of the viewing experience are sought by viewers. So, before describing how it is experienced, we wanted first to learn whether television viewing was something that people wanted to do.

People report "wanting" to watch television over 90% of the time—this in sharp contrast to their "wanting" to work only 15% of the time. Only when reading, eating, or talking did people report "wanting to do" these things more often than watching TV (Table 6).[9] In short, television viewing was among the most freely chosen of activities. Also of note is the relatively high total incidence (19%) of subjects indicating that they wanted to watch television because they "had nothing else to do." In no other "activity," except for the nonactivity of "idling" (not shown)—or doing nothing—did subjects more frequently use this explanation for involvement in an activity.

A WORD ABOUT TELEVISION CONTENT

Most of the analyses that follow involved the collapsing of all viewing occasions into one category of experience that we call *television viewing*. Although we and our colleagues have collected content data in some ESM studies and report on some of the experiential differences by content later in this chapter, content data were not collected from the adult workers.

Actually, a number of media scholars have recommended that researchers do precisely what we have done, that is, emphasize "exposure" and "social context" variables, rather than content, as the more neglected and basic aspects of media use appropriate for study (Katz, Blumler, & Gurevitch, 1974).[10] This approach is also supported by re-

TABLE 6
Reasons for Doing Seven Major Home Activities
(Percentage of responses)

	Television	Reading	Eating	Cooking	Chores	Talking	Grooming
Had to do	4.4	3.7	17.6	55.6	64.4	11.2	52.8
Wanted to do	90.2	94.1	96.3	80.9	59.6	95.2	75.7
Nothing else to do	19.0	10.3	5.4	7.8	4.2	13.2	2.5
	113.6[a]	108.1	119.3	144.3	128.2	119.6	131.0

[a]Columns add to over 100% because more than one motive at a time could be checked.

searchers who believe that the activity and experience of viewing are often more important variables to consider than content.[11]

Glick and Levy (1962) have concluded, for example, that the "main gratification from TV is simply in watching, regardless of content, and it is only as a more or less secondary consideration that program choices are made" (p. 50). Or as Leo Bogart (1972) wrote,

> There are powerful indications that the *activity* experience accounts for a good deal more of audience behavior than the symbolic content. Mass media are associated with particular parts of the day's routine or with particular recreational needs. Television viewing, for example, takes place at any given time of day in relation to the cycle of work and sleep, quite apart from the number of stations or the character of programming choices before the viewer. (p. 212)[12]

In other words, viewing choices are determined much more by scheduling and viewer availability than by content (Webster & Wakshlag, 1983). Robinson (1981), for example, reported a .43 correlation between amount of viewing and available free time. Furthermore, Wilensky (1964) and Steiner (1963) showed that education makes only slight differences in what most people view. Support for the study of television viewing without a focus on content also comes from EEG studies.*

HOW TELEVISION IS EXPERIENCED RELATIVE TO OTHER DAILY ACTIVITIES

The pages ahead describe how people experience viewing and how these states compare to those that coincide with other activities. We also wish to establish whether the viewing experience varies for different demographic groups or whether most groups experience television in much the same way. In other words, how uniform are the specific pleasures of viewing?

If television is experienced the same way by most people, one might conclude that the nature of the viewing experience is linked closely to the nature of the medium as well as to the similar motivations that place people before the set in the first place. If, however, people report widely

---

*Weinstein, Appel, and Weinstein (1980) claimed that when subjects looked at a blank page versus a blank TV screen, the pattern of EEG rhythms differed in much the same way as patterns elicited from printed and televised content. Krugman (1971) also concluded in his research comparing EEG responses to print and video that the "basic electrical response of the brain is more to the medium than to the content differences" (p. 7). For a literature review of media studies using the EEG see Rothschild et al. (1986).

different experiences with television, one might conclude that the medium itself has less uniform effects and/or that differences in what people bring to viewing substantially shape the experience.

Television viewing will be contrasted with other activities in a number of different ways. The comparisons for the first analysis focus on four major primary types of activity plus a "total activity" category that includes all primary activity reports after subtracting those given while watching TV.*

The four activities were: working at work (all work activity on the job, excluding socializing, coffee breaks, and lunch); public leisure (dining out, parties, sports and games, club meetings, and cultural and entertainment events); idling (waiting, not doing anything, daydreaming, resting, and lying in bed); and meals.

Table 7 presents a rank ordering of averaged individual self-report means. Activities whose means were significantly different from television watching are noted with asterisks. For this analysis, a single mean was calculated for each subject's self-reports on each variable and in each activity regardless of how many signals he or she may have received in each activity.[13]

Concentration, Challenge, and Skill.   The mean levels of concentration, challenge, and skill were significantly lower for watching television than the average levels for all other activities combined. Furthermore, viewing television is the least challenging and skilled activity. Respondents report greater skill while eating than when viewing.

Although it seems clear that most television viewing does not require a concerted application of skill, viewing seems to be conceived of in this way because people take it completely for granted that they have acquired a variety of cognitive abilities as well as knowledge about television that permits them to successfully decode televised information. Still, it is generally quite easy to view television. Some decoding processes go on almost automatically (Hawkins & Pingree, 1986) and, thus, the act of viewing requires only so much cognitive effort to accomplish.

Mood and Activation States.   Most notable among the findings in Table 7 is that television watching is experienced as the most relaxing of all activities. The degree to which people feel "relaxed" during viewing and the extreme infrequency of "tense" responses with this sample as well as with others demonstrates that in real life, television viewing is stressful

---

*In all analyses where television viewing experiences are being studied, we are referring to *primary* reports of viewing only, *not* secondary reports, unless otherwise specified.

TABLE 7
Rank Ordering of Individual Self-Report Means for Selected Activities[a]
(from Csikszentmihalyi & Kubey, 1981)

Response Variables	TV Watching $n = 93$	Total Activity[b] $n = 93$	Working at work $n = 93$	Public Leisure $n = 71$	Idling $n = 79$	Meals $n = 82$
Concentration	4	2*	1**	3	6**	5
	4.94	5.29	6.03	5.23	3.83	4.75
Challenge	6	2**	1**	3**	5	4
	2.49	3.77	4.84	3.72	2.58	2.65
Skill	6	2**	1**	3*	5	4**
	3.74	5.36	6.38	4.90	3.91	4.63
Mood						
Cheerful	3	4	5	1**	6**	2
	4.89	4.85	4.73	5.50	4.44	5.04
Relaxed	1	5**	6**	2	4**	3
	5.36	4.83	4.54	5.28	4.86	5.20
Sociable	5	3	4	1*	6*	2*
	4.74	4.86	4.82	5.62	4.47	5.14
Activation						
Alert	5	3**	2**	1**	6**	4**
	4.76	5.29	5.57	5.76	4.07	5.27
Strong	5	4**	2**	1**	6*	3**
	4.48	4.79	4.95	5.09	4.24	4.94
Active	5	3**	1**	2**	6	4**
	4.06	4.79	5.08	5.02	3.97	4.60

Note: Higher means refer to more positive states.

[a]Total number of signals for all subjects for each activity were as follows: TV 344; Total minus TV 4,447; Working at Work 1,189; Public Leisure 116; Idling 411; and Meals 257.

[b]Total activity refers to all activities minus television watching.

*Activities whose means are significantly different from TV watching means on a _t_ test (two-tailed) by a factor of $p < .05$.

**$p < .005$

only very rarely. The finding calls into question how concerned we need to be when warned that television causes tension, anxiety, or fear in viewers. As is seen here, ESM studies have revealed only the most occasional evidence of such experiences among adult respondents, and with children ranging in age from 10 to 17.

It is also noteworthy that in some samples examined, about 25% of the time subjects report feeling no closer to one pole or the other on the bi-polar variables of happy–sad, cheerful–irritable, friendly–hostile, and sociable–lonely (i.e., the modal television response chosen tends to be number "4," that is, "do not feel either"). Still, respondents generally use the full range of possible responses and, as noted earlier, they much more frequently report feeling relaxed than tense.

To continue, activation states while viewing are very low. Respondents report feeling significantly less "alert," "strong," and "active" when viewing than the baseline "total activity" figures. Respondents also reported being significantly less "active" and "alert" while viewing than while reading ($p < .01$) regardless of whether they were viewing or reading alone or with the family (not shown). Only when idling do people report feeling less active than when viewing.

To achieve a fuller understanding of the viewing experience we next compared it to a wider range of activities. In this comparison, mean responses and rankings for television viewing and 15 other typical daily activities are presented (Table 8). The self-report variables used here were the two clusters of affect and activation and the variable, "wish to do something else." In this analysis, the actual values for each raw signal were used.[14]

As can be seen, television viewing ranked next to the bottom of the list on both affect and activation. Respondents gave lower reports only when resting. It must be noted, however, that the affect means reported for

TABLE 8
Mean Affect, Activation, and Motivation Responses and Rankings
for Selected Activities

Activities	n	Affect[a]		Activation[b]		Wish Something Else	
		Mean	Rank	Mean	Rank	Mean	Rank
All Activities	4,656	5.03		4.85		3.20	
Television	344	4.86	15	4.29	15	1.94	6
Reading	181	4.87	13	4.55	14	2.56	8
Eating	257	5.47	4	4.94	8	1.77	3
Talking	423	5.49	3	4.94	8	2.59	9
Cooking	121	5.10	7	4.94	8	2.53	7
Chores	189	5.01	8	4.93	11	4.53	16
Hobbies[c]	176	4.87	13	5.14	3	2.86	11
Resting	180	4.22	16	3.37	16	1.81	4
Grooming	210	4.99	9	4.91	12	2.82	10
Working	1,189	4.91	12	4.98	7	4.33	15
Sports	58	5.43	5	5.52	2	1.88	5
Transit	263	4.97	10	5.08	4	3.75	13
Idling[d]	156	4.92	11	4.69	13	4.08	14
Shopping	88	5.12	6	5.08	4	2.94	12
Socializing	32	5.62	2	5.08	4	.90	1
Lovemaking	11	5.75	1[e]	5.59	1	.91	2[e]

[a]Affect = cheerfulness + friendliness + happiness + sociability.
[b]Activation = active + strong + alert + excited.
[c]Sewing, knitting, and gardening are included.
[d]Does not include resting and lying in bed as in Table 7.
[e]Low rankings (1,2, etc.) denote more positive states or higher motivation.

reading, hobbies, working, and idling, although ranked higher, are almost indistinguishable from the television mean.

As for our measure of intrinsic motivation, working, chores, and being in transit were the activities people wished most not to be doing. Television watching, on the other hand, ranked in the upper third of activities that people wanted to do and was surpassed only by socializing, lovemaking, eating, resting, and sports.

In order to visualize these similarities and differences, the 16 activities are projected in three dimensions in Figure 7.[15] To illustrate intrinsic motivation, the "wish to do something else" means from Table 8 were inverted by subtracting each mean from a constant. Means for the entire sample of activities are denoted by an $\bar{X}$.

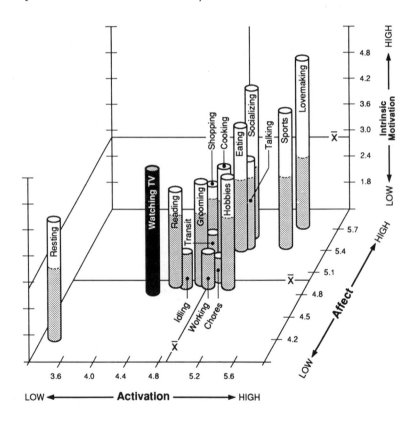

X̄ Mean response for all activities

---- Mean Intrinsic Motivation for all activities

FIGURE 7. The subjective landscape of adult activities.

As can be seen, television viewing is on the same affect plane with a great many activities: reading, idling, working, transit, cooking, hobbies, grooming, and chores. Clearly, eating, talking, socializing, sports, and lovemaking are more enjoyable.

On the activation plane, television viewing is lower than all other activities but resting. Respondents are most activated in sports and lovemaking.

Subjects report being quite intrinsically motivated to watch television as well as to socialize, to play sports, to eat, and to rest. Again, the degree to which people indicate low motivation for work and chores is striking.

Because almost all television watching took place in the home, it is useful finally to look at differences in the quality of the home viewing experience compared to other home activities. This set of comparisons also includes variables that have not been previously discussed and it should be noted that the comparisons in the three figures to follow held up regardless of whether subjects were viewing alone or with family members. Once again, t tests were used to distinguish between television watching and other activities.

In Figure 8, we see that viewing is reported as being lower on challenges, skills, and stakes than anything else done at home. Reading is only somewhat higher on challenge and stakes but it requires significantly greater skill to do. Again, people do want to watch television. This is illustrated by the rather low placement on wish to be doing something else (lower than reading, and significantly lower than cooking, grooming, and chores, but not nearly as low as eating and leisure).[16]

Figure 9 shows that viewing involves relatively little concentration, whereas reading requires significantly more concentration ($p < .001$) than any other activity. This corresponds with findings from Salomon (1981, 1983, 1984) and Salomon and Leigh (1984), who use the self-report measure of Amount of Invested Mental Effort (or AIME) that shows that children invest less attentional effort in television than in reading.

Another dimension of experience that dramatically differentiates television viewing from other activities is the sense of control people report. Subjects reported feeling very little control during viewing, significantly less than in each of the seven other activities. Finally, in Figure 10 we see once again that viewing is quite low on both activation and affect, but high on relaxation.

Respondents carried the pagers across a variety of different weeks over the course of 1 year and no substantial variations whatsoever were found in these reported experiences of television by time of year.

As for experiential differences between primary and secondary viewing, we have consistently found that when television viewing is second-

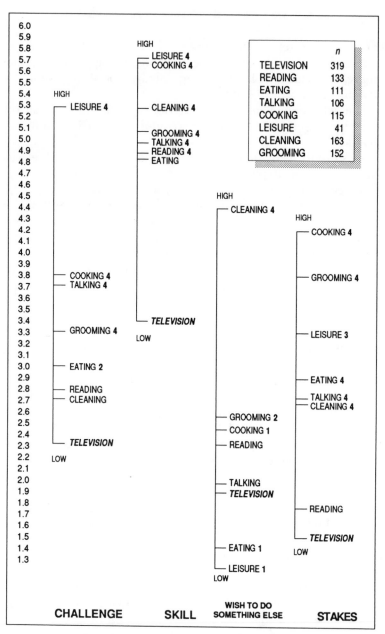

FIGURE 8. Television viewing experiences compared to experiences during other activities at home. Numbers 1–4 denote the significance level for *t* tests comparing the differences between television viewing and other activities.

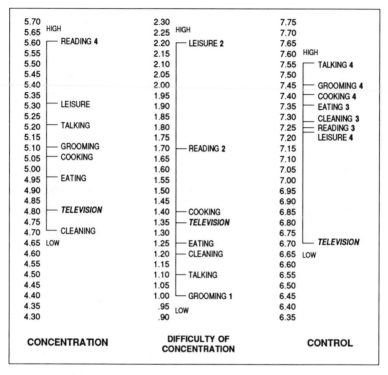

1 p<.1   **2** p<.05   **3** p<.01   **4** p<.001

FIGURE 9.   Television viewing experiences compared to experiences during other activities at home. Numbers 1–4 denote the significance level for *t* tests comparing the differences between television viewing and other activities.

ary, the reported experience tends to be very similar to whatever the primary experience is without a secondary activity involved. However, with viewing as secondary, primary activities do tend to be experienced somewhat more passively and involve somewhat less concentration. In short, the experience becomes somewhat more "TV like" but not so much that it is more like television viewing than the primary activity in question.

DO DIFFERENT GROUPS OF PEOPLE
EXPERIENCE TELEVISION DIFFERENTLY?

Are these findings applicable to most people or only to some? To answer this question, the experience of television viewing was examined by age, sex, race, income, education, and marital status across each of the self-report variables.

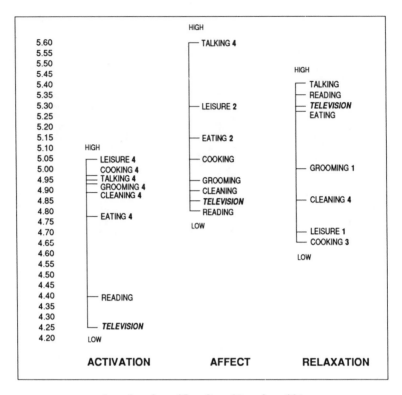

1 p<.1   **2** p<.05   **3** p<.01   **4** p<.001

FIGURE 10.   Television viewing experiences compared to experiences during other activities at home. Numbers 1–4 denote the significance level for *t*
tests comparing the differences between television viewing and other
activities.

In short, it was found that different demographic groups report experiencing television in much the same way. All the groups studied reported that the television viewing experience was relaxing, unchallenging, passive, and involved relatively little concentration.

The few demographic differences in experiential reporting are briefly summarized here along with explanations for the differences. (For the
interested reader, Appendices F and G present the means on activation
and affect for five demographic variables and for all activities, TV viewing, working, and meals.)

Sex.   Women generally report significantly higher affect than men, but
during television viewing there is no difference. Women's viewing is
slightly more active than men's—a result, in part, of the higher frequen-

cy of secondary activities such as cooking, cleaning, and child care that accompanies more of the females' primary viewing. The women also tend to view less, and as discussed in chapter 8, the viewing of light viewers tends to be more active.

Race.   Black subjects reported feeling somewhat more active during viewing than Whites. Differences in television content may be partly responsible. However, in all likelihood, a more powerful factor is that a relatively high proportion of the Blacks are divorced or separated women with dependents. Compared to the White subjects in the sample, they more frequently watch TV while performing the active tasks of household chores and taking care of children and thus their viewing is reported as being more active.

Age, Marital Status, and Income.   No substantial differences were found.

Education.   The only notable difference here is that the more educated respondents (those with at least some college) reported significantly greater "wish to do something else" while viewing compared to the less educated subjects (means of 1.4 vs. 2.7, $t = -2.96$, $p < .005$, not shown). We offer the following explanations. First, some of the more highly educated may feel that television viewing is a waste of time. Some educated people are "snobbish" about partaking in mass culture and in being critical of television's "low brow" mass appeal and commercial nature, a person can make himself feel superior (Fowles, 1982; Gans, 1974). In order to reduce cognitive dissonance, educated persons may report a higher wish to do something else when viewing.

Second, more educated respondents' viewing may be more guilt-ridden. Studies from England (Himmelweit & Swift, 1976), Japan (Furu, 1971), and the United States (Steiner, 1963) show that middle-class viewers tend to report more guilt about their viewing than less affluent groups.

Finally, people with more education are likely to be accustomed to processing information more complex than what they experience during the typical TV program, and may therefore wish that they were doing something else. It is worth noting, however, that Neuman (1982) found little variation in the number of analytic or interpretive responses made to television as a function of education level. He concluded that television may be a "cultural leveler." Or as Wilensky (1964) concluded, "education has a lot more to do with how people *feel* about TV than what they *do* with it" (p. 193).

HOW TYPICAL ARE THE FINDINGS
ON THE VIEWING EXPERIENCE?

Even though the demographic groups just discussed report experiencing television in much the same way, it might be argued that the patterns reported only hold true for the sample of adult workers, or for the particular historical moment in which the study was conducted. Secondly, of how much significance is television content?

A Cross-National Comparison

To answer the first question, the results from three additional ESM studies are compared with those from the study of working adults.

The Samples

The Italian adolescents are a group of 47 high school boys and girls from Milan, studied in 1985 by Professor Fausto Massimini and his team from the Psychology Department at the Medical School of the University of Milan.

The U.S. adolescents include 201 high school boys and girls from the suburbs of Chicago, nominated by their teachers as being academically talented. They were studied from 1985–1988 by Csikszentmihalyi.

Finally, the sample of aged Canadians, studied in 1982–1983 by Professor Roger Mannell and Jiri Zuzanek at the University of Waterloo, Ontario, included 92 adults of both sexes between 55 and 82 years of age, with a median age of 68 years.

Preparation of the Data

In Figure 11, the television viewing experiences of these four groups are compared on five dimensions of experience: concentration, activity–passivity, happiness–sadness, relaxation–tension, and challenge. To facilitate the comparison across the samples, the raw data were transformed to individual z scores, and then averaged.

This procedure involves finding the mean score on each self-report variable for each person across all reports for the week and assigning the value "0" to that score. Each individual score is then recoded so that those one standard deviation above the person's mean will have a value of 1.0, those one standard deviation below will have a value of -1.0. The values thus obtained are comparable across different individuals and different groups, and reflect on a normalized scale the relative devia-

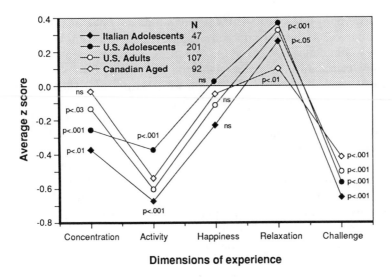

FIGURE 11.   Television viewing experience compared across four samples.

tions from the average level of experience. Thus, the average z score on the five dimensions of experience represent the average for each group when watching television, based on the mean of each individual in the group. The significance levels reported denote the probability that the difference between the television watching mean for each group and the mean for all other reports for that group is due to chance.

Findings

Concentration when viewing television was below average in all four groups. The difference was not significantly different from the weekly mean for the older Canadians, but was significant ($p < .03$) for the U.S. adults, extremely significant ($p < .001$) for the U.S. adolescents, and quite significant ($p < .01$) for the Italian teenagers, who when watching television were .4 of a standard deviation below their normal level of concentration.[17]

All four groups reported being significantly more passive when watching television than they were in general over the week of sampling. The differences on this activity dimension across all samples were significant at least at the .001 level. The Italian adolescents were again the lowest, their average level of activity being three quarters of a standard deviation below that for the rest of the week.

On the happiness ratings, there was similarity once again: lower reports on average than usual, but not significantly different from the rest
of the week. Relatively speaking, the U.S. teens seemed most happy
during viewing and the Italian teens the least happy.

Every group experienced viewing as relaxing, and the differences
were statistically significant for each sample. Of all the samples, the two
U.S. groups reported television as the most relaxing activity while the
Canadian seniors found it least relaxing. But again the similarities are
more impressive than the differences.

The four groups also consistently reported that watching television
offered very few challenges. On this variable the samples averaged over
half a standard deviation below the respective means for all activities.

It is noteworthy that older Canadians reported the highest level of
relative concentration and challenge and the lowest level of relaxation.
This is explained by the fact that older adults, particularly compared to
young adults and teenagers, watch significantly more information and
news programming that tends, at least for adults, to require more concentration (Kubey, 1980).

Also, the use of z scores makes a difference. Television viewing is
scored as somewhat more challenging, requiring more concentration,
and as being less relaxing *relative* to the older respondents' other daily
activities that tend to be somewhat more sedentary than those of younger respondents.[18]

Discussion

Although the 447 respondents used two different languages, came from
different cultures, and covered most of the life span, and even though
the data were collected by different investigators at various points in
time, the findings agree to a remarkable extent. They confirm that the
subjective experience of watching television has a general unitary character comprised of a strong sense of relaxation, average reports on the
happy–sad variable, and low levels of concentration and activation, as
well as low levels of challenge.*

Of the observable differences in Figure 11, that of age appears to be
somewhat more pronounced than the differences between the cultures,
but even these deviations from the common pattern are small compared
to the similarities. Furthermore, findings from other ESM databases
denote very similar general patterns.

---

*Although he analyzed different kinds of data, Wilensky (1964) similarly concluded
that responses to television were relatively uniform: "The usual differences in media
exposure and response among age, sex, and class categories . . . have virtually disappeared
in the case of television" (p. 195).

Although Stefan Hormuth and Marco Lalli (personal communication, August 11, 1989) used somewhat different measures, let us consider the results from their analysis of ESM data collected from 80 German university students (see Figure 12) and from 25 adults from the general German population. In both studies, television viewing was intrinsically motivated and subjects reported feeling about as good when viewing as when reading. As in the other ESM studies, the German respondents also reported substantially better feelings during social activities (talking, playing games, etc.) and when doing hobbies than when watching TV. Once again, work was least intrinsically motivated, least liked, and least enjoyed. These results were virtually identical whether comparisons

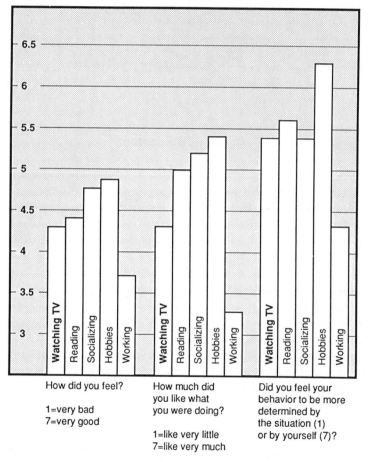

FIGURE 12. The experience of television compared to four other general activities in a sample of German respondents (adapted from Hormuth and Lalli, personal communication, August 11, 1989).

were made during the day or evening. (For more information about the procedures and samples involved, see Hormuth, 1986, in press.)

We suspect that the viewing experience would be reported in much the same way were data available from a much wider variety of countries, although there is certainly more frequent large group viewing in some less-developed countries and we know from our existing samples that, at least in small groups, the viewing experience is made more positive by the presence of other people (see chapter 6). Furthermore, as already noted, the sample of foreign students who were unaccustomed to television tended to concentrate more when viewing and derived a more activated experience than those who had been exposed to television all their lives.

Nevertheless, the consistency of the patterns we have found may suggest the anthropological notion of the so-called "psychic unity of humankind." At least as far as television viewing is concerned and the samples studied, human consciousness operates in similar ways irrespective of differences in age and culture. When using a medium that offers entertaining stimulation but involves little physical activity or highly challenging mental involvement, human responses are relatively uniform.

Variations by Content

Of how much significance is television content? Here we report on recent ESM data collected from a very large, randomly stratified sample of 483 Chicago suburban area students, ages 10–15, from whom data were collected in eight quarterly waves over a 2-year period concluding in March of 1987. We wish to thank Reed Larson for making these data available and for performing the analyses.

The Sample and How the Data were Prepared

Selection of subjects for this study was stratified so that the final sample included an equal number of students, half boys and half girls, in each quarter of the year from the fall of fifth grade to the winter of ninth grade. The students came from schools in two White, suburban communities, one middle class, the other working class (see Kubey & Larson, 1990; Larson, Kubey, & Colletti, 1990, for further details).

In this sample there were 19,054 ESM self-reports and just over 2,300 instances of television and VCR viewing. We divided TV content into 18 different program types but chose to look closely only at those 10 program types that each constituted 2% or more of all viewing occasions. In doing this, we were still able to account for 96.4% of all viewing occasions. The program types that were infrequently reported and excluded were such fare as mini-series, documentaries, variety programs, general children's programs, specials, and science fiction.

Differences in Experience by Content

Table 9 displays the z scores on the variables of affect, activation, and "wish to do" for the 10 major program types.

Although there were differences by program type, analyses of variance run separately for affect, activation, and whether respondents wished to be doing what they were doing resulted in no significant difference across these programs. With many other types of general activities, significant ANOVAs have been found when comparing experiences across different sub-categories of activity.

Affect. Except for viewing movies, music videos, and adult comedies, television fare was again experienced at or below the affect mean for all activities.

Activation. As with all the other samples, all television fare was scored negatively on activation. Not surprisingly, the most activated television experience with a z score of −.01 was watching music videos. Only a few occasions of teenagers dancing or tapping their feet in accompaniment to the music help explain this result. The least activated types of television program were news (−.30) and dramatic series (−.35), both program types geared more to adults than movies, videos, cartoons, or

TABLE 9
Mean z Scores of Subjective State for Selected Television Content

	% of Total TV Viewing	Affect	Activation	Wish to Do
Adult comedies	15.8	.01	−.09	.34
Child comedies	9.0	−.03	−.11	.31
Cartoons	14.4	−.09	−.10	.28
Dramatic series	10.8	−.26	−.35	.43
Game shows	2.6	−.19	−.15	.24
All movies on TV	24.7	.05	−.02	.46
Music videos	4.5	.01	−.01	.35
News	2.9	−.27	−.30	.07
Soap operas	2.4	−.14	−.25	.21
Sports	9.3	−.04	−.08	.38
F test		.94	1.28	1.29
p value		.53	.18	.18

comedies. The affect scores for news and dramatic series were also quite low.

Wish to Do. On this variable, as with adults and all other respondents studied, viewing television is something people report wanting to do. Except for news (.07), which is discussed next, all the z scores fell within a relatively narrow range from lows of .21 for soap operas and .28 for cartoons to a high of .46 for movie viewing.

Ironically, the subjects reported wanting to watch dramatic weekly series even though they do not enjoy them much. Teenagers reported wishing to watch adult programs such as "Dallas" or "St. Elsewhere" but, given the more mature themes of some such programs, it is likely that young adolescents cannot as readily identify with the characters or storylines and thus do not seem to enjoy this kind of program.

News Viewing

Young adolescents reported few occasions of news viewing (less than 3% of all viewing occasions), and viewing news was the least motivated and least positive of all television experiences for them. The children and young adolescents often watched the news as captives: in many instances their parents were also watching and the students frequently reported wishing to do something else.

Demographic Differences

Demographic differences in the use and experience of content for this group of respondents were predictable and largely limited to age and sex. Cartoons and children's situation comedies were watched less by— and provided significantly less involving and enjoyable experiences for—the seventh to ninth graders than was the case for the fifth and sixth graders. For these programs, self-reports of affect, activation, concentration, and "wish to do" were all significantly lower among the older children.

The only strong difference by sex was in sports viewing. Boys consistently wanted to view sports and enjoyed viewing sports more than girls, with resulting higher affect, activation, concentration, and wish to do.

VCR Versus Traditional Television Viewing

When analyzing VCR versus nonVCR viewing, similarities again outweigh differences (Kubey & Larson, 1990). The vast majority (72%) of

VCR use among the adolescents involved the viewing of movies. However, only slight experiential differences between VCR viewing of movies and regular viewing (nonVCR) of movies on TV could be discerned. The z scores on attention and wish to do something else were virtually identical (not shown).

These results demonstrate that for this sample, the VCR has not substantially altered the subjective experience of relatively similar content. We should add, however, that the most positive type of television experience for this sample was watching a movie on a VCR with other members of the family. This should not surprise us as such viewing occasions are generally planned in advance, often involve a small rental fee, and involve selection of a preferred movie. We also know that people feel better in virtually every activity—including TV viewing—when they are with other people than when alone.

However, given that the VCR has enabled viewers to view more movies and other preferred content than ever before, the overall experience of television among households with VCRs has almost certainly improved.

Sex and the Experience of New Video Media

Although the experience of most forms of traditional TV content did not vary much by demographics, there were substantial variations in reported affect when sex of respondent was taken into account and when examining the experiences of these adolescents with some of the newer forms of video entertainment (Kubey & Larson, 1990). In the three types of new video "media" studied—VCR viewing, video games, and music videos—boys consistently reported higher affect than did girls. These sex differences were greatest with video games and music videos and somewhat weaker when watching via a VCR. In contrast, for the traditional media of television, music, and reading the differences in affect by sex were smaller.

Because video games are generally designed for boys and often focus on aggressive competition and the destruction of spaceships or people (Dominick, 1984), it is not surprising that many more boys gravitated to this medium than did girls (by a ratio of 10 : 1 for the seventh to ninth graders) and that they also enjoyed video game play more.

Music videos are similarly targeted more to males than to females. Content analyses of music videos has shown them to be thick with aggression and sexuality—young, scantily clad women are often featured (Sherman & Dominick, 1986). A great many of these visual promotions of rock music are clearly sexist and oriented to a male audience (Brown, Campbell, & Fisher, 1986; Deiter & Heeter, 1989). This no doubt helps explain why boys enjoy watching music videos much more than do girls and why, in contrast, there is little difference by sex on reported affect during traditional music listening unaccompanied by video.

Although the differences are not so great as with games and music videos, boys also reported higher affect than the girls during VCR viewing. Here again, an examination of some of the movies viewed by the respondents reveals a targeting to males (e.g., sophomoric "peeping Tom" films such as *Porkys* as well as violent and horror movies) and it is not surprising that boys enjoy this kind of material more than girls.

DISCUSSION

The Consistency of the Television Viewing Experience

The similarity in reported experiences among different demographic and cultural groups persuades us that the experience of viewing is largely the result of the nature of the medium as it is constituted in the nations from which the samples come as well as the relatively similar needs that people in all cultures seek to gratify through viewing.

For all of the groups studied, television viewing was an unchallenging but freely chosen activity, distinguished by feelings of relaxation and low levels of mental investment, activation, and skill. Although relaxation in reading and many other leisure pursuits is associated with involvement, the very hallmark of TV viewing is relaxation without involvement or effort.

There is little evidence to suggest that adults, children, or adolescents felt tense or frightened during their television viewing. The large sample of nearly 500 U.S. adolescents, for example, reported feeling tense or nervous during less than 6% of television viewing occasions. The incidence was even lower in the adult sample. These findings may be of particular relevance to research teams that study how fear is induced in viewers or how it may be ameliorated (e.g., Cantor & Reilly, 1982; Gerbner & Gross, 1976; Sparks, 1986; Wilson, Hoffner, & Cantor, 1987; Zillmann & Wakshlag, 1986). This is not to say that various televised materials do not occasionally frighten children or adults, but rather that arousal and tension during viewing does not appear to be a very frequent phenomenon. Such effects seem to be rather short lived and so we pick them up only infrequently when sampling in real time.

Although it has been shown that people report viewing to be quite passive and involving relatively little concentration, we are not saying that viewers are not thinking about and interpreting what they are view-

ing. On the contrary, individuals must be conscious and at least somewhat mentally aware in order to track even the most simple of television
programs—such as a cartoon of a cat chasing a mouse—although some
such viewing may be nearly automatic. So although viewers may report
low concentration and low activity this does not mean that they have
turned their minds off completely, are incapable of understanding what
they are viewing, or that they are not possibly engaged in a critical
"reading" of what they are viewing.

Television, Reading, and Marshall McLuhan

At the same time it must be recognized that how a medium of communication presents information does help determine the skills an audience
member needs to decode that information. Different media require different forms and levels of interaction from the audience. This was in
part the insight contained in McLuhan's dictum, "the medium is the
message."

But McLuhan argued that television was a medium that demanded
more active involvement than the reading of books. His claim was based
on the assumption that the sensory decoding of visual images takes more
effort than following the linear presentation of written words on a page.
Because viewers must reconstruct the screen image from many points of
light, McLuhan thought, viewers are more involved and more free to
construct their own messages and experiences than readers, who must
follow a predetermined "hot" sequence of signs set down by the author.
To the contrary, we would argue that the reception of signs is generally
more fixed in television and in cinema than in print. Indeed, detailed
information about what something or somebody looks like is more
quickly and effortlessly communicated by a picture (it is worth a thousand words goes the saying) than by print.

Viewers often are involved in their viewing, but McLuhan was wrong
about why television is experienced as it is, as well as about how much
relative mental effort is typically involved in reading and watching television. McLuhan also failed to recognize that perception involves more
than simple sensory decoding. Interpreting a message can require a
great deal of cognitive processing—matching stimuli to memory contents, recognition, classification, evaluation, and judgment—and on that
score reading requires more effort, activity, and involvement than watching television.

One has to work harder and use more of one's mental capacities to
read. This is why we have consistently found that people report con-

centrating much more during reading than during TV viewing. But the effort of concentration required is also why we find that people report wishing to do something else more when reading than when viewing.

The reader confronted with a string of abstract signs must first translate them into words and then translate the words into visual images, emotions, ideas, and events. For example, a reader who has never seen the film, when presented with the adjectives describing the Tin Man in *The Wizard of Oz*, will ultimately construct an idiosyncratic image of what the Tin Man looks like and how he moves. A television viewer, on the other hand, is presented with a more complete visual and auditory message on the screen that generally requires less effort to decode or interpret. Viewing film or television one knows immediately what the Tin Man looks like and how he moves, and people's perception of him will be much more alike relative to print. By the same token, once one sees *The Wizard of Oz* in film or on television, it becomes difficult to imagine the Tin Man looking and behaving differently from the Jack Haley characterization.

In general, then, people's perceptions of television or film content are more likely to be similar to one another than people's perceptions of printed information. This is among the reasons that film and television are likely to have greater homogenizing influences relative to print.

The activity of reading also leaves much more room for freedom and control because the reader can stop at any time, retrace steps, reread a passage, meditate on it, and think of alternatives and consequences before returning to the text. The reader also determines at every moment the speed at which information is received. The viewer of film or television, by contrast, must follow the temporal sequence of what is being viewed. Viewing with a VCR can mitigate this feature, but for the most part the tempo of images is outside the viewer's control.

Given the various structural features of the medium, plus the factors that influence content—such as the market forces that determine so many nuances of programs—it should not surprise us that with regard to the model set forth in the first chapter, the average television viewing experience can be deemed somewhat more ordered (negentropic) than disordered (entropic) but low in terms of complexity.

Most televised communication does not conflict with the average viewers' goals lest audience members suffer disorder in experience and refuse to watch. Simultaneously, to reach the widest audience possible, much content is purposely made easy to decode. Or as Walter Goodman wrote in the *New York Times* (1989), "It is an axiom of commercial television that the mass audience's powers of concentration must not be taxed. . ." (p. H31).

Activation—or arousal—is low during viewing because the information being processed does not require concentrated attention or great effort to interpret. People frequently report feeling slightly happy during viewing but on average, *not* any happier than usual. They *do* report feeling quite relaxed both because the activity is so effortless and because the message content provides order and is generally in line with the viewer's goal to relax.

Reading is about as relaxing and affectively rewarding as television viewing but reading involves a good deal of concentration and is reported as significantly more active. These facts are particularly important because they tell us that a person need not reduce concentration and feel passive in order to experience relaxation. Rather, relaxation in leisure can be achieved in more active ways.

Television Viewing as an Altered State of Consciousness

In the final section of this chapter we compare and contrast the television viewing state to other psychological states.

Day Dreaming and Night Dreaming

It is more than a coincidence that the "activities" that appear most similar to television watching, particularly in activation and cognitive reports, are "idling" and daydreaming. Daydreaming can be compared to television viewing in that both are virtually effortless tasks (ease of concentration) with no compelling need to direct behavior toward a specific goal (nothing at stake) (Klinger, 1971). As is the case with television viewing, EEG studies have shown that brain wave patterns during fantasy and free imagery exercises correspond to low cortical activity (Klinger, Gregoire, & Barta, 1973; Kripke & Sonnenschein, 1978). Furthermore, both television viewing and daydreaming often seem to involve a blank stare.

Television watching and daydreaming are also those "activities" that people most frequently report doing when there is "nothing else to do." In other words, both activities help to pass or fill open time. In fact, some instances of TV viewing could be conceived of as special cases of daydreaming where rather than fantasizing on one's own, one taps into other people's (TV writers) ideas and fantasies. Indeed, it has been suggested that some people use television in order to legitimize their daydreams (Faber, Brown, & McLeod, 1979) or, in the case of heavy viewers, to substitute others' fantasies for their own unpleasant internal life (McIlwraith & Schallow, 1983).

Night dreaming, too, can be compared to television viewing in that both can be conceptualized as visual fantasy activity closely tied to wish fulfillment. As Carpenter (1972) wrote: "Television extends the dream world. Its content is generally the stuff of dreams and its format is pure dream."

Finally, television viewing states might also be compared to hypnotic states, at least in that hypnosis is often induced with the aid of visual fixation on a moving stimulus, not entirely unlike the viewing of moving images on a television screen.[19] In fact, a number of theorists have suggested that an involved television viewer is less defended and more suggestible—as in hypnosis (Gans, 1980; Hilgard, cited in Mandler, 1978; Himmelweit, Oppenheim, & Vince, 1958; Tart, 1972). And studies by Graham have shown that heavy television viewers are more readily hypnotized (Graham, Rudnick, & Battista, 1983).

These comparisons and our findings suggest that under certain conditions, particularly during uninterrupted and extensive viewing, the televiewing experience might qualify as an altered state of consciousness. Recall also that relaxed postures, frequent oral activities, and relaxation are common during viewing. These aspects along with the comparability of television viewing to day and night dreaming and hypnotic states lead us to further posit that television viewing may often permit an "adaptive regression."

A Psychodynamic Explanation

Television Viewing as an Adaptive Regression

In classical psychoanalytic theory, *regression* generally referred to a pathological return to modes of behavior or thinking characteristic of earlier levels of development, and was generally considered to be outside the control of the ego. Shortly before Freud's death in 1939, however, ego psychologists began to believe that the ego could retain control over primary process thinking, including regression.[20]

The adaptive regression, then, is a process by which a person may restore psychological equilibrium by taking one psychological step backward (as in sleeping and dreaming for 8 hours) in order to take two steps forward (16 hours of waking life and productivity). In an adaptive regression, an abstract painter might relax ego functions and engage in a purposeful and controlled regression that brings her safely into contact with primary process material. This is in marked contrast to the permanently and pathologically regressed psychotic.

All of the altered states of consciousness just discussed, as well as many forms of leisure, may involve such adaptive regressions (Hartmann, 1958) or "regressions in the service of the ego" (Kris, 1952), and except for daydreaming, television may well provide one of the least expensive and most effective waking retreats for those weary or frustrated by reality demands.

Furthermore, repeated viewing of the same television program or movie, like hearing the same fairy tale told many times, may similarly offer the viewer a means of adaptation and a sense of mastery similar to dreaming the same daydream many times in response to daily frustrations. As with a repeated fairy tale, repeat viewing of television programs can provide a stimulating yet ordered and comfortable experience for the viewer. This is one of the primary reasons that many people view the same television program or film many times.[21] As with the reading of fairy tales before bedtime, television shows are also typically watched after productive and maintenance activities have been completed and before going to sleep. Moreover, as with fairy tales, many television programs are familiar, filled with fantasy material, and end happily and tie up loose ends at the end of each program.

Oral Dependence, Depression, and Viewing

The application of psychoanalytic theory and the concept of regression to TV viewing was extended by the observations of Gerhardt Wiebe (1969), who noted that media use often coincides with the resumption of infantile postures, taking without "deference" to the giver, immediate gratification, and the sense of experience without accommodation. A psychiatrist, Eugene Glynn (1956) similarly posited that television provides solace to orally dependent characters whose needs center on the wish for someone to give comfort.[22] For Glynn, television provides nearly everything the dependent person wants: "warmth, sound, constancy, availability," and no need to cope with "the other" (p. 178).

But although television viewing may often constitute an adaptive regression, there is only sketchy evidence from our studies to suggest that people who may be more orally dependent watch more TV. (Kris, 1952, held that even placing a finger near or in the mouth was a sign of a "controlled regression.") There is no evidence to suggest, for example, that heavier TV viewers (i.e., the heaviest viewing third of the sample) eat or smoke more frequently than light viewers (the lightest viewing third of the sample).[23] Heavy viewers, however, were twice as likely to report "drinking" as a main activity and were 25% more likely to report *thoughts* about eating and drinking than light or moderate viewers.

Heavy viewers also reported greater "satisfaction" than light viewers when with family members and while simultaneously eating or drinking ($t = -1.6$, $p = .10$).

Evidence is presented in a later chapter that people who experience their lives more negatively or who may suffer from depression—which in psychoanalytic terms is often thought to be related to oral character dependencies, conflicts, and fixations—are more inclined to turn to television. The medium might well be popular among depressed persons because they can use it as a source for the "external supplies" necessary for the ordering, regulation, and maintenance of the self and experience.

In chapter 7 an attempt is made to determine whether people use television to provide psychological order and as a retreat from reality demands and entropic states or whether there is evidence to support the position that viewing itself causes psychological entropy. We also examine whether viewing induces passivity and relaxation and to what degree people may feel passive and relaxed before viewing—conceivably turning to television as an activity that mirrors both their state of mind and their mood.

But before tackling those topics, we wish to consider how families use and experience television and try to assess whether television may be a boon or a hindrance to the life of the family.

ENDNOTES

[1]Szalai's (1972) diary sample of 1,394 working men and women from 44 United States cities averaged 1.7 hours per day of primary and secondary TV viewing—20% more than our figure. Robinson (1977) also reported somewhat higher daily viewing for individuals in urban employed households. These discrepancies between ESM findings and those of Szalai and Robinson are due largely to the fact that we did not sample after 10 p.m. Using data from 1985, Robinson estimated U.S. viewing to be about 2.2 hours per day (Samuelson, 1989).

We should note that our estimate as well as those of Szalai and Robinson are substantially lower than Nielsen estimates and those of Bower (1985) for the entire adult viewing audience, not just workers. Nielsen estimated 4.1 hours of viewing per day for the 1987–1988 season using "Peoplemeters" which tend to give the company estimates of about 1 hour less per week than the audimeters the company used to use. But Nielsen's estimates, using both "audimeters" as well as "Peoplemeters," overestimate viewing because Nielsen only measures whether a television is on, not whether someone is viewing it, and research suggests that televisions may be on without being viewed for as much as a third of the time (Collett, 1986). Had the Nielsen company required viewers to "punch-in" on their "Peoplemeters" every 15 or even every 30 minutes, we believe that they would have been more likely to obtain more accurate measures.

Bower estimated just under 4 hours of daily viewing for all adults and that figure was drawn from personal estimates of viewing that *excluded* weekday daytime viewing. Bower's method of having respondents estimate what percentage of time they view in each 1 hour interval of the day could be subject to reporting inaccuracies and inflation.

[2]The mean number of primary and secondary TV signals per person was 4.5 (the median was 4). Although 11 persons indicated no primary or secondary TV viewing, examination of the checklist data from the second side of the ESF shows that of these 11, only 4 reported no viewing during the entire week of sampling. As primary TV viewing reports alone are used in many of the analyses to follow, it should also be noted that the mean for primary TV reports was 3.2 per person, the median was three. Over 75% of subjects reported four or fewer primary occasions of viewing per week.

[3]The positive correlation with income was largely the result of the poorest 12 respondents viewing less TV on average than the rest of the sample. Even though sex was controlled for—along with age and education—the preponderance of women in the lowest income group cannot help but play a role in the direction of the relationship.

[4]Additional analyses showed that there was a slight rise in viewing on, and immediately after, the hour and half-hour and a slight drop off before each of these two time intervals. This indicates that viewers are more likely to be viewing at the beginning of programs but that they do not always watch for an entire show.

[5]This figure is higher than the 30% to 50% range reported in diary method studies. Because diary methods do not catch people in the midst of their activities, persons often must recall what they were doing many minutes later and the precision of the accompanying reports, especially those of secondary activities, may suffer from this delay. Videotape and film studies of viewing, on the other hand, may cause some subjects to be more aware of their behavior and thus they may behave differently. Finally, there is only limited comparability between any two studies' method of coding and definition of accompanying activities. Perhaps the ESM coding is more comprehensive.

[6]The predominance of talking and eating behavior with television viewing has also been observed by Bechtel et al. (1972) and by Allen (1965).

[7]Robinson (1969) has similarly noted that secondary viewing occurs most in countries where a high percentage of the population owns TV sets. In addition to our research, Television Audience Assessment, Inc. (1981), Szalai (1972), and Robinson (1969) have each used diary methods while Allen (1965), Anderson and Lorch (1983), Bechtel et al. (1972), and Collett (1986) used videotape or film to record viewing behavior in the home or laboratory. Having examined many of these studies, Comstock et al. (1978) concluded, as have we, that television watching is a "discontinuous, often interrupted, and frequently nonexclusive activity" (p. 147).

[8]These data were collected by Malik (1981).

[9]The notion that reading is done more willingly than viewing (Singer, 1980) is given only marginal support by these data. Furthermore, subjects reported a greater wish to be doing something else while reading at home than when watching TV at home.

[10]Studying television viewing in this way could be compared to studying eating behavior without concern for the types of food consumed. Or as Joshua Meyrowitz (1985) has written: "By concentrating popular and scholarly attention primarily on message content, our approach is often not that different from a hypothetical attempt to grasp the impact of the automobile by ignoring the issue of new patterns of travel and by focusing instead on a detailed examination of the names and faces of passengers" (p. 20).

[11]Among those who have advanced this position are: Dorr (1980); Hirsch and Panelas (1981); Lindlof (1982); McLeod and Reeves (1980); Rosengren and Windahl (1972); Steiner (1963); and Wilensky (1964).

[12]Bogart has similarly written that "Viewing is a pastime activity indulged in for its own sake rather than its content" (p. xvii). In further support, Goodhardt, Ehrenberg, and Collins (1975) posit a "duplication law of viewing" and claim that the best predictor of what

a viewer will watch tomorrow is whichever channel his or her set is tuned to today. The A. C. Nielsen Company's research confirms that approximately half the viewers of a program come directly from the preceding show on the same network. Also see Raymond Williams' (1974) concept of audience and programming "flow."

Paul Hirsch (1977b) has noted that "[Television] sets are turned on every day for approximately the same number of hours, irrespective of which programs are scheduled" (p. 403). Comstock et al. (1978) concurred: "The decision to view is typically more influential than the decision what to view" (p. 11).

[13]In this way, disproportionate individual influences from selected respondents who may have received more or fewer signals in a given activity are effectively ruled out. Note that the n's range from 71 to 93—only those subjects who reported doing an activity at least once could be included in the analysis. For the purpose of comparability, every subject was also required to have at least one instance of primary TV viewing—hence the same n of 93 for working at work, total activity, and TV.

[14]Repeated analyses of this type have demonstrated that the magnitude of differences rarely changes whether grand means are generated from individuals' means or from raw signals. Only in those rare instances where the number of total signals is low and a few subjects are responsible for many of the reports have results differed.

[15]The diagram is for illustrative purposes and not perfectly accurate. A few activities had to be moved slightly so that they weren't blocking or being blocked by the illustration of another activity.

[16]Home leisure includes playing games or a musical instrument, listening to radio or records, doing art work, dancing, exercising, entertaining guests.

[17]The reason this difference is not more statistically significant is because the number in this sample (i.e., 47) is the smallest of the four.

[18]Note that the inverse relationship between challenge and concentration on the one hand and relaxation on the other is quite common in ESM studies (i.e., most activities that require more concentration coincide with lower relaxation). Reading, however, stands out as a major exception to this rule.

[19]Of interest is the claim by Anderson and Collins (1988) that there is "no evidence that television has a mesmerizing effect on children's attention caused by color, movement, and visual changes" (p. 4), even though Anderson et al.'s (1979) own research shows that as children watch for longer than 10 seconds, their bodies tend to relax, their heads drop forward, and their mouths drop open. Mulholland (1973) reported identical bodily and facial relaxation. Although physical relaxation is not proof of an altered state or a state akin to hypnosis, it cannot be disregarded either.

[20]It should be noted that Freud (1905/1960) himself suggested that humor was often an invitation to common regression. Freud was also aware that people could discharge or gratify repressed impulses through identification with other people's activities whether they be fictional or real. Ironically, such activity would now be considered by some to constitute a "regression in the service of the ego."

Other scholars who have considered the psychoanalytic properties of media use include Bettelheim (1976, 1985); Feshbach (1976); Gussen (1967); Mendelsohn (1966); and Warner and Henry (1948). Wolfenstein and Leites (1950) explored the potential of movies to induce fantasies and to function as daydreams, whereas more recently, Meyrowitz (1985) has tried to show how regression in everyday life may be encouraged by the electronic media. (See also Munsterberg, 1916, for comparisons between film and dream states.)

Montani and Pietranera (1946) have characterized the movie-going experience in terms of regression in this poorly translated statement: "Darkness [of the movie theater] which lowering the resistances, helps the identification and regression and prepares an oscillating surrounding between dreams and reverie. It is in this surrounding which on the screen, there passes visions and fancies of the unconscious thought expressed in its own language" (p. 188).

[21]Tannenbaum (1985) reported having accidentally stumbled upon the finding in one survey that 40% of viewers had watched the exact same situation comedy episode only a few days before on a different station. He has also demonstrated a strong preference for repeat viewing under experimental conditions.

[22]Lindlof (1982) has suggested that reclining and sitting postures during television viewing may enhance cognitive susceptibility to ideation. Schramm, Lyle, and Parker (1961) concluded that "when a child sucks his thumb and immerses himself in television, we can guess that television is substituting for the warmth of a mother relationship." Also in this context, one cannot resist noting that Harlan Ellison (1969) entitled his collection of critical essays on television, *The Glass Teat.*

[23]In Freud's (1946) *Mourning and Melancholia* the oral character is *literally* oral (i.e., exhibiting an undue amount of behavior centered on the mouth and alimentary system). However, Gottheil and Stone (1968) have confirmed an oral trait factor consistent with psychoanalytic descriptions but did not find evidence of a positive relationship between oral trait and actual mouth habits.

CHAPTER 6

Television and the Quality
of Family Life

TV has ruined American home life. People no longer sit around and visit.
Everywhere you go you have to outtalk TV. TV people have entered your
home and life more than people who should be friends and companions.
—one of Gary Steiner's (1963) interviewees

When the TV set is on, it freezes everybody . . . Everything that used to go on
between people—the games, the arguments, the emotional scenes, out of
which personality and ability develop—is stopped. So when you turn on the
television, you turn off the process of making human beings human.
—Bronfenbrenner (1973)

The television atmosphere in most households is one of quiet absorption on
the part of the family members who are present. The nature of the family
social life during a program could be described as "parallel" rather than
interactive, and the set does seem quite clearly to dominate family life when it
is on.
—Maccoby (1951)

Television seems to have changed the ways in which family interaction
occurs. When the set is on, there is less conversation and less interaction. . . .
There is more privatization of experience; the family may gather around the
set, but they remain isolated in their attention to it.
—National Institute of Mental Health (1982)

One of the longstanding, unresolved controversies in mass communication research is whether the use of television and other media interferes with the conduct of family life. For Frankfurt School theorists a
central fact of capitalism was the decline of the family as an agent of
socialization. In this view, the socialization role of the family is partly
passed on to the media and as a result, the audience becomes passive and
one-dimensional (Horkheimer & Adorno, 1972; Marcuse, 1964).

Indeed, since the first days of its massive popularity in the early
1950s—and in the days since—television has been conceived by some to
constitute an overwhelmingly dominant presence in the home—a pres-

ence that interferes with family interaction and the process of socialization itself.[1]

Other observers consider the television set to be a relatively unthreatening home furnishing.[2] In fact, there is a fair amount of research suggesting that viewing may be linked to more frequent and positive family interactions.[3] As early as 1949, Riley, Cantwell, and Ruttiger claimed that television's presence in the home enhanced family togetherness because it provided one of the few opportunities for family members to spend time together, helping to close the gap between adults and children. In this view, television viewing is conceived of as being well integrated with the rest of everyday life and posing little threat to human welfare. Wilensky (1964), however, was dubious about families watching "violent, escapist television" and advised that "students of the media who stress the absorption of television into the warm bosom of the family and peer group ponder what is being absorbed most effectively by whom with what effect" (p. 183).

There are many explanations for these differing views. For one, researchers often examine different aspects of a phenomenon and only see part of the puzzle. And when it comes to television, scholars and critics are sometimes prone to arrive at singular conclusions about television's impact when in reality, behavior associated with television is quite complex. With regard to the family, some of this complexity was captured by Coffin's (1955) conclusion over 30 years ago that "Television is both credited with increasing the family's fund of common experience and shared interests and blamed for decreasing conversation and face-to-face interaction" (p. 634).

In this chapter we shed light on whether the quality of family life is threatened by TV or whether television viewing might play a positive role within the family context.

FINDINGS

Family Interaction During Viewing

As is apparent from the quotes introducing this chapter, developmental psychologists such as Eleanor Maccoby and Urie Bronfenbrenner have expressed concern that family life is dominated by TV. Bronfenbrenner is especially concerned about socialization processes and the psychological development of children. Explicit in these concerns is the assumption that when people turn on the TV they do little else but watch. We already know from the findings in the previous chapter that people do often engage in other activities while watching television and that talking is among the most frequent of accompanying activities. But how much do people talk with family members when watching TV?

Subjects reported talking to other family members during 21% of all primary and secondary viewing that took place with the family.[4] The comparable figure for all non-TV familial activities was 36%. But even though a proportions test between these two percentages was highly significant ($p < .001$), it would be inaccurate to say that family TV viewing is always "parallel" or that family interaction in the form of conversation is even twice as likely to occur when television is not being viewed.

Family Experiences With and Without Television

The next question is whether experience is altered by the kind of people one views with and whether viewing with the family is substantially different from solitary viewing. We start by looking at how typical familial experiences differ from family experiences *with* television.

As can be seen in Table 10, the viewing of television involves a qualitatively different familial experience from being with the family and not watching. When television is viewed with family members, people report feeling significantly less challenged, less skilled, more relaxed, less alert, less strong, and less active than in non-TV family activities.

TABLE 10
Subjective States While Watching Television with the Family,
Compared to Family Interaction Without Television,
and Television Watching Alone (from Kubey, 1989c)

Response Variables	TV Watching with Family n = 206	Being with the Family without TV n = 933	Watching TV Alone n = 108
Concentration	4.81	5.01	5.08
Challenge	2.60	3.58**	1.90*
Skill	3.44	4.93**	3.37
Mood			
Cheerful	4.92	5.02	4.59*
Relaxed	5.38	5.01**	5.11
Sociable	4.95	5.11	4.10**
Activation			
Alert	4.67	5.22**	4.69
Strong	4.37	4.75**	4.39
Active	3.91	4.81**	4.00

Note: Comparisons between means were made by *t* tests.
*$p < .05$; **$p < .002$; two-tailed.

However, viewing with the family is clearly a more positive experience than viewing alone. When television is viewed with family members, it is a significantly more challenging, cheerful, and sociable experience than when viewed alone. Family viewing is reported as more challenging than solitary viewing because family interaction and accompanying secondary activities such as talking create a more demanding situation and one in which it can be more difficult to view.[5]

How people experience being with the family when reading, an activity that is much more difficult—if not impossible—to accomplish while simultaneously talking, was also examined. As with television, people reported feeling significantly more relaxed ($p < .004$), passive ($p < .004$), and less challenged ($p < .05$) while reading in the presence of family members than when interacting with them. However, there was no drop in perceived skills or in alertness or "strength" when reading with family present as was the case when people watched television with their families.

In summary, television viewing is modified by the social context in which people view but the general experiential trends associated with viewing remain intact regardless of context. In this sense, the nature and quality of familial experiences are altered by the presence of television in the direction of less activation and cognitive activity. It stands to reason, then, that families that spend substantial portions of their time together watching television are likely to experience greater percentages of their overall family time feeling relatively passive and unchallenged compared with families who spend small proportions of their time watching TV.

But some of these trends are as relevant for a family that spends much of its time together reading. Furthermore, at least with television, family members are sharing the same experience and are more likely to talk and share observations with one another than if everyone in the household was reading by themselves.

Amount of Viewing and Familial Life

Time With the Family and at Home.   The heaviest viewing third of the adult sample as measured over the week of sampling was no less likely to spend time with their families (vs. being alone) than the lightest viewing third ($\chi^2 = 3.7$, $p = .82$)* Heavy viewers did spend relatively more time

---

*The term *light viewers* always refers to that third of the sample that watched the least amount of television over the week. *Heavy viewers* always refers to that third of the sample that watched the most television for the week.

at home than the light viewers ($\chi^2 = 2.53$, $p = .11$), and when at home, the heavy viewers were also more likely to be alone than the light viewers ($\chi^2 = 3.7$, $p = .06$, Yates' correction).

Experiences With the Family. Heavy viewers' affective experiences with their families in non-TV activities were no worse than light viewers'. In fact, the heavy viewers reported feeling significantly more "free" (vs. constrained) during non-TV activities with family members than did light viewers ($t = -3.6$, $p < .001$). Furthermore, heavy viewers were no more likely to be "alienated from the family" as measured on Maddi's Alienation Index (Maddi, Kobasa, & Hoover, 1979).

However, the light viewers did report significantly higher activation ($t = 2.1$, $p = .04$) when with family members in non-TV activities than did the heavy viewers. So, not only is the familial television viewing experience less active when compared to non-TV family activities, but for heavier viewers, non-TV family time is itself experienced as being less active as well. This is probably the combined result of heavier viewers being somewhat less active than light viewers to begin with and the possibility that the often passive and drowsy TV viewing state spills over into more of the heavy viewers' familial experiences (*passive spillover* is discussed in the next chapter).

Differences by Marital Status. When all respondents' familial experiences were compared with respect to marital status, interesting differences emerge. First, the married adults, especially those with children, watched significantly more television, stayed at home more, and spent less time with friends than adults who were single or without children. Furthermore, as can be seen in Table 11, the married respondents' moods with family members in non-TV activities were better in relation to more TV viewing.*

Just the opposite phenomenon was observed for single respondents. Negative correlations were found between amount of viewing and level of reported happiness, friendliness, relaxation, and satisfaction during time with family members. Two of these five correlations were statistically significant even when controlling for age, sex, income, and education. For example, the correlation for single respondents between amount of viewing and their reported happiness during family time was $-.39$ ($p = .05$). These trends in the correlational findings are also observed for the heaviest and lightest viewing thirds in the t test com-

---

*In this table and in Table 12 to follow, all primary and secondary instances of television viewing were removed from the analysis of "family" experience in order to avoid a confound.

TABLE 11
Correlating Amount of TV Viewing and Mean Mood Responses
During Time With Family Members for Single and Married Subjects[a,b]
(from Kubey, 1989c)

	Single (n = 29)		Married (n = 54)	
Response Variables	r	p two-tails	r	p two-tails
Friendly	−.41	.04	.25	.08
Happy	−.39	.05	.19	.19
Relaxed	−.24	.23	.18	.20
Satisfied	−.29	.15	.14	.75
Wish something else	.28	.16	−.22	.12

[a]Single means for each subject were used.
[b]Controlling for age, sex, income, and education.

parisons in Table 12.[6] The trends for the divorced and separated respondents, it should be added, were similar to those for the single respondents.

Why might heavy viewing young, single adults feel worse with their families than light viewing young adults?[7] First, heavier viewing singles (as well as the heavier viewing divorced and separated individuals) felt worse generally than the light viewing singles and thus, feeling worse with the family must be understood as part of a larger trend. Second, as is discussed in chapter 8, television is more frequently viewed in response to negative internal states for a greater number of single, young, and divorced and separated respondents, than it is for married respon-

TABLE 12
Comparing Light and Heavy TV Viewers' Mean[a] Mood Responses
with Family Members by Marital Status (from Kubey, 1989c)

	Single			Married		
Response Variables	Light Viewers	Heavy Viewers	t	Light Viewers	Heavy Viewers	t
n	63	66		230	212	
Friendly	5.3	4.4	2.6***	5.1	5.2	−.7
Happy	5.4	4.4	3.2***	5.2	5.4	−1.8*
Relaxed	5.5	4.7	2.4**	4.9	5.1	−1.7*
Satisfied	4.8	4.2	1.8*	4.9	5.1	−1.9*
Wish something else	2.1	3.1	−1.9*	2.5	2.0	1.8*

[a]Means were generated from raw signals from the lower third (light viewers) and upper third (heavy viewers) of the sample.
*$p < .10$; **$p < .05$; ***$p < .01$; two-tailed.

dents. For married people, in contrast, viewing is more socially determined and related to time spent with the family. Indeed, married respondents' viewing is much more frequently done with the family (71% vs. 38% for single adults). Because they more frequently view alone, single individuals' moods play a significantly larger role in the decision to view than is the case for married respondents who more frequently view because someone else in the family has turned on the set or in order to be with another family member who will be viewing.

Adolescent Subjects and Heavy Viewing.   Similar trends were found in two adolescent samples. First, the rate of television watching was positively correlated with the amount of time teenagers spent with their families and negatively correlated with the amount of time they spent with friends. This was the case for both an older adolescent sample of 9th to 12th graders (Larson & Kubey, 1983) and for the male and female subsamples of the young adolescent sample discussed toward the close of the previous chapter (Larson, Kubey, & Colletti, 1990). Furthermore, for the older adolescents, the amount of time spent with television was also positively correlated with adolescents' moods with family members and negatively correlated with moods with friends.

In general, these and other findings reflect the relationship of television to what we have called *adult-structured domains* (Larson & Kubey, 1983). For example, the amount of time spent watching TV was also positively correlated with the amount of time spent in the classroom and with better school performance as measured by grade point average and controlling for aptitude.*

As with most of the married adults, then, more frequent use of television by teenagers was associated with more time spent with the family and with better feelings with the family. For both adolescent groups and for our married adult subjects, there is little support for the idea that heavy television viewing signifies poor family relations. If anything, more time spent with television appears to connote a preference for spending time with the family.

---

*The polarity of these correlations was reversed when doing the analysis for the amount of time spent listening to *music*. Here the correlations with school performance and time spent in class were both negative. More music listening was also correlated with feeling *worse* with the family and feeling significantly *better* with friends—the opposite trend as with amount of television viewing. These findings coincide with Lull's (1985) observation that the message of much rock music is at variance with the socialization aims of the school and parents, and with Roe (1983) who has shown that the heaviest music listeners are frequently individuals who do less well in school and turn to music as a medium that reinforces their independence from the school and adult values.

SUMMARY AND DISCUSSION

That talk accompanied viewing with the family over one fifth of the time—compared to one third of the time for other family activities—suggests that it may well have been an overstatement for the National Institute of Mental Health (1982) to conclude that when people view with their families "they remain isolated." Similarly, Bronfenbrenner (1973) overstated when he concluded that television "freezes everybody" and that viewing causes everything that goes on between people to stop. In fairness to Maccoby, however, it should be recalled that her conclusions were based on the state of American television viewing in the late 1940s and 1950 when viewing was more of an event and, by most informal reports, less likely to be interrupted by talking or other secondary activities.

Findings generally lend support to the view that television viewing harmonizes with family life. Heavy viewing adolescents and married adults spent more time with their families generally and felt better with their families than did light viewing respondents.

Even in adolescence, when we find that the frequency of family television viewing drops off from what it was in childhood, it is still a prevalent activity, continuing to offer the opportunity for children to share common experiences with their families.

The groups for whom heavier viewing was not generally associated with more positive familial experiences were those adults who were single, divorced, or separated and it was suggested that for these respondents, loneliness and negative mood states play greater roles in the decision to view than is the case for married subjects.

Clearly, heavy viewing of television was not shown to be the uniformly negative phenomenon vis-à-vis the family that some have suggested. Rather, that heavy viewing is often in accord with more positively experienced familial relations may be overdetermined. People who enjoy time with their families may be more inclined to watch TV together, and time spent watching together may reinforce and enhance family solidarity. For the family that wishes to be together, television offers an opportunity to readily share the same experiences. In contrast, other activities that family members do together often require preparation and planning, a cash outlay, or nearly equal skills, background, or shared interests. Television requires virtually none of these and it is understandable that family members who watch more TV together spend more time together generally.

For many subjects, time spent with the family and with television helps provide psychological order. For those who live alone and spend more time by themselves, television can become an even more important source for the provision of psychic order. Maslow (1954) set belonginess and love as the third most basic need in his seven-tier hierarchy and it is no surprise that people who are in less contact with others use television to substitute for the satisfaction of this basic human need.

It should also be kept in mind that much American television content is itself supportive of mainstream, conventional values (Gitlin, 1972; Parenti, 1986).* In fact, a series of studies reviewed by Gerbner, Gross, Morgan, and Signorielli (1986) provides evidence that television may actually narrow or "mainstream" the political and social outlooks of heavy viewers. Heavier use of television has also been correlated with a "syndrome of conventionality" (Weigel, 1976; i.e., conventional social attitudes and values are often those of the heavier television viewer).

In this view, "like-minded" viewers are inclined to gravitate to television's conventional perspective on the world. This congruence between viewer and content may help provide order in experience while reinforcing mainline attitudes by extolling the virtues of basic institutions such as the family, church, and school, and values such as honesty, hard work, and self-advancement. In this regard it is noteworthy that among the items from Maddi's alienation index that generated the most agreement from the heavy adult viewers—and differentiated them significantly from the light viewers—was: "I work to support myself and family, and that's important."

Ultimately, the evidence on whether the medium might disrupt family life is mixed. On the one hand, heavier use of television was associated with somewhat more positive familial experiences for most of the respondents in three separate studies. On the other hand, families that spend a lot of time watching television together spend relatively more time passively with one another and heavier viewers' non-TV family time was also shown to be more passive than that of lighter viewers.

What this bodes for the psychological and behavioral ecology of the family or for the development of children is not simply assessed. The difficulty lies in part in that we do not as yet have longitudinal ESM data. But even if we did, it is nearly impossible to know how family life might have proceeded in any given family or set of families if less television had been viewed. Which came first, a problem in the family or television

---

*Although television is a commercial medium, dominated by the rhythms and values of a post-industrial consumer society, it still reflects the concerns of a Puritan people (Goethals, 1981; Hirsch, 1980; Newcomb, 1974; Newcomb & Alley, 1983). Moral messages can be discerned at the conclusion of most dramatic and comedic presentations. Good triumphs over evil, the forces for social cohesion defeat the perpetrators of chaos.

viewing? What would the heavy viewing families have done instead of watching TV? Conversely, what would happen to light viewing families if they viewed more?

It may also be the case that for some families, parallel or separate experience during television is quite functional. In some households, television viewing may serve as an "atmospheric barrier" helping to keep families together by keeping them apart (Rosenblatt & Cunningham, 1976). And as we and others have suggested, television may be among the few things that some families can (or will) regularly do together.

Still, it is certainly the case that some families, or some individuals in families, might profit by spending less time with television and more time in direct interaction with one another and engaging in more active, challenging, and creative pursuits either together or alone. In this regard, parallel viewing is certainly problematic when a parent (often the father) consistently ignores a child because the parent would prefer to watch television. Not a few adults similarly feel that their spouses (again, more frequently the husband) would rather watch television than talk with them or listen. Not a few people have to compete with TV shows and celebrities for the attention of other members of their family. Television viewing can also be thought to compete with how much attention one pays to one's own life versus the time one pays to the lives being led on the screen.

But even in these examples, it may be too easy to immediately point a finger at television. In thinking about such matters we should keep in mind the husband or father who purposely hides behind his evening newspaper to avoid interaction with the family. Such behavior occurred before television and no doubt before the advent of the newspaper as well.

ENDNOTES

[1]Among those who subscribe to this view are Bronfenbrenner (1973); Goldsen (1977); Maccoby (1951); Mander (1978); and Winn (1977).

[2]Among those who hold to this position are Bechtel et al. (1972); Bramson (1961); Comstock et al. (1978); and Fowles (1982), among others.

[3]A host of observers (Brody et al., 1980; Faber, Brown, & McLeod, 1979; Foley, 1968; Friedson, 1953; Glick & Levy, 1962; Katz & Foulkes, 1962; Katz & Gurevitch, 1976; Lull, 1980; Lyle, 1972; Robinson, 1972b) have suggested that greater family solidarity may be achieved via television-induced interaction and conversation as well as shared laughter, sorrow, and anger. Friedson (1953), for example, concluded that children preferred television to other media because it provided contact with the family.

[4]Many of the findings to follow are reported elsewhere (Kubey, 1989c).

[5]These findings follow the trend of all "alone" experiences, which are generally more

negative than "family" experiences regardless of what a person is doing. In other words, as a function of being alone or with the family, television watching is modified in much the same manner as most other activities. One exception is the higher level of challenge accompanying family viewing—a variable that does not typically differentiate solitude.

The TV viewing experience is also often enhanced by involvement in secondary activities. For example, when eating is reported as secondary to TV, all subjective self-report ratings improve—especially activation states.

[6]Different units of analysis were used in Tables 11 and 12. In Table 11 "person"-level analyses were employed. Here, each person's applicable reports were summed and averaged. In Table 12, analyses were done at the "signal" level (i.e., the total number of applicable reports were used). The former method is more strict and less likely to produce significant results because the number of cases is smaller, but as we mentioned earlier, for many kinds of comparisons, signal-report level analyses have proved reliable and when compared to person level analyses, the results are virtually identical.

[7]With regard to these analyses it is important to clarify that being with one's "family" means different things for single versus married respondents. Family almost necessarily implies "family of origin" for single people, whereas for married people, time spent with family generally refers to "family of procreation" (i.e., spouse and possibly children).

This means that because many single respondents live alone, when they get together with family members they do so most frequently in their parents' homes or in public (i.e., only occasionally in their *own* home). The vast majority of the married persons' family time, in contrast, does occur in their own homes. Furthermore, even though age was controlled for in the correlations just cited, an age factor may still be operative as 77% of the singles were 30 years old or younger and 97% were 45 or below (mean age = 27.9 years), whereas for the marrieds, 36% were above 45 and only 17% were below 30 (mean age = 41.3 years). Put another way, heavier viewing young adults (ages 18–30) felt worse with their families than did light viewing young adults (the correlation between amount of viewing and affect with family for young adults was $r = -.33, p < .05$).

CHAPTER 7

Viewing as Cause, as Effect, and as Habit

A body at rest tends to remain at rest.

—Newton's First Law of Motion

To find an association between watching television and a particular mood or cognitive state does not by itself imply a causal connection. Television viewing occurs in real time and any single episode of viewing could conceivably cause, or be caused by, any number of mental states.

Does television viewing result in negative moods or is it a functional solution to negative experiences?[1] Whether television viewing causes certain things to happen in people or whether these same "things" are what cause people to view is the subject of this chapter.

Actually, to be able to link any particular set of emotional or cognitive states with television viewing using ESM data will mark something of an achievement. For as critical as the direction of causality is to understanding media behaviors, no one to our knowledge has previously attempted to test whether such relations exist outside the lab or beyond responses to survey questions. As noted earlier, there have been excellent eth-

119

nographic studies of television behavior in the home but they have not attempted to understand or explain how people feel before, during, or after viewing.

Some of the validity problems inherent in many laboratory studies of media behavior have already been mentioned. As for surveys, the question arises whether people are generally cognizant of how they feel affectively or cognitively before or after they view. This problem in using surveys to understand why people actually use the media is emphasized by Zillmann and Bryant (1985):

> People usually pay little attention to why they choose what they choose when they choose it . . . the large majority of people, are likely to attribute their choice to factors other than the actual determinants. (p. 163)

Instead of having respondents try to remember past experiences and moods or attempt to explain their behavior, the ESM permits people to simply report on what they are doing and how they are feeling. These reports can then be used to map patterns of use that may elude the subjects themselves.

The goal, then, is to begin to untangle the relationships between moods, cognitive states, and viewing behaviors in real time.

The first problem was to determine whether particular states coincided with the act of viewing or whether people already felt particular ways before turning to TV. In other words, television viewing could conceivably have been found to be relaxing only because people already felt relaxed before they began to view.

The next step was to examine how people felt before, during, and after television viewing and for comparison, these analyses were plotted against similar time-sequence profiles for other forms of leisure. The question here was whether people felt differently while viewing than they did before or after viewing, and whether the television sequences were different from those coinciding with other activities.

The third question was whether there were characteristic changes in moods and cognitive states as a result of people viewing for longer periods of time. We already know that people feel relaxed when they view. But does more viewing result in more relaxation?

The final set of analyses focused on how people felt before, during, and after their heaviest and lightest evenings of viewing. The question was whether certain emotional states increased the likelihood that people would watch a lot of television, and whether there was any evidence to suggest that people felt differently after heavy viewing.

HOW DO PEOPLE FEEL BEFORE WATCHING TELEVISION?

The first question to resolve was whether TV viewing actually induces the feelings of passivity and relaxation as reported in chapter 5, or whether respondents feel more passive and relaxed before they begin to view. To provide an answer, we first compared feelings reported during signals immediately preceding viewing TV, against those reported by the same persons on another evening at home, at roughly the same time of day and in the same environment, but not prior to viewing.

Little evidence was found in these analyses that people feel any more or less relaxed or passive before TV viewing than they do before engaging in other activities. There was evidence, however, that people felt somewhat less happy and satisfied before TV viewing than before other activities, although these were not statistically significant differences.

EXPERIENTIAL STATES BEFORE, DURING, AND AFTER VIEWING

The next issue is quite similar and concerns the sequences of mood that occur before, during, and after viewing. In order to compare these sequences with those associated with other leisure activities, we also conducted analyses for sports and general "leisure" activities. The procedures and data preparations involved were fairly complex and are presented in the accompanying note.*

Procedures and the Handling of Data. Due to limitations in the data and the various procedures described here, the sample sizes for these analyses were small and the reader needs to recognize that although significance tests were applied, one can only conclude so much from such data. Fortunately, the largest number of sequences available for comparison was for the activity that we are most interested in—television viewing ($n = 40$). As a result, we can be more confident in these findings than for activities meant only for comparison: sports ($n = 25$) and leisure ($n = 17$). (The leisure activities involved were composed of the following: entertaining friends or attending a party; doing art work, hobbies, or practicing for a performance; and watching a sporting event, play, or movie or listening to live music.)

On average, before and after responses occurred within 1.2 hours of the "during" observation. In each sequence, we set a criterion such that each before and after report had to occur within 2½ hours of the free-time activity under study. In order to permit a fair comparison and because different activities typically occur with greater or lesser frequency earlier or later in the evening (e.g., cooking and eating occur before TV viewing, whereas preparing for bed typically occurs after) the frequency of before and after activities had to be balanced by weighting and in a few instances randomly removing a small number of observations.[2] Before and after observations were also limited to activities (or secondary activities) other than the free-time activity under study. Statistical comparisons for the six variables to follow employed t tests.

Findings

Challenge.   Figure 13 shows that when people watch TV, the mean reported level of challenge is significantly higher ($p < .01$) both before and
after viewing. In contrast, when people become involved in sports ($p <
.001$) and leisure, reported challenges are clearly far higher during the
activity than before or after.

Concentration and Difficulty of Concentration.   As with challenge, concentration falls off during television viewing and then rises again afterward ($p < .05$). In contrast, concentration increases during the two comparison activities (Figure 14), especially for sports.

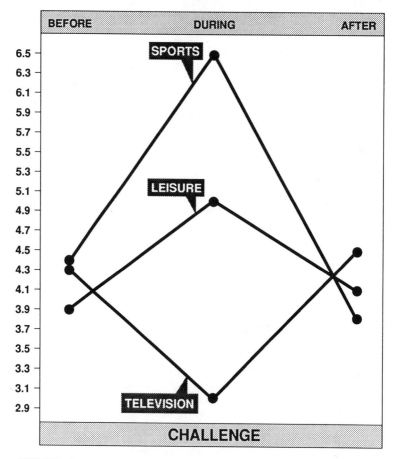

FIGURE 13.   Mean responses before, during, and after television, sports,
and leisure.

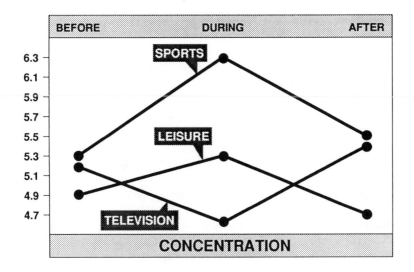

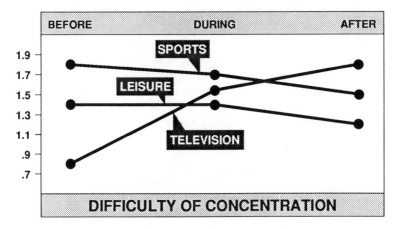

FIGURE 14.   Mean responses before, during, and after television, sports, and leisure.

There is no evidence in this comparison to suggest that television impedes concentration after viewing as some critics have suggested. However, self-reports of *difficulty* of concentration did rise significantly ($p < .05$) during viewing from the level reported before and instead of dropping back down, the level after viewing was even higher than it had been during. The finding suggests that spending time with television might make concentration more difficult afterward. In contrast, in an identical analysis of 25 similar reading sequences, it was found that difficulty of concentration *decreased* after reading from the level before or during.

Activation. For the comparison activities, the level of activation (active–passive, alert–drowsy, strong–weak, excited–bored) increased from before to during (Figure 15). During television viewing, however, reported activation dropped off quite significantly ($p < .01$) and did not return to its previous level. There does appear to be a downward time trend in the data as presented in Figure 15, but a general time of day effect would appear to be only partly responsible for these results as the correlation between time of day and activation in non-TV activities is only $-.15$ ($p < .001$).* Nor after other non-TV activities is there a similar report of lowered activation.

With our colleague Reed Larson we have also found significantly lower alertness after television viewing compared with other activities in a sample of nearly 500 children and young adolescents. Furthermore, this finding held up, as it did with the adults, even after numerous attempts to explore possible confounds in the data (Larson & Kubey, 1989).

The less-activated viewing state tends to "spill over" into at least some of the non-TV experiences occurring afterward.[3] That any state or mood, particularly one as notable as passivity during viewing, might be maintained for a time afterward is supported in a previous ESM study by Larson, Csikszentmihalyi, and Graef (1980) in which extreme moods were shown to be at half strength 2 hours later.

Affect. In Figure 16, we turn to the affect cluster (happy–sad, cheerful–irritable, friendly–hostile, sociable–lonely) and find substantially better moods during the comparison activities than during viewing, and roughly equal shifts from before to during and from during to after. For television viewing, however, there is a decline in affect from before to during and a further decline from during to after. There appears to be no time of day effect insofar as the correlation between time of day and affect in home activities generally, is not at all strong.

---

*A potential problem in such time-sequence analyses concerns whether there are certain characteristic changes in mood and activation states that coincide with later hours regardless of the activity. This was controlled for, in part, by the balancing procedure described earlier but also by learning which self-report variables were most vulnerable to change as a function of time. This was accomplished by correlating the time of day, after 4:30 p.m., with each of the self-reports given at home for each variable. To avoid confounds, when correlating time with self-reports in all activities, television and reading reports were removed. Not surprisingly, the strongest relationship was a negative correlation of $-.21$ ($p < .001$, $n = 642$) between time of evening and reported alertness. In short, people simply grow more drowsy as the evening progresses.

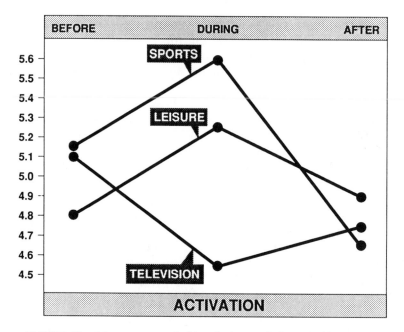

FIGURE 15.   Mean responses before, during, and after television, sports, and leisure.

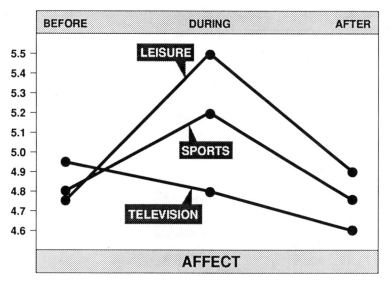

FIGURE 16.   Mean responses before, during, and after television, sports, and leisure.

In short, other forms of leisure give every appearance of helping to raise moods during involvement, but this is not the case for television viewing. Moreover, correlations indicate that the lower activation after viewing is related to the simultaneous reports of less positive affect after viewing.

Relaxation.   In Figure 17 we see that there is a rise in relaxation from before to during television viewing and a more substantial difference ($p < .05$) between during and after. Although subjects were more relaxed during viewing than before or after, they did not report feeling more relaxed after viewing than they did before. Again, there appears to be no general time of day effect for this finding as the correlation between relaxation and time of day was extremely low ($r = .04$, $n = 642$) and insignificant.

There is a significant and striking rise in relaxation from before to during for the very small number of leisure activity pairs ($p < .01$), but no comparable decline afterward. In fact, respondents reported feeling as relaxed after leisure as they did during. In contrast, if there is any

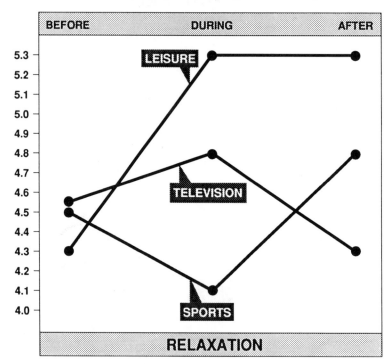

FIGURE 17.   Mean responses before, during, and after television, sports, and leisure.

recuperative relaxation function to be observed for television watching, it appears to occur only at the time of viewing. There is no evidence in these analyses to suggest that television viewing offers emotional rewards that extend beyond viewing.

DO EXPERIENCES CHANGE
WHEN TELEVISION IS VIEWED OVER TIME?

In this next section, any two successive occasions of television viewing were examined. The procedure involved comparing all instances of two consecutive ESM self-reports of television viewing from the same person while at home and occurring no more than 2½ hours apart. Because of concern about time-of-day effects, a group of consecutive "control" activities was also selected for comparison.*

Two types of analyses were performed. First, for each variable in each comparison, paired t tests were used to test the difference between Time 1 and Time 2. Second, a repeated measures analysis of variance was calculated to test (a) the overall difference between the two types of activity being compared; (b) the effect of time, namely, a treatment effect; and (c) an interaction effect. All 21 self-report variables were examined but only those 9 which were most revealing are presented here.

Findings

Figure 18 shows that the overall level of challenge is substantially and significantly lower for television than for the control activities. Challenge also drops off from Time 1 to Time 2, but not significantly. "Wish to be doing something else" also exhibits a large rating difference between

---

*Procedure. The "control" activities also consisted of any two consecutive ESM reports, occurring at home, of the same primary activity other than TV viewing or reading. There were 56 pairs of observations included in the TV viewing group, and 46 pairs in the control group.

Although subjects did not necessarily engage in the same activity (whether it was TV viewing or control) continuously from Time 1 to Time 2, the "checklist" data from side 2 of the ESF indicates that continuous television viewing activity occurred in many instances. Some subjects did stop watching TV on occasion to do other things or to fix a snack or answer the telephone. At the very least, the Time 2 observations denote occasions of TV viewing or the control activity when the total amount of viewing or control activity for that day was cumulatively higher than at Time 1. (The most common non-TV and nonreading control activity occurring twice in succession at home was cooking.) Successive occasions of reading were studied in the same manner but there were only 16 consecutive pairs of observations available for analysis.

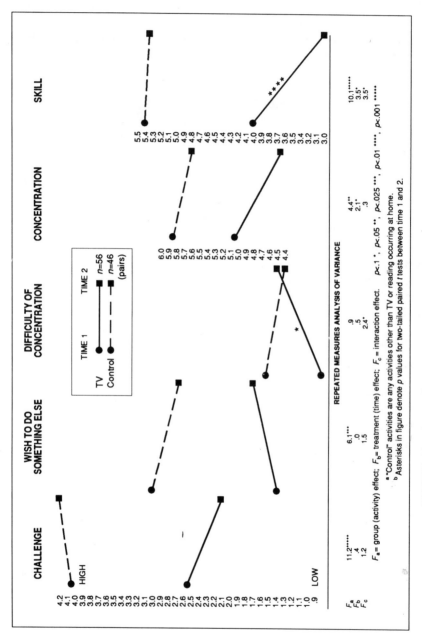

FIGURE 18. Comparing mean responses for two consecutive reports of television viewing versus other activities.[a,b]

[a] "Control" activities are any activities other than TV or reading occurring at home.
[b] Asterisks in figure denote p values for two-tailed paired t tests between time 1 and 2.

F_a = group (activity) effect; F_b = treatment (time) effect; F_c = interaction effect. $p < .1$ *, $p < .05$ **, $p < .025$ ***, $p < .01$ ****, $p < .001$ *****

activities, but there is a slight increase with time for viewing and a slight drop for the control activities.

Difficulty of concentration rises for TV viewing from Time 1 to Time 2 and there is a small interaction effect indicating that concentration may become more difficult to direct as the person continues to view over time relative to concentration becoming somewhat easier in the control activities. Concentration is itself significantly lower during viewing than during the control activities ($p < .05$) and there is also a general time effect. Finally, for skill, we see a very large difference between activities. In addition, the level of reported skill falls off markedly ($p < .01$) from Time 1 viewing to Time 2 viewing.

In Figure 19, the level of affect for television viewing and for the control activities is virtually the same, but there is an interaction effect ($p < .05$) indicating that relative to other activities, affect may drop with prolonged viewing. An even larger interaction effect is observed for satisfaction. Television viewing is shown once again to be much more relaxing than other activities ($p < .01$) but people do not report being more relaxed at one time than the other.

To summarize, at Time 2, people reported applying less skill to the activity of television viewing. Concentration dropped, whereas difficulty of concentration simultaneously increased. The wish to do something else also increased slightly, whereas affect and satisfaction fell over time. For the comparison activities, however, this was not the case. Much the same experience was reported at Time 2 and at Time 1, or there was improvement over time. Only for concentration was there a similar decrease over time for the control activities.

The findings indicate that the experience of viewing tends to become less rewarding as it is viewed for longer periods of time, although this was not the case for other household activities.

The same type of analysis comparing TV viewing and reading suggests that the decrease in concentration and increase in difficulty of concentration over time with television viewing may be noteworthy. For reading, concentration increased from Time 1 to Time 2 whereas it simultaneously became less difficult to concentrate over time.

The same trends were found when time of day after 4:30 p.m. was correlated with self-reports made during viewing and reading. For reading, as the evening progressed, people reported concentrating more but ease of concentration improved. For television viewing the pattern was the opposite—concentration declined but became more difficult.[4] Not only was concentration lower during viewing than reading, but concentration during TV appears to drop further over time and it simultaneously becomes more difficult to concentrate.

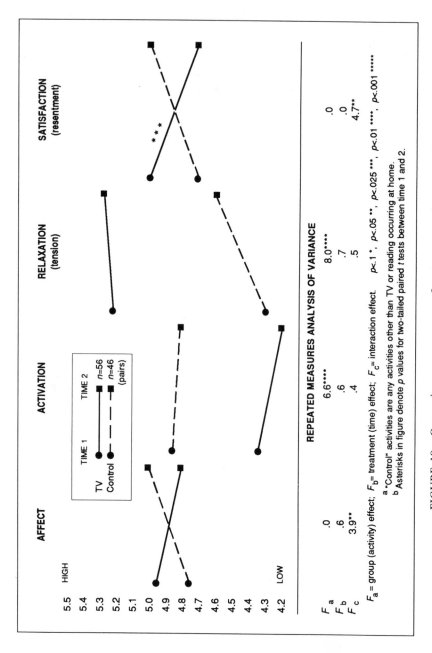

FIGURE 19. Comparing mean responses for two consecutive reports of television viewing versus other activities.[a,b]

EXPERIENCES AND ACTIVITIES BEFORE, DURING, AND AFTER A HEAVY VERSUS A LIGHT NIGHT OF TELEVISION VIEWING

Do People Feel Differently Before a Heavy Night of Viewing?

Television is viewed for many reasons. But referring back to the model in chapter 1, it would seem that viewing would be particularly likely to occur when people needed to increase order in experience (i.e., when their recent experiences were negative or difficult to reconcile with their goals). To test this assumption, the following analyses compared nights in which people watched television extensively with nights in which little or no television was viewed. The question was whether people felt differently before a night of heavy viewing.[5] To obtain an answer, viewers' subjective states before and after a heavy (or "high") night of TV viewing were compared with states before and after a light (or "low") night.*

Table 13 shows that people experienced significantly more negative moods before a heavy night of television viewing than before a light night. Most striking is that the differences on these variables were smaller and nonsignificant in the morning before a high or low night. The larger affective differences were only present in the afternoon, close in time to the onset of heavy viewing. There was some evidence, however, that people felt significantly less control during the morning before a heavy night than before a light night and there is some evidence to suggest that lack of control earlier in the day could lead to more negative moods later in the day.

Because of the significant differences on the items friendly–hostile

---

Procedure. Each person's daily evening record, past 6 p.m., of primary, secondary, and checklist reports of TV viewing was examined in order to locate the highest and lowest nights of TV viewing. Only weekdays were used in order to maintain comparability. A number of subjects watched approximately the same amount of TV every night and were therefore not included in the analysis. The criteria required that a person had to have at least three times as many reports of TV on a heavy evening as on a light evening to be included.

Once the heavy and light nights were established, it was a relatively simple matter to select the next day as the "day after" a high or low night. After selecting high and low nights, the days before and after could be broken down by morning, afternoon, or evening as raw reports for each subject were used.

For the analyses to follow, the few occasions of primary and secondary TV viewing occurring before 6 p.m. were eliminated in order to reduce confounding influences. In each comparison and time frame, t tests were used to compare how the same people felt either before or after a high and low night of television viewing. Some of these findings are reported in Kubey and Csikszentmihalyi (in press).

TABLE 13
Mean Responses Before a Heavy and Light Night of Television Viewing
in All Non-TV Activities[a] (from Kubey & Csikszentmihalyi, in press)

Response Variables	7 a.m. to noon			12:01 p.m. to 6 p.m.		
	Heavy	Light	t	Heavy	Light	t
n	98	115		149	167	
Concentration	5.0	5.7	−1.9	5.0	5.1	−.4
Hard to concentrate ..	1.7	1.6	.4	1.7	1.7	.0
Self-consciousness	2.3	3.0	−1.5	3.1	2.7	.9
Control	6.9	7.6	−2.3*	7.4	7.5	−.7
Challenge	3.6	4.3	−1.7	3.7	4.1	−1.1
Skill	5.5	5.9	−1.0	5.6	5.7	−.3
Wish something else ..	4.1	4.2	−.3	3.8	3.8	−.3
Stakes	3.8	3.7	.3	3.7	3.7	.0
Activation	4.8	4.9	−.6	4.9	4.9	−.4
Alert	5.4	5.5	−.8	5.4	5.6	−.7
Strong	4.6	4.9	−1.8	4.8	4.9	−.5
Active	4.9	4.8	.6	4.9	4.9	.0
Excited	4.3	4.3	.2	4.3	4.3	.0
Affect	4.8	4.9	−1.1	4.7	5.1	−2.9**
Friendly	5.0	5.2	−.9	4.9	5.4	−3.1**
Happy	4.7	4.8	−.4	4.9	5.2	−2.2*
Cheerful	4.6	4.7	−.4	4.5	4.9	−2.4*
Sociable	4.7	4.9	−1.5	4.7	5.0	−2.3*
Relaxed	4.7	4.7	.4	4.5	4.7	−1.1
Creative	4.5	4.7	−.8	4.5	4.6	−1.2
Satisfied	4.6	4.7	−.5	4.6	4.9	−1.7
Free	4.6	4.4	.9	4.7	4.7	.0

[a]Secondary TV viewing was excluded from all "before" data.
*$p < .05$; **$p < .01$; two-tails.

and sociable–lonely, it was suspected that the results might be confounded by a higher incidence of people being alone before a high TV night than before a low TV night. Indeed, a parasocial motive to viewing does appear to be at play. People were somewhat more likely to be alone before a high night of viewing than before a low night ($\chi^2 = 3.54$, $p = .11$). Such a finding initially qualified the results in Table 13 but further analyses showed that although social context does play a role, the differences in affect hold up across both social contexts of being alone and being with others. These differences were also consistent across the days of the week and for every demographic group tested.

Although there is some evidence that people may feel worse an hour or so after viewing television than after other leisure activities, there is stronger evidence that negative affect precedes rather than follows heavy viewing. It is more appropriate to conclude, therefore, that television viewing is more a response to negative affect than a cause of it—at least in the short term.

Additional support for this conclusion comes from the fact that no significant differences were found the morning after a heavy and light night of viewing, although a variety of factors, particularly the mere passage of time, may be responsible for the fact that no differences were found the day after.

Do People Engage in Different Activities Before and During a Heavy and Light Night?

People did tend to be alone more before a heavy night of viewing than before a light night and not surprisingly, they also spent significantly less time talking. That loneliness leads to television viewing has been noted frequently (Danowski, 1975; Davis & Kubey, 1982; Hess, 1974; Meyersohn,1965).

The medium clearly offers parasocial experiences. TV programs are well stocked with familiar faces and voices and viewing can help people maintain the illusion of being with others even when they are alone.

Not surprisingly, during a light TV night, more time was spent in activities outside the home such as driving, walking, sports, and club meetings. Less time was spent cooking. When home activities only are considered, the activities more frequently occurring on a low TV night are somewhat more active (preparing to go out, doing laundry, and sewing) and creative (art work, hobbies, playing a musical instrument). On heavy TV nights, the same people more frequently report talking, cooking, and "just relaxing" or lying in bed as their main activity (the latter two being frequently accompanied by secondary TV viewing).

Do People Feel Differently in Non-TV Activities at Home on Heavy and Light Nights?

People reported much greater wish to do something else ($p < .001$) during non-TV activities on heavy viewing nights than on light nights.* The finding can be interpreted in two ways: The wish to do something else may itself help drive television viewing on heavy TV nights, or heavy television viewing may make people wish to avoid non-TV activities more. It is also possible that both phenomena are operative.

Subjects also reported feeling less challenged, less strong, and less

---

*All instances in which television was being viewed in accompaniment with another activity were eliminated from this analysis.

creative on heavy nights in non-TV activities. This is partly the result of the different kinds of activities engaged in but may also be the result of the *passive spillover* effect in that some of the most distinguishing experiential aspects of viewing are maintained for a period afterward.

SUMMARY AND DISCUSSION

Before interpreting the many findings in this chapter, let us briefly recount them. First, reports of happiness were found to be slightly lower than usual before people began to watch television, and significantly lower in the afternoon before an evening of heavy viewing. The results indicate that lower affect earlier in the day is a much better predictor than any of the other self-report variables, including passivity or tiredness, of heavier viewing at night. People were also significantly more likely to be alone both before and during a heavy night of viewing.

The act of viewing, in contrast to sports and the general leisure activities studied did not appear to substantially improve affective states. Viewers did become more relaxed (or less tense) during viewing but there was no evidence that television acted to promote higher relaxation after viewing. To the contrary, people reported feeling relatively less relaxed, happy, and satisfied after viewing than after the other activities studied. Only after highly relaxing but cognitively demanding general leisure activities did people continue to report feeling relaxed.

Activation before viewing was as high as before other activities, but it fell off perceptibly during viewing and tended to remain low afterward. The highly passive act of viewing television appears to cause some adults, as well as adolescents and children, to continue feeling significantly more passive and less alert after viewing.

In comparisons of two successive occasions of television viewing, Time 2 viewing was reported as less challenging and involving less concentration and skill than Time 1. Although high relaxation was reported at both observations, satisfaction decreased significantly and it was harder to concentrate at Time 2. In contrast, in an examination of two successive occasions of reading, people reported concentrating more at Time 2 than at Time 1, although they also concentrated with less difficulty at Time 2.

Subjects did appear to watch television more heavily in reaction to negative affect and to being alone, but viewing appeared to do little to improve affect—only tension was relieved and only while viewing lasted.

The findings demonstrate that people use television in personal adaptation. Heavier television viewing is partly a response to solitude and to more negative affective experiences earlier in the day, and the heavy viewing evening may be one in which subjects opt for personal indulgence in order to escape reality demands, not wishing to do anything more demanding than watch TV.

The Experience of Television Viewing and Reading and Comparability With Other Studies

To further interpret these findings, we examine how the activity of television viewing and reading compare psychologically both in our research and the research of others.

Brain Activity and Attentional Inertia.   As shown in chapter 5, reading is significantly more demanding cognitively: it is more active and involves more alertness, more concentration, more challenges, and more skills than television viewing. Furthermore, these differences were significant regardless of whether persons viewed or read alone or with the family.[6]

A number of EEG research findings comparing the two media harmonize quite well with our results in showing that reading produces somewhat more beta activity ("fast waves" associated with increased mental activity and attention) than television viewing, which causes somewhat more alpha activity ("slow waves" associated with relaxation and less mental arousal).[7] Krugman (1971, 1977), for example, concluded that "the [EEG] response to print may be fairly described as active . . . the response to television as passive" (1971, p. 7).

Television can involve us and attract our attention but it does so without effortful concentration. In other words, in terms of concentration, television viewing is a low-involvement activity. The paradoxical consequence is that low-cognitive effort by the viewer may make it harder, not easier, to continue concentrating. With time, people may miss being challenged and actively involved and may feel somewhat worse and more passive as a result.

We are not alone in finding that people concentrate less the longer they view television. EEG research supports the ESM findings and in a different kind of study, Husson and Krull (1983) found that attention in children—measured as amount of time subjects had their eyes on the screen—dropped over a 1-hour period.

Anderson et al. (1979) reported a result different from that of Husson and Krull, although one that may be compatible with ours nonetheless. They concluded that television often induces "attentional inertia" (p. 339) (i.e., "the longer people look at television, the greater is the probability that they will continue to look"). Anderson and Lorch (1983) suggested that this "inertia" may be indicative of *increased* "cognitive engagement," although we hasten to note that "looking" does not necessarily connote *concentration*. For example, Anderson et al. (1979) also reported that on those occasions when a single episode of looking at the TV lasted longer than 10 seconds, "we often observed the child's body relax, head slouch forward, and mouth drop open. The posture might then be maintained continuously for several minutes . . ." (p. 340). Mulholland (1973) also reported postures and facial musculature relaxing with prolonged viewing. Such behaviors suggest that the form of attention or concentration associated with television viewing may be of a special kind.

As for EEG studies, Mulholland (1973) and Reeves, Thorson, Rothschild, McDonald, Hirsch, and Goldstein (1986) reported that more alpha waves, indicating lower cortical arousal, also coincided with prolonged viewing. Krugman (1971) similarly reported exponential decreases in left-brain dominance with repeated brief exposures to TV ads. Left-brain activity is generally associated with linear and sequential cognitive functions such as speaking, reading, and mathematical calculation. The perception of images is thought to be largely a right-brain function. Thus, for Krugman (1971, 1980), Mulholland (1974), and others, left-brain activity is equated with high involvement and gross-eye movements, and right-brain activity with low involvement and a motionless or focused eye as with TV viewing.

The Importance of Eye Movement and the Advent of High-Definition TV. Eye movement may well be a crucial factor in understanding some of the experiential differences among television viewing, reading, and other media. Reading, for example, requires constant, active eye movements. Watching a movie on a large screen also typically involves active visual searching and scanning. By contrast, because the screen is much smaller, television is viewed with much less eye movement. Along with other factors, this helps to explain why the television viewer may be "involved" but why it is a different form of attentional involvement, one requiring little concentration or active, intentional control.[8] As suggested in chapter 5, some instances of prolonged viewing may involve an altered state of consciousness.

Eye movements may also prove important to understanding how people will experience high-definition television (HDTV). HDTV is likely to produce changes in how television is viewed and experienced because the greater detail and quality of the picture will allow viewers to sit twice as close to the same size television screen as has been the case with traditional screens where one sits further away in order for picture imperfections to disappear. Furthermore, the HDTV screen aspect ratio will be considerably wider (Kubey & Barnett, 1989). The traditional television set has a short-to-long side ratio of 3 : 4, or 0.750, whereas the companies pioneering HDTV have settled on a screen approaching the aspect ratio of *Cinemascope* with a ratio of 0.562.

As Lachenbruch (1989) has concluded, "The combination of closer-viewing distance and wider screen will have the effect of putting the viewer 'in' the picture, because the screen will occupy a much greater proportion of the field of vision" (p. 19). Sitting closer to a wider screen will also necessarily require more horizontal eye movement than sitting far away from a more square-like screen. Because the nature of eye movements is related to the nature of the television viewing experience and because it seems likely that viewers will engage in more active scanning of the new screen, the HDTV experience may involve greater cognitive activity than did traditional television viewing.

Why Television Viewing Is Habit Forming

How do our findings fit within the context of the larger culture in which viewing and the television industry itself are embedded? First, watching television is exceedingly easy to do and this surely helps explain why it is relaxing. The consistent reports of low concentration and the low level of cortical arousal in EEG studies both point to a mentally undemanding activity. With experience, processing television almost certainly becomes more automatic and this further explains why the medium places few demands on attentional resources.

Viewers are steadily reinforced by viewing in that they remain relaxed throughout, but as they view for longer periods of time, they become somewhat less likely to invest themselves in the enterprise—mental effort is less likely to be used in processing the information appearing on the screen.

It seems likely that the very lack of involvement and activity and the physically passive nature of viewing, particularly as it is continued over time, contributes to the lack of activity afterward as well as the lowered feelings of happiness and higher reports of wishing to do something else.

Passive spillover and the somewhat decreased enjoyment of television as viewing continues over time may also be the result of the three similar processes of *habituation, desensitization,* and *satiation* (Klapp, 1986; Linz et al., 1984). Each denotes a loss of responsiveness as novelty wanes. But because television viewing remains effortless and relaxing and helps order experience under most conditions, people often continue to view even if they are enjoying it less or have lost some appetite for the experience.

Viewing encourages more viewing, and although it occurs at a low level of emotional intensity, viewers grow attached to the screen. During viewing, people also come in contact with their own fantasy life and with other peoples' ideas and fantasies presented in an entertaining and palatable form, allowing temporary distraction and escape from personal concerns. Indeed, Singer (1980) has concluded that "If TV has a potential addictive power it arises from the fact that it reduces negative affect" (p. 50).[9] Easy escape from aversive states, and the relaxing viewing state itself both help provide order in experience and are among the primary factors that make it easy for people to develop and sustain a television habit.

Developing a viewing habit is made even easier by the fact that television is extremely inexpensive and available every day regardless of the hour.[10] In simple operant conditioning terms (Skinner, 1969), when people view they experience an immediate reward in the form of distraction and relaxation within seconds of turning on the set, and come to associate that improvement in emotional state with viewing.[11] In fact, children as young as 4 and 5 learn to use television to alleviate aversive states (Masters, Ford, & Arend, 1983).

Television viewing is unquestionably habit forming. It may even be addictive, although there are those who claim otherwise (Smith, 1986). Much depends on how one defines addiction. In any case, there is considerable anecdotal evidence that people experience symptoms akin to withdrawal when television is removed. The following examples illustrate what happens to some people when they suddenly stop watching television. We must caution, however, that most of the "experiments" listed were not conducted by social scientists but by newspapers or television companies.[12]

In 1977 the *Detroit Free Press* offered $500 to 120 families before 5 finally agreed to give up television for 1 month. Similar experiments have been run by the *Denver Post* (Ryan, 1974) and by the BBC in England. In each of these "experiments" as well as one conducted in West Germany in 1973, many TV abstainers allegedly reported increased boredom, nervousness, and depression. Domestic violence, smoking, and the use of tranquilizers were also reported to have increased. Winick (1988), who methodically studied families whose TV sets were in repair, also reported finding greater anxiety and aggression in families and more boredom and irritation among those who live alone.

Recollections from people whose only TV set broke down provide similar evidence for an addiction claim (Steiner, 1963):

"The family walked around like a chicken without a head."
"It's like a lost friend."

"It was terrible. We did nothing—my husband and I talked."
"I screamed constantly. Children bothered me and my nerves were on edge. Tried to interest them in games, but impossible. TV is part of them." (p. 99)

It should come as no surprise that the removal of television from a household might be disruptive. After all, viewing helps to provide relaxing feelings with minimal effort and viewers rarely report moods that connote psychological disorder. Once a television habit is formed and people become accustomed to using television to structure a significant proportion of their experience, it is no wonder that disorder in consciousness would increase if such a simple means of ordering is suddenly removed.

The Orienting Reflex, the Design of Television Programs, and the Structuring of Attention and Experience

A further explanation for why viewing is habit forming lies in how the medium elicits our attention via the orienting response. The orienting reflex, first described by Pavlov (1927), is our instinctive visual response to any sudden stimulus in the environment and it has been shown that television's "primitive visual elements" do elicit orienting responses as measured by the EEG (Reeves, Thorson, & Schleuder, 1986).[13]

Singer (1980) has applied the orienting response to television this way:

The TV set, and particularly commercial television with its clever use of constantly changing short sequences, holds our attention by a constant sensory bombardment that maximizes orienting responses. . . . We are constantly drawn back to the set and to processing each new sequence of information as it is presented. . . . The set trains us to watch it. (pp. 50–51)

But although it is normal for people to habituate and exhibit decreased responsiveness over time to such stimuli, in the case of television viewing, it seems that the reflex never reaches a state of complete habituation. Thus, it is easy for our eyes to remain transfixed on the screen even though we concentrate less and derive less satisfaction from the experience.

Television programs, after all, are carefully designed for dramatic action to peak immediately before the onset of advertisements that are so chock-full of special effects, flashy colors, movement, and sex that even an overworked orienting reflex may still respond.

Producers of TV ads are especially aware of the need to attract the viewer's attention via movement and rapid montage when selling what they call "low-involvement" or "low-interest" products such as toothpaste or breakfast cereals—products that the viewer is likely to consider mundane and otherwise ignore. TV ads play on the orienting reflex by casting these low-involvement products in highly paced dramatic montages and in unusual and improbable situations. As a result we are regularly presented with singing toilets, dancing raisins, or a new but not particularly unusual car parachuting from an airplane or sitting atop a mile-high summit. Not surprisingly television ads are by far the most expensive TV fare to produce and contain many more separate pieces of film and technical events (zooms, pans, slow or reverse motion, etc.) than the entertainment or information programming they *seem* to interrupt.

To be sure, the visual pace of television advertising has had an impact on the entire industry. The late TV producer Quinn Martin observed that "as commercials got people used to absorbing information quickly, I had to change my style to give them more jump cuts or they'd be bored. . . . The whole art form has speeded up" (interviewed in Newcomb & Alley, 1983, p. 62).[14] Kubey's (1989b) ongoing research on television production decision-making processes has revealed that virtually everyone in the television industry ardently believes that the audience attention span is growing shorter, and that to hold the audience, television editing must be even faster paced and present more and more exciting visual material.

The orienting reflex, which helps to keep people viewing, combined with the ease with which television materials are assimilated, helps explain why viewing is often automatic[15] and why "attentional inertia" (Anderson et al., 1979) sets in. In fact, in the days before the advent of VCRs and a high density of remote control channel changers, Paul Klein (1971) concluded that it was the laziness (or inertia) of the viewer that helped explain why a weak TV program could still receive a strong Nielsen rating as long as it followed a hit show. Of course both the national networks and local TV stations further encourage sustained viewing by making every effort to hold viewers throughout a program and for as much of the day or night as possible by incessantly promoting the next scheduled program with what TV professionals call "teases."

Television Viewing and Optimal Experience

A great deal of our thinking, reading, and learning involves successive efforts to attend, while the viewing of television and films is less likely to require effort. In one sense, attention is controlled from *inside* when the person invests psychic energy to decode a complex message, or from *outside* by the moving film or television image as these media tend to relieve the person of effortful control. This concept of "workless" or "involuntary" attention (Krugman, 1971; Munsterberg, 1916) helps explain why it is so easy to focus attention for long periods of time on the ever-changing image, and why much television watching can be properly characterized as passive, relaxing, and automatic.

Truly rewarding experiences, in contrast, almost invariably require concentrated involvement and interaction with complex information. The things that give people "natural highs"—playing music, a close game of tennis, an intense and meaningful conversation with a friend, a job well done—all require that we pay attention, that we look, listen, and act with care and skill.

The "flow" state, the episodes when life is heightened and when one is deeply involved and mental energy is highly focused, is in many ways the opposite of the viewing experience.* In flow experiences, people report very high concentration but ease of concentration—they feel active, strong, and in control. Concentration is so focused during flow activities that people typically report a diminished awareness of their surroundings and they lose track of time ("time flies"). The state is also more likely to occur when there is rapid, positive feedback about how one is doing in an activity.

Flow tends to occur when persons are confronted, or choose to confront themselves, with demanding opportunities for action (or challenges), which they feel capable of matching with their skills (Csikszentmihalyi, 1975, 1978, 1982). As illustrated in Figure 20, high challenges and low skills typically result in anxiety, whereas high skills and low challenges cause boredom—and often anxiety, as well, when boredom is great enough.

Flow activities involve a near equal pairing of high challenges and high skills, but as the figure indicates, the higher the skills and challenges, the more likely it is that flow will occur. In other words, challenges and skills can vary somewhat more with respect to one another at these high levels without impeding flow experiences.†

In the figure, sports and hobbies are but two examples of the activities likely to involve flow states. The key to flow is that the activity permits

---

*The word "flow" is a "native category." People often describe themselves as being "in flow" when functioning optimally and deeply absorbed in an activity. Flow states are comparable to the transient moments of self-actualization that Abraham Maslow (1967) called "peak experiences."

†The original flow model was refined by our Italian colleagues, Massimini and Carli (1986), who established that flow only occurred when challenges and skills were balanced and above a certain level (i.e., above average). In the model presented here, we have gone one step further to posit that although skills and challenges still need to be matched generally, the higher they are, the less balanced they need to be.

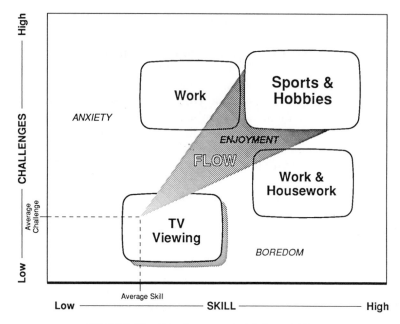

FIGURE 20.   The flow state and daily activities.

the person to experience high challenges and to apply matching skills. In other words, if a person packing groceries can continually find new challenges in the activity and more creative and innovative ways to keep accomplishing the job more quickly or with better results, then this job, too, can readily involve flow states.

Flow is often a force for personal growth and learning because to keep experiencing it, one needs to continue to challenge oneself and to do this, one must keep developing greater skills. In this sense, the flow diagonal as illustrated in Figure 20 refers back to the model discussed in chapter 1, in that for cognitive complexity to grow, challenges and skills must also grow. But as suggested by Figure 21, people cannot live by complexity alone, and a certain amount of order (and redundancy) must be constantly striven for lest one feel confused and anxious, or even lose hold of reality.

The highly focused attention and deep involvement of flow states are also directly associated with the loss of a sense of time and this helps explain why many leisure activities and some work activities can be "cleansing and restorative"—flow experiences help distract one from the other things going on in one's life and "wipe the slate clean" (Larson & Kleiber, in press).

Television also provides distraction and involvement, but with TV

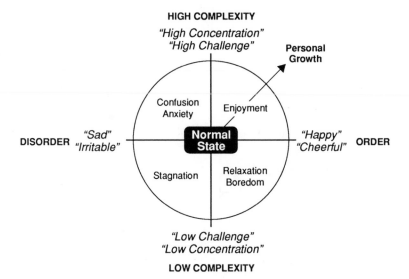

FIGURE 21.   A model for the effects of information on experience. Subjective complexity and order are the two main dimensions in how a message is experienced. Depending on the relative magnitude of these two vectors and the type of information involved, a person may experience anxiety, confusion, relaxation, boredom, stagnation, or enjoyment (or any other emotion). The condition most suited to personal growth is when both complexity and order are high.

there is generally a pairing of low challenges with very limited use of skills. Thus people usually do not concentrate very much and they feel relaxed and passive. In fact, adult respondents report nearly equal high challenges and high skills during only 3% of television viewing experiences. In comparison, the same respondents report low challenges and low skills during 70% of viewing occasions.

For the small number of 10 reports when television watching was in the flow condition of high challenges and high skills, the associated levels of concentration, affect, and motivation were a half standard deviation above the weekly mean. Clearly, then, viewing can be very involving and associated with high affect. But an incidence of 3% means that this occurs infrequently at best.

However, there are media activities that are much more likely to engender flow or flow-like experiences than television viewing (Figure 22). For example, the ESM research with adolescents has shown that video game play is quite activating and involves much higher reports of affect than does television viewing (Kubey & Larson, 1990). Video play is highly challenging, requires skill, and offers rapid feedback and thus

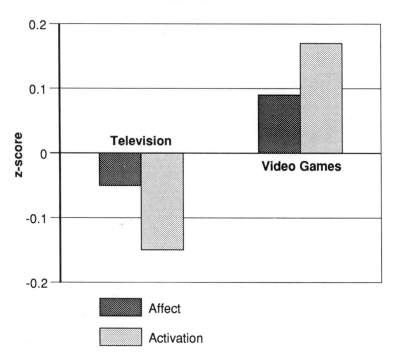

FIGURE 22.   Comparing mean affect and activation responses while watching television viewing and playing video games.

possesses all of the key structural elements necessary to experiencing
flow. Because many video games are also programmed to increase in
difficulty as the player's skill increases, video games offer unusual opportunities for flow and there can be little doubt that these same structural
features, and the flow experiences they engender, explain much of the
popularity of video games.

As economist Milton Friedman is fond of repeating, "there is no free
lunch." The exhilaration of flow must be paid for in a psychic curren-
cy—namely, active attention adapting to and interacting with challenging and complex stimuli. Put another way, one needs to experience a
sense of personal efficacy in an activity for flow to occur.

In contrast, television viewing allows us to order experience and be
occupied without greatly investing ourselves or using much mental energy, but then we get what we paid for—an illusion of activity that appears to
leave many viewers feeling no better—or worse—after viewing than they
did before. Yet because of its low psychic costs and the enormous visual
energy it contains, television viewing readily becomes habit forming.

Television Viewing, Passivity, and Guilt

For many then—perhaps for most—television viewing involves the relaxing passing of an evening but with little lasting reward. Indeed, many people feel mildly guilty about viewing. Consider the following quote from a heavy viewing college English instructor interviewed by Marie Winn (1977):

> I find television almost irresistible. When the set is on, I cannot ignore it. I can't turn it off. I feel sapped, will-less, enervated. . . . So I sit there for hours and hours. . . . I remember when we first got the set I'd watch it for hours and hours, whenever I could, and I remember that feeling of tiredness and anxiety that always followed those orgies, a sense of time terribly wasted. It was like eating cotton candy; television promised so much richness, I couldn't wait for it, and then it just evaporated into air. I remember feeling terribly drained after watching for a long time. (pp. 21–22)*

Previous attitudinal research (Bower, 1973, 1985; Furu, 1971; Himmelweit & Swift, 1976; Steiner, 1963) confirms that guilt about TV viewing, especially excessive viewing, is fairly common among American, British, and Japanese respondents and is greatest for middle-class viewers. It has also been shown that this guilt is often tied to passivity, namely, the feeling that one should have done something more productive than sitting or lying in front of the TV, while chatting idly or increasing one's daily consumption of calories. In fact, compared to six other possible typical leisure activities, 31% of Steiner's (1963) subjects, said that viewing television was the one that best fit the description, "I really should have been doing something else." The figure jumped to 42% for college educated subjects. Forty-nine percent picked TV as the activity that best fit the phrase, "Am I lazy!"

In other words, viewers know that they could have done something more productive. It makes sense, then, that after viewing, people are less likely to feel as good about themselves as they do after sports or leisure.

---

*Although it is rarely mentioned, the small speaker and low quality of television sound reproduction in many existing TV sets and, especially, increased volume during commercials may also contribute to the tiredness and irritation viewers informally report during and after a binge of viewing. It has even been suggested that the quality of light emanating from television sets could play a role in feelings of tiredness during and after viewing (Kubey, 1979; Mayron, Mayron, Ott, & Nations, 1976; Narkewicz & Gravens, 1966; Ott, 1973).

Furthermore, the high passivity of the viewing state is not readily shaken as one moves on to a new activity.

To the degree that guilt and discontent over television viewing are tied to passivity, and passivity is maintained after viewing, it makes even more sense that people are often not pleased with the amount that they view. People feel more passive and relatively less relaxed and satisfied afterward because television viewing is only a marginally effective solution; it distracts and removes us from stress and the demands of reality only temporarily.

ENDNOTES

[1]The former position has been advanced by Berlyne (1971); Conrad (1982); Gerbner and Gross (1976); Maccoby (1951, 1954); Mander (1978); Roszak (1968); and Winn (1977), among others.

The latter position, that television is used in response to negative emotional states, has been advanced by Brody, Stoneman, and Sanders (1980); Faber, Brown, and McLeod (1979); Foley (1968); Fowles (1982); Friedson (1953); Glick and Levy (1962); Hirsch (1977a, 1977b); Hirsch and Panelas (1981); Johnstone (1974); Katz and Gurevitch (1976); Pearlin (1959); Rosenblatt and Cunningham (1976); Singer (1980); and Tannenbaum (1980).

[2]A few subjects also contributed more than one set of observations for a specific activity. The demographic characteristics of those subjects contributing to the sequences followed the general trends of the larger sample. However, because of unequal contributions per subject, the analyses were performed twice—once with corrective weightings. As there were no instances of excessive contribution from one person or group of persons, no substantive differences were found in reanalyses. For this reason the results of the unweighted analyses only are presented. Also, for the sake of clarity, presentation of the actual findings in the five figures that follow has been simplified. For additional details on these analyses see Kubey (1984).

[3]A concept similar to passive spillover is Zillmann's (1971, 1978, 1980) notion of *excitation transfer* wherein arousal engendered by media stimuli lingers and can intensify subsequently experienced emotions. Excitation transfer helps explain theoretically how erotic arousal can lead to affiliation, lovemaking, hostility, aggression, and other states after viewing or why some people may engage in more intense interpersonal interactions than normal after seeing a highly emotional film or play. See also *spreading activation theory* (Collins & Quillian, 1969; Quillian, 1969) and *priming effects* (Berkowitz & Rogers, 1986).

Passive spillover may also help explain the findings from others' research showing that children who watch more television tend to be significantly more overweight than lighter viewing children, even after controlling for a myriad of possible intervening variables.

[4]As the evening progressed past 4:30 p.m., reported concentration increased slightly during reading—the correlation with time of day was positive ($r = .20, p < .10, n = 65$), although this was not the case if one was watching television. Just the opposite trend occurred for difficulty of concentration, where the correlation with time of day for TV was positive and significant ($r = .15, p < .05, n = 205$), whereas concentration during reading did not become any more difficult with time.

Quite striking was the reversal of how much was reported to be at stake when reading and viewing. As reading continued later into the night, significantly more was perceived to be at stake; but significantly less was at stake during TV viewing. A similar pattern occurred for challenges.

[5]There are a handful of studies bearing on this question, but none that we know of that has been performed outside the laboratory. Tannenbaum (1980), for example, observed subjects over a period of 1 day in a laboratory experiment and concluded that people often used TV after work as a means of adapting themselves to the rigors of the day. Bryant and Zillmann (1984) also showed experimentally that viewers seek certain kinds of programs to alter or adapt to unpleasant mood states such as stress and boredom. Wakshlag et al. (1986) similarly showed that experimentally varied working conditions resulted in different television program preferences. Christ and Medoff (1984) reported a counterintuitive finding that annoyed individuals avoided television viewing more than did people who had been praised.

[6]In contrast, mood states while watching television and reading were quite similar although in the large ESM study of adolescents, girls reported feeling better affectively during reading than boys, whereas boys reported more positive affect during television viewing than did girls (Kubey & Larson, 1990).

[7]See, for example, Appel et al. (1979); Mulholland (1974); Peper and Mulholland (1971); and Walker (1980). Rothschild et al. (1986), in reviewing these and other EEG studies of television viewing, concluded that there are often problems in such research. The sample sizes are frequently quite small and the length of time studied extremely short. In some instances there also seems to have been an overemphasis on the frequency of alpha relative to beta during viewing.

[8]Consider these comments from Emery and Emery (1976):

> The evidence is [that] TV not only impairs the ability [of the viewer] to attend, it also, by taking over a complex of direct and indirect neural pathways, decreases vigilance—the general state of arousal which prepares the organism for action should its attention be drawn to a specific stimulus. . . . The continuous trance-like fixation of the TV viewer is then not attention but distraction—a form akin to daydreaming or time out. (pp. 73–74)

It should be noted that the Emerys' conclusions were based on scattered findings, especially Krugman's (1971) research on a single subject that showed that the longer a person views TV the slower brain wave activity becomes.

[9]Dental patients who viewed a TV comedy were sufficiently distracted as to report significantly less pain than a control group during standard dental procedures (Seyrek, Corah, & Pace, 1984). As Singer (1980) has written: "It [television] is simply the easiest, most nondemanding resource ever available for shifting one's attention away from contemplating one's miseries" (p. 50).

[10]If traditional TV viewing is immediately gratifying, viewing with the aid of a video recorder may be even more so. The VCR allows viewers to record programs of particular interest and to "time-shift" viewing to a preferred viewing time. The "speed search" capability along with a remote control also allows viewers to skip undesired commercials and other program features, thereby better obtaining gratification.

[11]As Thorndike (1932) said, "relief stamps in the preference" in instances where an action relieves the person from an aversive state and "pleasure stamps in the preference" when positive states are induced.

Similarly, in Zillmann and Bryant's (1985) "theory of affect-dependent stimulus arrangement":

Actions incidentally taken and selections incidentally made during states of aversion that terminate or reduce the hedonically negative experience will leave a memory trace that will increase the likelihood for similar actions and selections under similar circumstances. . . . The actions or selections that provide relief from aversion are negatively reinforced . . . and thus placed in a superior position for reenactment under similar conditions of aversion. (p. 159)

[12]It is curious that newspapers often pay people to stop using a rival medium. Imagine the outcry if a television station encouraged people to stop reading newspapers for a week.

[13]Lynn (1966) has provided evidence that orienting responses coincide with decreases in alpha amplitudes and that lowered alpha generally denotes greater cortical arousal.

Zillmann (1982), Zillmann and Bryant (1981) and Zillmann, Hezel, and Medoff (1980) have suggested that the orienting response to visual cues in television may facilitate learning. It is also important to note that Anderson and Lorch (1983) have concluded that viewers are as likely to follow aspects of a story on television as be attracted and held to the screen by the message structure. Although there can be little doubt that content is critically important to holding audience attention, Reeves, Thorson, and Schleuder (1986) have pointed out that "it is the form, not the content, of television that is unique" (p. 274). Actually, the television form may not be truly "unique." Film form is obviously quite similar except perhaps for the rapid montage occurring in TV advertisements. And, of course, films are often shown on TV. What does differentiate television and film is the combination of the form, the small screen, and the settings in which viewing occurs.

[14]This description of TV viewing, it must be noted, is most applicable to television in the United States and other developed western nations. Although western-style television predominates throughout the world, TV is not so rapidly paced in some countries. There have been informal reports, for example, that some foreign visitors to the United States experience difficulty adjusting to and understanding the rapid montage that has become so common in American television and film.

[15]Automaticity is discussed by Berger (1980); Donohew, Sypher, and Higgins (1988); Hawkins and Pingree (1986); and LaBerge and Samuels (1974), among others. Note that there is also automaticity with reading, but we see no likely relationship between that process and the orienting reflex.

CHAPTER 8

The Causes and Consequences of Heavy Viewing

The only thing which consoles us in our troubles is diversion, and yet it is the greatest trouble of all. For it is chiefly that which prevents us from thinking of ourselves.

—Pascal (1900/1941)

It has long been assumed that the amount of time people spend reading books or newspapers, or listening to the radio is indicative of the importance these same media play in their lives. By the same token it is also assumed that relatively stable characteristics of personality and lifestyle coincide with the use of particular media.

In the previous chapter some of the causes and effects of heavy television use were examined. In this chapter we build on those findings, and on the assumptions just presented, and consider the potential causes and consequences of heavy viewing. Specifically, we want to know whether levels of viewing are related to particular moods, particular moods in certain activities, general personality characteristics, and the percentage of time invested in activities other than television viewing.

AMOUNT OF VIEWING AND AMOUNT OF TIME
SPENT ON OTHER ACTIVITIES

In a variety of studies in different nations, television has been shown to decrease the amount of time spent with friends, doing housework and hobbies, sleeping, and reading. In fact, according to John Robinson (1977), the medium's impact on American life has been responsible for a greater rearrangement of life activities than any other 20th-century innovation including the automobile.

Using a variety of different methodologies, especially diary and time-budget reports, Robinson (1972, 1981) and others have shown that television most displaces time devoted to media that are "functional equivalents": magazines, newspapers, and especially radio and movies.[1] Television viewing not only decreases the use of these alternatives, but it also increases the total use of mass media by as much as 40% (Robinson & Converse, 1972).

Many of these studies have compared TV owners' time use to that of nonowners. Today, given that only about 2% of U.S. households are without TV,[2] it makes more sense, at least in the United States, to study the *amount,* or proportion, of time spent viewing in relation to involvement in other activities. Using ESM data we can do just that.*

Time Spent at Home, Alone, Talking, and Walking

Although heavy viewers did not spend more time alone across all environments, they did spend substantially more time alone at home than light viewers ($\chi^2 = 3.67$, $p = .06$). As a result, light viewers were twice as likely to be found talking at home and they spent comparatively less time at home generally than did heavy viewers. Light viewers were also more

---

*In the analyses that follow we are measuring proportion of time spent viewing. Recall that the data used to construct this measure were collected in response to randomized signals from 1 week in each subject's life. As a result, the viewing measure is only an estimate.

As described earlier, the proportion of viewing measure was constructed as follows. Each respondent's total number of primary, secondary, and checklist reports of television viewing were summed and divided by the total number of reports given during the week. As a result, the measure is on a ratio scale that ranges from .0 to .75 with a standard deviation of .17.

Although the full array of scores is used in each correlation (with controls for age, sex, income, education, and because it is related to amount of viewing, length of time spent with company), in a good many of the comparisons to follow only the heaviest and lightest viewing thirds of the sample are compared. These two groups were not substantially different in demographic makeup from the sample as a whole.

than twice as likely to report preparing to go out. Because television viewing is a homebound activity, more viewing also means more time with family and less time with friends, in public, and in transit.

Light viewers also spent relatively more time walking and standing—more than twice as much time as the heavy viewers. This was because more time spent sitting or lying in front of the TV simply reduced the proportion of time spent in vertical or more active postures.[3]

Time Spent Reading and Playing Sports

The amount of reading did not vary a great deal by amount of viewing.[4] But contrary to what some might expect, more television viewing is not at odds with involvement in sports. Rather, heavy viewers were more likely than light or moderate viewers to be engaged in athletics.[5] This is because watching televised sports may encourage athletic activity in some viewers. A more powerful factor is that athletically active people enjoy viewing sports on television and, hence, watch more TV.

Sex Differences in Time Use

Another key factor in viewing levels is simply the amount of time available to view. For men, amount of viewing was negatively correlated with amount of time actually spent working ($r = -.50$, $p < .001$) (see also Wilensky, 1964) and time spent in transit ($r = -.50$, $p < .001$). These findings may be the result of substantially more of the men being in higher status occupations and driving their own cars to work. Because the men had greater control over the amount of time spent working and time spent commuting, amount of viewing varied more with the amount of time spent at work and in transit than it did for the women whose lives were more regimented by predetermined and fixed work hours and mass transit schedules. For men, amount of viewing was also significantly related to feeling more "free" (not constrained) generally ($r = .46$, $p < .01$) and more free ($r = .51$, $p = .002$) and relaxed ($r = .35$, $p < .05$) during work. For some of the men, then, a more carefree attitude at work appears to be associated with a preference for an effortless leisure activity at home.

No significant differences were found between light and heavy viewers in the percentages of time spent in child care, pet and garden care, laundry, or grooming. Robinson and his colleagues[6] found that television owners spent about 5 to 6 minutes less time on average in each of these activities than non-TV owners. Of course we were not studying non-TV owners, nor can time usage to the minute be estimated with the ESM.

AMOUNT OF VIEWING AND THE EXPERIENCE
OF EVERYDAY LIFE

We turn now to the question of whether people who watched more or less television reported a different overall quality of experience during the week of sampling.[7] As can be seen in Table 14, the heaviest viewing third of subjects reported lower moods and lower relaxation in non-TV activities than did light viewers.* Differences were strongest on the friendly–hostile variable ($t = 2.6$, $p < .01$) and on cheerfulness versus irritability ($t = 2.5$, $p < .025$). Heavy viewers also reported less concentration ($t = 1.7$, $p < .10$) and less control ($t = 2.0$, $p < .05$) and somewhat less challenge, skill, stakes, alertness, strength, and satisfaction than light viewers.

The differences between light and moderate viewers on these variables are quite similar to those for light versus heavy viewers, whereas the difference between moderate and heavy viewers is small. In other words, there is not a strong linear relationship. Put another way, had the analysis been run comparing light viewers against both moderate and heavy viewers, the confidence with which we can specify differences between the groups would have been greater.

Although the correlations between amount of viewing and overall affect in all activities during the week are negative for the sample as a whole, the findings actually only hold up for women. Among the various demographic groups, the level of viewing of the divorced and separated was the most strongly related to negative experiences in the rest of life, even with all the standard demographic controls (friendly–hostile: $r = -.64$, $p < .025$; cheerful–irritable: $r = -.71$, $p < .01$; and satisfied–resentful $r = -.73$, $p < .01$).

A scatterplot of the relationship between amount of viewing and the cheerful–irritable variable for the divorced and separated respondents (Figure 23) helps to illustrate that for this subsample, the same people whose experiences are more frustrated and disordered are also the same people who watch more television. (Note that, in another ESM study, a small group of clinically depressed adolescents watched twice as much television as a group of "normal" teenagers; Mokros, Merrick, & Poznanski, 1987.)

For the divorced and separated subjects, amount of viewing was also correlated positively with amount of challenge during the week ($r = .42$) and correlated negatively with amount of skill ($r = -.32$). In other words, more viewing was related to perceiving relatively more challenge and less

---

*These data represent aggregated individual self-report means across all activities minus primary and secondary television viewing.

TABLE 14
Mean Responses During All Activities for Light
and Heavy TV Viewers[a,b]

Response Variables	Light TV Viewers n = 38	Heavy TV Viewers n = 39	t
Concentration	5.6	5.0	1.7*
Hard to concentrate ..	1.3	1.5	−.8
Self-consciousness	2.0	2.4	−.7
Control	7.6	7.0	2.0**
Challenge	4.1	3.5	1.5
Skill	5.8	5.2	1.4
Wish something else ..	3.3	3.0	.9
Stakes	3.9	3.4	1.1
Activation			
Alert	5.5	5.3	1.1
Strong	5.1	4.7	1.5
Active	5.0	4.9	.8
Excited	4.5	4.4	.5
Affect			
Friendly	5.4	5.0	2.8***
Happy	5.3	5.0	1.8*
Cheerful	5.1	4.7	2.5**
Sociable	5.0	4.8	1.7*
Relaxed	5.0	4.7	1.7*
Creative	4.6	4.5	.4
Satisfied	5.0	4.7	1.4
Free	4.8	4.8	−.2

[a]Light and heavy viewers represent the lower and upper thirds of the subject pool for amount of TV viewing.
[b]All instances of primary and secondary television viewing were removed.
*$p < .1$; **$p < .05$; ***$p < .01$; two-tails.

skill during the week—a condition that according to the flow model is associated with anxiety. Indeed, the correlation between amount of viewing for the week and the relaxed–tense variable for these subjects was −.62 ($p < .05$).

For some subjects, then, television is viewed more heavily in response to unpleasant subjective experiences. For the married men with higher incomes, however, more television viewing was related to better affective experiences.

A number of explanations can be offered. First, the men have a greater number and variety of opportunities for coping with stress and nega-

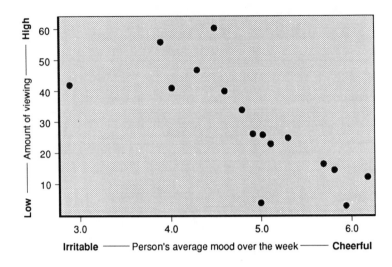

(n=16; r =−.71; p =.002, two-tailed test)

FIGURE 23. Correlation between amount of television viewing and mean cheerfulness for divorced and separated respondents.

tive affect. They are more likely to have family members around with whom to talk and do things, and with greater income and more people about, a greater variety of activities is possible. Second, because they are married and have children they are generally less lonely. More of their viewing is done *with* the family. In contrast, the divorced and separated subjects, most of whom are low-income women who live alone, are more inclined to use television to combat loneliness and other negative feelings.

But although some results held up only for certain groups, there were trends that applied for almost every major demographic group: Concentration, difficulty of concentration, and alertness were all rated more negatively during the week in relation to the amount of viewing. Challenge, skill, control, and self-consciousness also tended to be rated more negatively with more viewing.

These findings suggest that heavy viewing may be part of a general preference for low complexity. This seems especially true for the subjects who did not go to college and for whom the correlation between amount of viewing and concentration during the week was −.38 ($p < .01$).

It is also probable that the spillover effect accounts for some of these differences. Television viewing itself was shown in chapter 5 to be extremely low on challenge, concentration, control, and alertness and by and large it is these same variables that the heavy viewers give lower reports on during non-TV activities during the week. In other words, because more of the heavy viewers' time is spent with television, more of their non-TV activities may be colored by the passive spillover from earlier TV viewing.

Clearly, amount of viewing does not have the same causes and consequences for all groups. As the uses and gratifications approach suggests, and as we see through the balance of this chapter, people use television in different ways to address different needs.

DO HEAVY VIEWERS FEEL DIFFERENTLY DURING VIEWING?

Comparing the experiences of light and heavy viewers as they watch television (Table 15), one sees that heavy viewers report a significantly less cheerful and sociable viewing experience and one that involves less control. This is due, in part, to the fact that a greater proportion of their viewing is done alone.

Heavy viewers were also lower on alertness, activity, challenges, and relaxation when they viewed, although the differences were not significant. They also report concentrating less while viewing, but concentration was more difficult. In short, the longer hours in front of the TV are less rewarding.

These findings may be at odds with Himmelweit and her colleagues' (1980) conclusion that the viewing of heavy viewing adults is more "involved" (i.e., reports that television is "exciting" and "absorbing"). Rather, the lower scores on alertness and concentration may be similar to those of Cline, Croft, and Courrier (1973) and Foss and Alexander (1987), who report heavy viewers often being less aroused or describing television as seductive but boring. In any case, the findings indicate a somewhat less mentally active—and possibly less aware and/or desensitized—heavy television viewing experience.

There are two primary explanations for these findings. First, heavy viewers gave lower responses on most of these measures even when not watching TV (Table 14). Second, more of their viewing is prolonged, and it was shown in chapter 7 (Figures 18 and 19) that concentration drops off during the course of viewing.

In summary, light viewers generally experience the rest of their life *and* television more positively than do heavy viewers. In both Tables 14 and 15, across virtually all 21 self-report variables, light viewers gave more favorable responses than heavy viewers.

Thus far, a number of possible reasons have been advanced for why

TABLE 15
Mean Responses During Television Viewing for Light
and Heavy TV Viewers[a]

Response Variables	Light TV Viewers n = 27	Heavy TV Viewers n = 38	t
Concentration	5.3	4.9	.8
Hard to concentrate ..	.9	1.3	−1.1
Self-consciousness	1.9	2.2	−.5
Control	7.6	6.5	2.4**
Challenge	3.1	2.0	1.6
Skill	3.7	3.5	.4
Wish something else ..	1.7	2.2	−1.0
Stakes	2.2	1.2	1.8*
Activation			
Alert	5.1	4.7	1.3
Strong	4.7	4.5	.5
Active	4.4	4.0	1.6
Excited	4.5	4.3	.7
Affect			
Friendly	5.3	5.1	.5
Happy	5.1	5.1	.0
Cheerful	5.3	4.7	2.2**
Sociable	5.2	4.6	2.1**
Relaxed	5.7	5.3	1.5
Creative	4.3	4.1	1.0
Satisfied	5.1	5.0	.6
Free	5.2	4.8	1.1

[a]Light and heavy viewers represent the lower and upper thirds of
the subject pool for amount of TV viewing.
*$p < .1$; **$p < .05$; two-tailed.

some people might view more television than others. Some watch more
simply because they have more free time or because they enjoy spending
time with their families. Others view more because they live alone and
are lonely. For some, the low complexity of viewing may harmonize well
with a general preference for less complexity, whereas for others, television is used as an antidote to a great deal of complexity experienced
earlier in the day. Still others have a strong preference for television
relative to the alternatives that are available. For some subjects these
alternatives may be perceived as being too discomforting, complex, or
challenging.

To be sure, any number and combination of these explanations can
apply to various individuals at different times, and this helps explain

why correlations are not higher. People use television to different ends at different times. No one views television for precisely the same reason all the time.

VIEWING AND ALIENATION

Nevertheless, there might be particular kinds of activities and particular characteristics of personality that are related to heavier viewing. For example, it was expected that alienation might be related to amount of viewing. In fact, a number of researchers have found evidence of heavy viewing being related to alienation.[8]

A week before experience sampling began, respondents filled out a questionnaire that included an abbreviated form of Maddi et al.'s (1979) alienation inventory. Each item in the inventory contributes to a score for context of alienation (i.e., self, family, or work).*

But in our analysis, across the three alienation contexts, only the variable of alienation from self† was correlated at all significantly ($r = -.17, p < .05$, one-tail) with amount of viewing. In fact, the relationship was nonexistent for men but stronger for women ($r = -.21$) and it was particularly strong for the Black subjects ($r = -.46$).

Among the strongest single-item correlations with amount of viewing across all subjects was Item 5: "The most exciting times in my day are those when I daydream or fantasize in my head." This item was more strongly correlated with amount of viewing for women ($r = -.27$), Blacks

---

*All of the individual alienation items can be found toward the end of Appendix C. For statistical purposes, each item was recoded so that a response of *greater* alienation yielded a *lower* score.

†*Alienation From Self.* In order to clarify what Maddi and his colleagues mean by alienation from self, and because this variable is discussed later, the items comprising the factor are noted here.

(Rated from strongly disagree [1] to strongly agree [7].) Starred items (*) are those statements where coding was reversed so that lower scores uniformly denoted higher alienation.

1. *Trying to understand myself and others is a waste of time.
2. When I try hard my efforts can accomplish much.
3. *Life is empty and has no meaning for me.
4. Most of the time I understand my own actions and thoughts.
5. *The most exciting times in my day are those when I daydream or fantasize in my head.
6. *I long for a simpler life than I have now, a life in which bodily needs are most important.

($r = -.41$), and those of less education ($r = -.29$) and less income ($r = -.25$). In other words, an affinity for fantasy seems to be at least slightly related to heavier viewing for the less privileged demographic groups in this sample.

DO HEAVY VIEWERS FEEL DIFFERENTLY THAN LIGHT VIEWERS DURING PARTICULAR ACTIVITIES?

Having learned earlier that heavy viewers felt worse during the week than light viewers, we became interested in determining whether there were particular domains of life where light and heavy viewers felt differently.

Ultimately, three independent "escape" or "distraction" hypotheses were proposed, each holding that negative moods in particular types of activities would be related to heavier viewing.

The *first* hypothesis, based in part on Hirsch and Panelas' (1981) finding that less-satisfied workers view more television, was that negative experiences at work would cause people to gravitate to television upon returning home.

Second, it was thought that negative experiences while interacting with other people might be related to heavier viewing. Many researchers have noted a relationship between the quality and quantity of social interaction and viewing habits. Strained personal relationships (Davis, 1975; Kline, 1971; McLeod, Ward, & Tancill, 1965), reluctance to cope with "the other" (Berelson & Steiner, 1964; Gutman, 1973; Swank, 1979; Wiebe, 1969), and reduced social interactions and loneliness (Bower, 1973; Danowski, 1975; Kubey, 1980; Steiner, 1963) have each been linked empirically or theoretically to heavier television viewing.

The *third* hypothesis was that heavier viewers would report feeling relatively worse than light viewers during idle time—"non-activities" such as waiting, sitting and not doing anything, or staring out of a window. This expectation was based on the theory that heavier viewers of television are more likely to be persons who experience aversive and unpleasant fantasies, thoughts, and feelings in open time and use television to substitute or distract from negative cognitive–affective experience (McIlwraith & Josephson, 1985; McIlwraith & Schallow, 1983; Singer, 1980). Heavier viewers might also be more "vulnerable" or "susceptible" to boredom (Hamilton, 1981; Zuckerman, 1975).

It was hypothesized that a relationship would be found between television use and the experience of idle time, especially because consciousness tends to become disordered, and is experienced negatively when left without a focus. That people who experience idle time more

TABLE 16
Correlates of the Amount of Television Viewing and
Reported Affect in Three Activities[a] (from Kubey, 1986)

	Working	Talking	Idling
n	107	98	88
Affect Variables			
Friendly–hostile	−.08	−.06	−.26**
Happy–sad	−.06	.02	−.22*
Cheerful–irritable	−.14	−.11	−.19*
Sociable–lonely	.01	.03	−.35***

[a]Controlling for age, sex, income, and education.
$*p < .05$; $**p < .01$; $***p < .001$; one-tailed.

negatively would watch more television made sense because television is among the most readily available ways to fill and structure open time. Furthermore, more than any other activity, viewing is done when people report having nothing else to do.

Table 16 summarizes tests of the three hypotheses and presents correlations between the amount of viewing and affect during work, talking, and idling. Mean scores on each self-report measure in each activity for each subject were correlated with the amount of viewing.* Contrary to expectation, there was no evidence to suggest that more television viewing was significantly related to more negative affective experiences at work or in direct encounters with other people (talking). However, the significant and negative correlations during idling "activities" support the third hypothesis in demonstrating that heavier viewers of television tend to feel somewhat worse on average than light viewers when doing "nothing."

The relationship between discomfort during idle time and amount of television viewing was particularly salient for those whose marriages had been disrupted or terminated and for those who were less affluent and less educated. Compared to single and married subjects, divorced and separated subjects exhibited a much higher negative correlation between amount of viewing and affect while not doing anything ($r = -.55$). These relationships were also stronger for Black subjects and for those of less income and less education.

---

*In creating these means, activities that included secondary TV viewing were eliminated in order to avoid a confounding relationship with the amount of viewing measure. The number of reports differ from one activity to the next because not all 107 subjects had reports in every activity category. Because age, sex, income, and education are controlled for in each correlation, the degrees of freedom are reduced by five.

As reported earlier, it was the female subjects for whom the level of television viewing was related to the personality measure of alienation from self, and it is again the females[9] for whom heavier television viewing is related to feeling more negative when left with nothing to do ($r = -.33$, $p < .02$). Level of viewing by Black subjects was even more highly correlated with alienation from self ($r = -.46$) than it was for women, and the negative correlation of viewing and affect during idling for Blacks was also quite high ($r = -.80$). Indeed, for these two groups, the correlation between alienation from self and affect in unstructured situations was particularly high (for women, $r = -.58$, $p < .005$; for Blacks, $r = -.66$). By comparison, for all subjects, the correlation between alienation from self and affect in unstructured activities was $-.32$ ($p < .01$).

Alienation from self seems to translate into negative experiences during idle time because it is during such time that people necessarily come into greater contact with the self. And as was seen in the individual items listed earlier, alienation from self denotes an existential turmoil that may well be characterized by anxiety and/or depression.

It is similar feelings (e.g., sadness and irritability) occurring in idle time that tend to be correlated with heavier use of television. Thus, for people who are alienated from self, television appears to offer a ready means of structuring attention that permits escape from the discomfort that occurs during idle time.

DOES SOLITUDE OR LACK OF STRUCTURE EXPLAIN AFFECT DIFFERENCES BETWEEN HEAVY AND LIGHT VIEWERS?

In addition to idling, exploratory analysis of a variety of other typical daily activities also resulted in a negative correlation between affect and amount of viewing during walking and standing ($r = -.25$, $p < .05$). There was also evidence that heavier viewers felt somewhat worse affectively, particularly more tense, while traveling by car or on public transportation. But during other activities such as housework, meals, and other leisure activities, there was no such relationship.

These activities that are experienced more negatively in relation to heavier viewing have two primary properties in common. First, like idling, walking and standing and being in transit are all frequently done alone. Second, idling and walking and standing are often unstructured. There may be little or no externally structured, goal-directed involvement. The person is typically between activities and is likely to be waiting, thinking, daydreaming, or scanning the environment.

Because these activities are often done alone, it remained to be seen whether it was the lack of structure or solitude in such activities that explained the results.[10] Thus, for the following analyses, two new broad categories of activity were created.

Unstructured activities included all reports of staring into space, waiting, walking, pacing, standing, sitting, riding in a car or bus or train (not driving), lying in bed, trying to sleep, fantasizing, daydreaming, and thinking. *Structured activities* included all reports of working, cleaning, general chores, cooking and baking, sewing and knitting, and hobbies.

In the upper half of Table 17 four *t* tests confirm that the heavy viewers experience significantly lower affect than light viewers when alone, in unstructured activities, and when with the family. There was very little difference between heavy and light viewers during structured activities.

In this analysis, both lack of structure and solitude were experienced more negatively by heavier viewers. In the bottom half of Table 17, additional *t* tests were employed to test whether being alone or with others (family, friends, coworkers) makes a difference under the two conditions of structure and lack of structure.[11]

Here, the largest difference between the mean affect of heavy and light viewers occurred when subjects were alone and in an unstructured situation ($t = 4.0$, $p < .001$). A second significant difference also occurred under unstructured conditions but when subjects were with oth-

TABLE 17

Mean Level of Affect for Light and Heavy Viewers by Social Context and Type of Activity (from Kubey, 1986)

	Light		Heavy		
	n	mean	n	mean	t
Alone	445	5.0	441	4.6	5.7***
With family	349	5.2	307	5.0	2.1*
Unstructured	242	5.1	212	4.5	5.2***
Structured	476	5.1	452	5.0	1.3
Unstructured/alone	83	4.9	71	4.2	4.0***
Unstructured/with others	117	5.3	114	4.7	3.0**
Structured/alone	120	5.0	123	4.8	1.6
Structured/with others	325	5.1	290	5.1	.7

Note: Unstructured activities are: staring into space, waiting for someone, walking or pacing, standing in place, relaxing, sitting, riding in a car, bus, or train, lying in bed—just relaxing, trying to sleep, fantasizing, daydreaming, thinking about the past or future. Structured activities are: cooking or baking, cleaning, chores at home, sewing or knitting, hobbies, working at work place. Structured and unstructured totals are slightly lower in bottom half because occasions when subjects were with strangers were eliminated.

*$p < .05$; **$p < .01$; ***$p < .001$; two-tailed.

ers ($t = 3.0$, $p < .01$). There was only a small but nonsignificant difference when subjects were alone and in structured activities. Finally, there was virtually no difference in reported affect between high and low viewers in structured activities with others present ($t = .7$).

Figure 24 illustrates these same differences and helps make it clear that it is unstructured activities in particular that are experienced more negatively by heavy viewers. They tend to feel worse when they are in unstructured situations whether they are alone or not, but especially when they are alone.

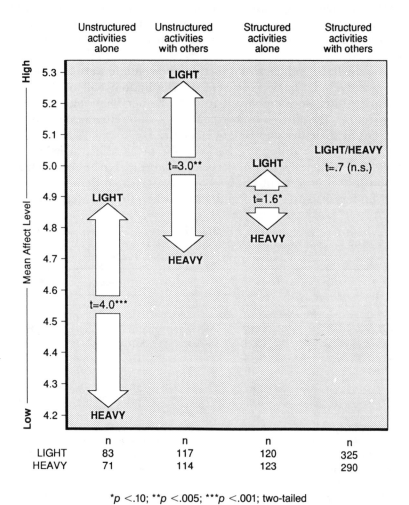

*p <.10; **p <.005; ***p <.001; two-tailed

FIGURE 24. Comparison of mean affect levels for light and heavy television viewers by social context and structured or unstructured activities (adapted from Kubey, 1986).

AMOUNT OF VIEWING AND AMOUNT OF SLEEPING

We turn finally to the study of sleeping behavior. These analyses were carried out both for comparison purposes[12] and in response to the National Institute of Mental Health's (1982) urging that researchers study viewing and its relationship to sleep and sleep disturbances.

The daily reports of sleep length, onset of sleep, and quality of sleep on each person's first ESF of the day provided the variables with which to work. We found that across all respondents, there was no correlation between amount of viewing and the three sleep habit measures (controlling for age, sex, income, and education). But in examining the data by demographic groups, similar patterns to those already described were noted once again.

With the usual demographic controls, Black, divorced and separated, and female subjects who watched more television were also found to have spent more time sleeping ($r = .69, p = .02; r = .47, p = .12;$ and $r = .27, p = .04$, respectively). Rather than one activity supplanting the other, as was suggested by Robinson (1972b), the data suggest that many of the same people for whom heavier viewing was related to an affinity for fantasy and who are most likely to feel badly in unstructured time, also spent more time sleeping. It may be that as they do when they watch television, some subjects sleep more in order to escape negative experience. There was little support for the notion that such results can be explained by heavier viewers simply having more time available to be at home and sleep and watch TV.

SUMMARY AND DISCUSSION

In studying the respondents' week of experiences and how these vary with the proportion of time spent watching television, we have concluded that for many subjects, heavier TV viewing is a means by which to order experience and cope with negative affect.

Over the week of sampling, heavier viewing was also related to lower reports of concentration, challenge, skill, control, and alertness, but higher reports of difficulty in concentration. Because television viewing itself is reported in much the same way, it was suggested that the passive spillover effect might be partly accountable. But heavier use of television also appears to be part of a general preference for less complexity among some viewers, especially those of less education. In a set of findings that lends support to this view, Wober (1986) reported that heavier viewers prefer stability and calm and score low on a modified version of Zuckerman's Sensation-Seeking Scale.

There was no evidence to suggest that heavy television viewing is more psychologically involving. Rather, heavy viewers spend more time with TV but find it is less rewarding. Heavy viewers' experience with the medium is also more likely to be low in concentration and alertness, and this suggests that some viewers may be less mentally alert and more desensitized when viewing.

Alienation from self also correlated with higher rates of viewing. This was especially true for Blacks, women, and the less affluent. For men, and those of higher income, there was no relationship.

This was not the only instance of a link between a negative psychological phenomenon and heavier viewing for these groups. In correlations between rate of viewing and overall affect, and affect in unstructured situations, negative relationships emerged for the less privileged respondents and those who had experienced divorce or separation.

Aversion to the Self in Isolation

It seems quite certain that a good many viewers turn to television in order to avoid negative experiences during uncommitted time. Television offers a ready opportunity to occupy the mind when nothing else is available, especially for those for whom idle time is burdensome.

Coupled with the findings that solitude is experienced more negatively by heavy viewers and that for the same respondents, a heavy night of viewing is preceded by and is concurrent with more solitude, it can also be concluded that one of the important motivating forces that drives television viewing is loneliness. This was especially true for the single, the divorced, and the separated.

It is not so much that viewing TV makes one feel more sociable. Rather, the negative feelings of loneliness that generally coincide with solitude are readily avoided while viewing. One need only recall how effective a radio or TV can be in quickly providing some psychological order and in reducing feelings of loneliness when one has to spend the night in a strange hotel room, or when the family leaves for a few days and one is suddenly left alone. In the case of television, the medium fills the room with familiar faces and sounds and one feels not nearly so alone.

Does Television Viewing Cause Intolerance for Unstructured Time?

Although it was concluded that feeling badly in unstructured and solitary time leads to the use of television, it must be noted that heavy viewing, and the rapid montage of much contemporary television, may also help reinforce an intolerance in the heavy viewer for daily moments that are not similarly chocked full of sight and sound. In other words, we cannot rule out that spending tens of thousands of hours watching television might not reduce a person's ability to give shape to free time. Indeed, in some individuals, it is quite conceivable that television viewing leads to a psychological dependence on the medium. Of course a good many other activities (e.g., reading, playing video games, working with a computer, or work itself) can also help provide a consistent stream of structured experiences that might lead a person to feel bereft when without such stimuli. Still, it seems likely that heavy viewing helps perpetuate itself. Some television viewers grow dependent on the ordered stimuli of television or similar entertainments and become increasingly incapable of filling leisure time without external aids. In fact, other researchers have concluded that for children, television programs may result in overstimulation and contribute to a shorter attention span, more impulsivity, less self-restraint, and less patience with the normal delays of daily living.[13]

Time Condensation, Real Life, and Life on Television

It is also possible that the condensation of time in film and television makes the normal speed at which we live seem slower relative to how people experienced their lives before the advent of these media. Events that normally occur over years, months, or hours take place in a matter of minutes on the screen. This could conceivably be related to reduced patience and an increased desire to keep one's life moving along at a faster clip. The constant pressure to hold the audience with more rapidly paced materials, and the domination of the medium by advertising conventions that emphasize short bursts of information, may also play a role.

Furthermore, television viewing may instill in many of us the notion that our lives are dull in comparison to the lives of the people on television who, whether in fiction or in reality, do important things and live lives that seem fascinating and out of the ordinary. Put another way, television competes with how much attention one pays to one's own life as against the time one pays to the lives being led on the screen.

Television offers us an alternative life and, thus, the medium may be particularly attractive to those who are alienated from their own lives and who dislike their own inner experience. In watching the more dramatic lives being led on the screen, one might expect that some people would become even more disaffected with their lives and that such negative feelings would motivate people to curb their viewing. No doubt this occurs from time to time. But in practice it may more commonly be the case that one can always find another program that is soothing and nonalienating and still holds one's attention and so, rather than turning the set off, it is as likely, or more likely, that the disaffected person will continue to view.

One could argue that for such individuals, leaving television and focusing on improving "real" life might best serve their long-term interests. But in the reality of the given moment, not a few people, perhaps most of us, will gravitate to television, or some other form of escape, because at least, then, the problem of negative affect or loneliness is quickly solved.

The Direction of Causality

The direction of causality in mass communication research is notoriously difficult to pin down and it is often an error to assume that it flows in only one direction. Rather, such findings as we have been discussing often represent interwoven lifestyle, personality, and experiential differences that cannot be separated.[14]

So, although it is likely that heavy television viewing could cause intolerance for unstructured time, there is also evidence that discomfort in unstructured time leads to heavier viewing; recall that in the previous chapter negative affect earlier in the day predicted heavy viewing that same night. Furthermore, a person already alienated from his or her own life, is going to be more prone to gravitate to television than someone who feels good about life and who finds daily living rewarding.

That people turn to television in an attempt to relieve the negative experiences of uncommitted time may also dovetail with McIlwraith and Schallow's (1983) finding that heavier viewers of television experience significantly more aversive and unpleasant fantasies and thoughts. Their research suggests a "full-headed" model wherein viewing is driven by an effort to escape from a discomforting and intrusive inner life rather than motivated by a scarcity of inner images and fantasies. Of course the scarcity of inner images could itself be aversive.

Whatever the exact reason or reasons, when they are left to their own devices and when external goals are lacking, heavy viewers from the aforementioned demographic groups seem somewhat less able to bring order to experience. When they have nothing to do, they are more likely to turn on the TV to help structure attention and to avoid the unpleasant experience of disorganization in consciousness.

The need for this kind of structuring and for escape has been related to heavy viewing for a number of groups in this sample and these are much the same groups for whom rate of viewing was related either to an affinity for fantasy or amount of time spent sleeping.

Each of us needs the occasional relief of fantasy, and the more frustrating the reality, the more urgent is the need for escape. Less-privileged individuals may also be less able to afford, or have readily available, as many alternatives for ordering experience and dealing with negative affect. Except for sleep and daydreaming, television is the cheapest and most immediately available escape imaginable.

Subjects from the more affluent demographic groups, on the other hand, seem less inclined to use television for escape. In fact, the heavier viewing of the more affluent subjects—of whom most are married and male—although generally unrelated to subjective reports, was more strongly related to a greater number of hours available for TV viewing. Furthermore, the affluent have more leisure alternatives than those with less disposable income, or many of the divorced and separated who cannot go out in the evening because they have work to do at home and/or children to look after.[15]

Self-Awareness, Self-Regulation, and Television Viewing

In combination with greater proximity to potentially disturbing unconscious material, some subjects may also feel especially disordered psychologically when alone and during idle time because it is during such time that people regularly take stock of themselves. During idle time, some members of the less-affluent and divorced and separated groups may become more aware than at other times that they are in debt, overworked, alone, or in a dead-end job.

Of course, the divorced and separated are also much more likely to live alone and to experience loneliness. When left with nothing to do and feeling badly, they are less likely to have another person to turn to and are left instead to turn to TV.

As discussed previously, television programs and commercials provide parasocial experiences and are cleverly constructed to hold the viewer's attention. By keeping attention focused on the screen and not on the self, the medium provides a much welcomed and soothing alternative to the gaping, potentially boring, and psychologically disordering voids of solitude and unstructured time. It is the very fulfillment of these functions that helps explain the enormous and worldwide popularity of the medium.

We must also consider the possibility that some heavy viewers may possess fewer inner resources with which to maintain emotional control and balance, a view espoused by Berelson and Steiner (1964), Lull (1980), and Villani (1975), among others.[16] In this view, television helps provide order for those who may be less able to supply it on their own. Those individuals with less assurance about the meaning of their world, or with fewer sources of support to confirm it, will use television to help maintain psychological stability.

It may well be that some people watch a great deal of TV because they lack the resources or the ability to provide order in consciousness when left to their own devices. The solution, however, may be illusory. The viewing state is one generally low in complexity, and most viewers, especially habitual ones, less frequently experience during viewing the intense concentration, skills, control, and challenges associated with more rewarding and enjoyable experiences. Viewing fills time in a relaxing way and helps distract us, but may only mask the causes of alienation and unhappiness.

Leisure Options and the Propensity Toward Heavy Viewing

Although in the final chapter we debunk the notion that education or wealth necessarily prepare a person to derive meaning and enjoyment from free time, it is the case that certain basic demographic and personality factors can limit one's leisure options and/or increase one's need for escape and dependence on television. To conclude the chapter, we briefly summarize six factors that this research, and the research of others, suggests are often related to heavier or less discriminate television viewing.[17]

Loneliness.   Those who lack structured interactions with other people due to unemployment, divorce, widowhood, personality factors, or declining health are more likely than others to turn to television for companionship, information, and escape. Older people who are widowed and/or retired, for example, are among the heaviest television viewers (Davis & Kubey, 1982; Kubey, 1980).

Availability of Free Time.   Not surprisingly, persons with substantial free time are among the most likely to view television heavily. Such people typically include unemployed and retired persons, "empty nest" parents, children, the institutionalized or seriously ill, and those of wealth who choose not to work.

Emotional Difficulties.   Persons with emotional problems such as depression and anxiety are more likely to gravitate to television for escape and distraction especially because such states come more to the fore during unstructured time while simultaneously making it more difficult to attend to more demanding forms of communication.

Youth.   Due largely to lack of experience, education, and self-control, children are among the most likely of groups to become indiscriminate heavy viewers of television.

Low Income. Low-income people have a much more restricted range of potential leisure activities to choose from. Among those activities generally unavailable to the poor are: travel, many sports, especially those requiring expensive equipment and/or instruction (e.g., skiing, golf, mountaineering), and attendance at performing and musical arts (theater, opera, symphony, ballet). In addition, book, magazine, and recorded music purchases may be restricted as may film and museum going. Low-income parents who are single, who live alone with their children, and who cannot afford child care, experience particularly serious restrictions on what they can do for enjoyment and leisure. Low-income groups are also less able to purchase expensive video technologies (VCRs, video cameras, video games) and personal computing equipment. Clearly, the most readily available and inexpensive forms of leisure remaining are radio listening and traditional television viewing.

Lack of Education. A factor that overlaps to a considerable degree with low income is lack of education. Education enhances a person's symbolic skills—the ability to derive information, meaning, and pleasure from more complex forms of communication. In order to participate, many forms of leisure require that psychic costs in the form of training and education be paid in advance. Television viewing, by contrast, does not require any special training.

ENDNOTES

[1]Only recently has the long reign of television been at all threatened by a new technology. Many owners of personal computers initially cut back significantly on television viewing (Rogers, 1983; Venkatesh & Vitalari, 1987). Doubtlessly, home and arcade video game play decreases time spent in traditional TV viewing as well.

For further studies of functional equivalency, see Bogart (1956/1972); Coffin (1955); Himmelweit et al. (1958); Murray and Kippax (1978); and Weiss (1969).

[2]In 1980, for example, the U.S. Bureau of the Census chose for the first time since 1950 to omit its question on TV ownership—after all, according to A. C. Nielsen, 98% of U.S. households had one or more TV sets by 1977. The number of TV sets per 1,000 persons in the United States is 571. Only Monaco has more per capita at 640/1,000 (United Nations, 1981).

[3]These patterns were confirmed in correlations. For example, rate of viewing is significantly and negatively related to the percentage of time spent walking and standing ($r = -.32, p < .001$) and in transit ($r = -.23, p < .05$), but positively related to the percentage of time spent with the family ($r = .18, p < .10$).

[4]See Bogart (1956/1972) and Coffin (1955) for reviews of studies that show that TV viewing supplants reading. See Belson (1967) and Robinson (1981) for studies showing heavier viewers to be more homebound.

[5]This finding complements Robinson (1977) and Csikszentmihalyi (1975), who also found a positive relationship between heavier viewing and greater outdoor activity and recreation.

[6]Robinson (1969, 1972a); Robinson and Converse (1972); and Robinson, Converse, and Szalai (1972).

[7]In one study, substantial proportions of variance in television program preference were accounted for by subjects' retrospective ratings of the emotion eliciting qualities of programs (Christ & Biggers, 1983). Experimental studies have similarly shown that type of negative affect is critical in determining a person's program selection (Bryant & Zillmann, 1984; Zillmann, Hezel, & Medoff, 1980). See Biggers (1983) for an emotion based theory of viewing.

[8]Some who have touched on the alienation concept with regard to television viewing include Gutman (1973); Hirsch and Panelas (1981); Kline (1971); McLeod, Ward, and Tancill (1965); Villani (1975); and Morgan (1983). These studies found that heavier viewers were more alienated and dissatisfied with life, finding it dull and routine. Klinger (1971) also concluded that people living empty, emotionally impoverished lives gravitate to television. Johnstone (1961), Katz and Foulkes (1962), and Robinson (1972b) have also linked alienation and "low self-concept" to amount of viewing.

[9]It must be recalled that the women in this sample are significantly more likely than the men to be divorced or separated. The female subjects were also far more likely to hold redundant, low paying, nonmanagerial jobs.

[10]The relatively high correlations on the sociable–lonely variable also indicated the need for further analysis along these lines.

[11]The same analysis was run with family members versus alone (as opposed to "with others") and nearly identical results were obtained.

[12]Robinson (1972b) previously found that one of the temporal effects of the introduction of television was a loss in the amount of sleep (6 minutes less each night on average for TV owners). Robinson hypothesized that sleep may be a functional equivalent of television viewing, citing parallels in brain-wave comparisons of sleep and TV viewing.

[13]See Gadberry (1980); Salomon (1979); Singer and Singer (1979, 1983); Singer, Singer, and Rapaczynski (1984); and Williams (1983).

[14]Bauer and Bauer (1960) correctly concluded 30 years ago in a review of mass communication research that in many instances "we do in fact find upon more extensive investigation that correlated variables 'interact,' i.e., that there is 'causation' in both directions" (p. 28).

[15]In support, for the divorced and separated subjects, the correlation between amount of viewing and time spent in public leisure activities was −.48 while the correlation with the time spent in housework and chores was .53.

[16]Support for such a view comes from other studies that show an affinity for television to be related to stress and anxiety (Pearlin, 1959), neuroticism (Hendry & Patrick, 1977; Nordlund, 1978), and to more negative appraisals of the quality of one's life (Morgan, 1983).

[17]See Bower (1985) and Comstock et al. (1978) for similar lists.

CHAPTER 9

A Brief Review of Major Findings: Reclaiming the Idea of Media Effects

Television is a new, hard test of our wisdom. If we succeed in mastering this new medium it will enrich us. But it can also put our mind to sleep.
—Arnheim (1935)

In the chapter to follow considerable thought is given to the broader meaning of our findings. But first it might be helpful to summarize briefly what these findings are and to consider a few of their more basic implications, especially in terms of what they suggest about current ideas concerning media effects and the "activity" of the audience. Reflecting on the findings reported in the previous four chapters, a number of conclusions stand out.

Television Viewing is a Passive and Relaxing, Low Concentration Activity. When viewing television, people report feeling more passive and less challenged and alert, while simultaneously concentrating less and using fewer skills, than in almost any other daily activity except resting and "doing nothing." Although there are occasional reports of people feeling tense, viewing rarely involves feelings of fear or anxiety (chapter 5).

171

Television May Both Promote and be a Hindrance to the Quality of Family Life. Heavier use of television viewing is related to slightly more positive experiences with family members (chapter 6). Television may also increase the total time that family members spend together. However, there was also evidence that people feel significantly less alert, less active, and less challenged when they view television with the family than when they are with the family and not watching television. Furthermore, light viewing subjects reported feeling significantly more active and alert when with the family in non-TV activities than did heavy viewers. Thus, in some families television viewing may be altering the general quality of family interaction toward greater passivity even when television is not being viewed.

Viewing is Often Driven by the Wish to Escape or Avoid Negative Affective States. Loneliness and negative affect in the afternoon were found to precede heavy viewing later the same evening (chapter 7). Heavier viewers also reported feeling significantly more negative affect during the week than did light viewers. It was concluded that television is often used as a substitute for social interaction and to ward off feelings of loneliness. Negative affect is more likely to cause viewing than the other way around. It was also concluded that people use television to help structure their experience and modulate moods and that the medium may serve a therapeutic function in this regard. In some instances, particularly prolonged viewing, it was suggested that the highly relaxing, low-concentration viewing state may be akin to an altered state of consciousness.

Viewers Tend to Feel Passive and Less Alert After Viewing. A passive spillover effect following television viewing was found among adults, children, and adolescents: People reported feeling more passive, less alert, and experiencing somewhat more difficulty concentrating after television viewing than they did before viewing or after other activities (chapter 7).

This finding raises concerns about the nature of the medium's ultimate impact on the quality of thinking and behavior, and whether television reduces the likelihood of engagement in active cognitive and behavioral activities after viewing.

Television Becomes Less Rewarding the Longer it is Viewed. Although television viewing is relaxing, one must generally continue to view to keep feeling relaxed and as the amount of time spent viewing increases, satisfaction in the experience tends to drop off for some viewers and so does the reported level of concentration (chapter 7). In general, the more people view the less they appear to enjoy it. Furthermore, the relaxing rewards only appear to occur during viewing and not afterwards. Viewing seems to provide relief from tension only temporarily.

Of primary concern here is that viewing may only mask the causes of negative affect and that with prolonged viewing, analytic skills may be less likely to be marshalled toward the screen. The longer they view, the less likely some people are to invest mental effort in the enterprise, and they may thus become less able—or less inclined—to engage in a complex analysis of what they view. These findings raise the possibility that viewers may be less guarded against and more susceptible to certain kinds of persuasive messages the longer they view.

Heavier Viewers Feel Worse than Light Viewers Generally, and Particularly When Alone or During Unstructured Time.   Heavier viewers generally reported enjoying television viewing less and feeling worse during the week than did light viewers (chapter 8). Some subjects reported significantly more negative feelings during both solitary and unstructured time and appear to be especially prone to using television to cope with loneliness, and to provide structure to experience.

Heavier viewing appears to perpetuate itself by causing psychological dependence in those who grow accustomed to having their experience so effortlessly structured. Both the relaxation and distraction that television so readily provides leads many viewers to become dependent on the medium.

RELATIVE TO OTHER ACTIVITIES, WHY DO PEOPLE WATCH SO MUCH TELEVISION?

Television is by far the most frequent of leisure activities, but respondents typically report feeling much more active and alert during other activities, especially sports and hobbies. But although other activities may be more enjoyable or invigorating than television, the opportunities for involvement are often constrained by costs, by the necessity of other people to participate, by the ability to engage intensely for only so long, and by the completion of the activity. In contrast, the only constraints on television viewing are free time and access to a set. Viewing is extremely inexpensive, one can readily watch alone, there is always another program available to view, and most people can watch for hours at a stretch without finding the experience noxious or too tiring. Viewing is almost always mildly rewarding in that it provides relaxation, distraction, and escape with minimal effort.

These distinguishing features of television viewing along with the general need for information and the need to feel connected to the rest of the culture and to partake in its stories, are among the primary reasons that television is watched as much as it is. But relative to many other leisure activities, because television is unchallenging, requires so little active mental concentration and skill, the immediate rewards are of low intensity.

CRITIQUE OF THE ACTIVE AUDIENCE CONCEPT: ON THE MINIMIZATION OF MEDIA EFFECTS

The findings demonstrate that there are general experiential effects associated with the use of television. And although for certain purposes one can conceptualize television viewing as active, it is unquestionably the case that people report viewing to be a passive activity.

Although it makes perfect sense that different people will bring different things to their experiences of the media, and although this approach to media studies has inspired much valuable research, some uses and gratifications advocates err in minimizing media effects and by overgeneralizing the assumption that audience members are always active simply because they choose what they are exposed to, and because they interpret messages in line with their needs and background.[1]

Actually, the idea that different people will use the same stimuli or entertainment in different ways is not a particularly new or startling one. Early in the 19th century, Goethe wrote in *Faust* (1808) that "Each loves the play for what he brings to it." And certainly anyone familiar with psychological tests such as the Rorschach or Thematic Apperception Test—developed in the early 1920s and middle 1930s—knows that different people see (or project) different things in response to the same ink blot, photograph, or drawing. But people also tend to see and experience very similar things and it should come as little surprise that with a much less ambiguous and prepotent stimulus such as television, although there will certainly be different reactions among different people, there will also be many similarities.

Uses and gratifications theorists too seldom think of these reactions (or gratifications) as effects and thus do not recognize the degree to which the mass media bring about rather uniform and immediate responses in substantial portions of their audiences. Indeed, in every sample we have studied, with different demographic groups and with subjects ranging in age from 10 to 82, and with groups from more than one country, it has been found that people consistently report their experiences with television as being passive, relaxing, and involving relatively little concentration.

People do actively choose to watch television in the vast majority of viewing instances, and we do not doubt that they may very well be "actively" interpreting what they view. But what is really meant by "actively interpreting"? Is there such a thing as an audience member *passively* interpreting television? In other words, in many conceptualizations of the active audience, there seems to be little nuance or variation in how active audience members might be. Can an audience member ever not be active or be less active? If the audience is always active how does that further our understanding?

We agree with Webster and Wakshlag (1983) and with Blumler (1979) that too many researchers conceptualize whether the viewer is active or passive in either—or terms when in fact, depending on what one means by activity, the same instance of television viewing might be properly described both ways.[2] Indeed, as shown in the present work, audience activity is a variable that can be measured rather than an absolute condition (see also Rubin, 1984; Windahl, 1981, in this regard).

There is also insufficient consideration in uses and gratifications approaches of how frequently television sets the audience's immediate agenda and concerns, and how readily it engenders immediate experiential effects.[3] For example, although it is true that moviegoers or television viewers come to the same film or television show with different backgrounds, needs, and expectations, these media are often powerful enough that once involved in an effectively produced drama, say a suspense plot, most viewers will care at exactly the same time whether the protagonist survives, whether a victim is rescued, and whether the villain is vanquished (Comisky & Bryant, 1982). Similarly, viewers of comedic and tragic fare often laugh or cry at the same time.

So, too, are television promotions and "teases" often capable of peaking curiosity sufficiently that some viewers will watch the 11 p.m. news or the next scheduled situation comedy when they had no intention of doing so when they first sat down to view. In fact, most everyone will report that at least occasionally they view more television than they had originally intended. And what about the simple fact that people watch as much television as they do? Aren't these media effects as well?

It is also important to recognize that prior instances of television viewing necessarily constitute viewers' prior *experiences,* and thus, prior television viewing helps shape audiences' needs and expectations. In fact we know that audience expectations and amount of previous experience with the medium are related to how viewers use and experience television. In other words, before the advent of the electronic media, people living in different parts of the country, or the world, would necessarily have had fewer commonly shared cultural experiences. To the degree that one is shaped by prior experience, this means that the mass media will have homogenizing or mainstreaming effects on viewers. (In just one of many possible examples, a recent national survey showed that over 50% of Americans knew who Judge Joseph Wapner of "The People's Court" was whereas only 12% knew who Chief Justice William Rehnquist of the United States Supreme Court was.) Frequent exposure to television over many years is certain to shape knowledge, and therefore what needs, attitudes, and expectations we bring to new encounters with televised materials. Indeed, Wilensky (1964) argued over two decades ago that even professors, intellectuals, and other "keepers of high culture" were spending great portions of time with the mass media thus "reducing their versatility of taste and opinion" while simultaneously being "tempted to play to mass audiences" (p. 190).

Let us also consider that if media "texts" do not result in some uniformity of response, how do we explain that new audiences gravitate to certain classic television programs and films year after year, whereas others are almost universally deemed worthless and never find large or appreciative audiences? It is certainly not the case that the sustained popularity of *It's a Wonderful Life* or "The Honeymooners," as just two examples, is due solely to random chance. Rather, these offerings are popular, as are so many other films and television programs, because they reliably resonate with and reinforce widely held human concerns, needs, and experiences.

The active audience approach also generally neglects to recognize that relative to print, certain cognitive and affective responses to television and film are much more likely to be uniform as a result of the pictorial nature of these media. As argued toward the end of chapter 5, different people reading *The Wizard of Oz* without having seen a filmed or televised version will visualize each of the characters much more idiosyncratically than will people who are exposed to the more complete characterizations offered on the screen.

Responses to film and television will also tend to be more uniform than those to print because the pace of information reception in film and television is dictated almost entirely by the medium. By contrast, when one reads, one can move along at a variety of paces. Thus, the reader is in more active control of reception and the resulting experience is more idiosyncratic. These facts—along with the natural inclination for the human-orienting response to react to particular kinds of televised material (as discussed in chapter 7)—represent just a few of the important ways in which television and film structure our experience.

Furthermore, if it were the case that people could more readily derive from some other activity the experience that they derive from television, it is likely that they would do so. In other words, people watch as much television as they do for a reason, and that reason must have to do with how television viewing characteristically affects them.

Granted that any effect is a function of an interaction between the stimulus and what the person wants to obtain from the encounter, as well as the person's needs, background, and psychological make-up. But this is also the case for many other stimuli that people encounter. If we were to minimize television's effects on this basis—and on the basis that people choose to expose themselves to the stimuli of television—we would, by necessity, have to also minimize the impact that many people have on us, or, for that matter, the power of books, or a college education, to influence how we think, feel, and behave. In other words, because we actively choose to enter a relationship or read a book or begin a college education and we start with a particular background and set of needs and with a particular set of expectations of what we will get for ourselves in these encounters, does that then necessarily mean that the person or the book or the education are less influential in our lives?

Put another way, is there something inherently different about the nature of our interactions with people or with education, and our interactions with media? Surely there are important differences, and this is precisely the point. The uses and gratifications approach often steers us away from building a theory of mass communication that reveals the nature of media effects generally, how they differ from other effects, or about the specific effects of a particular medium. What is it about mass communication, or a particular television program, or about how a particular medium is situated within a particular social formation, that makes it different from another medium, another program, or a particular medium in some other social formation, both in terms of how people typically interact with it and are influenced by it?

The uses and gratifications approach made important contributions in sensitizing researchers to the idea that different people used different media in different ways in different situations and that many people used the same medium in similar ways. Neglected was the fact that many people are *affected* by the same medium in similar ways and that there are general media effects. It is our sense that approaches that seek to explain such effects hold the greatest potential for the development of mass communication studies.

AN APPROACH TO THE ACTIVE AUDIENCE CONCEPT,
CIRCA 1916

It might be enlightening to conclude the chapter with the observations of Hugo Munsterberg (1916), an early psychologist and media observer who dealt incisively with some of the questions about audience activity that we have been discussing.*

In writing about theatrical plays and films, for instance, Munsterberg—like the uses and gratifications theorists—observed that the audience's background and previous experience were crucially involved in the process of reception:

> They [the images and scenes of a play] must have a meaning for us, they must be enriched by our own imagination, they must awaken the remnants of earlier experiences, they must stir up our feelings and emotions, they must play on our suggestibility, they must start ideas and thoughts, they must be linked in our mind with the continuous chain of the play, and they must draw our attention constantly to important and essential element of the action. (p. 72)

But as we have argued, much of the control of attention rests with what is presented to the audience. Here, Munsterberg focuses on theatrical effects:

> The actor who speaks holds our attention more strongly than the actors who at that time are silent. Yet the contents of the words may direct our interest to anybody else on the stage. We watch him whom the words accuse, or betray or delight. Every gesture . . . brings order and rhythm into the manifoldness of the impressions and organizes them for our mind. (pp. 76–77)

Of course, with film and television there can be little question but that

---

*Munsterberg's observations are rarely brought to bear in current empirical mass communication research even though his work is frequently republished and analyzed in contemporary books and essays on film theory. Indeed, a number of early film theorists' writings are highly relevant to those concerned with audience psychology and the impact of television on viewer attention.

Some of the most seminal writings of Munsterberg as well as many of the most notable early and modern film theorists (Pudovkin, Eisenstein, Arnheim, Bazin, Metz, and Kracauer) can be found in Mast and Cohen's (1979) *Film Theory and Criticism.* These same theorists are also each given a separate chapter in J. Dudley Andrew's (1976) *The Major Film Theories.* Munsterberg's (1916) book on film, *The Photoplay,* was republished in 1969 by Dover Press, New York, as *The Film: A Psychological Study.*

our attention is even more dependent on the cues of what we are shown than is the case with a play. Here Munsterberg wrote about silent films, which he called "photoplays":

> But it is evident that with the exception of the words, no means for drawing attention which is effective on the theater stage is lost in the photoplay. . . . Our whole attention can now be focused in the play of the face and of the hands. . . . Everything is condensed, the whole rhythm is quickened, a great pressure of time is applied, and through that the accents become sharper and the emphasis more powerful for the attention. We might sit through the photoplay with the voluntary intention of watching the pictures with a scientific interest in order to detect some mechanical traits of the camera, or with a practical interest, in order to look up some new fashions. . . . But none of these aspects has anything to do with the photoplay. If we follow the play in a genuine attitude of theatrical interest, we must accept those cues for our attention which the playwright and the producers have prepared for us. (pp. 80–81)

A final quote from Munsterberg may well be among the most elegant in all of mass communication theory. It explains another of the great appeals of film (and television), one that until now we have only touched on, and that perhaps we could only expect would be noticed by an insightful observer who in his earlier life had never seen moving lifelike images projected on a screen. For Munsterberg, then, in film (and television):

> The massive outer world has lost its weight, it has been freed from space, time, and causality, and it has been clothed in the forms of our own consciousness. The mind has triumphed over matter . . . The photoplay shows us a significant conflict of human actions in moving pictures which, freed from the physical forms of space, time, and causality, are adjusted to the free play of our mental experiences and which reach complete isolation from the practical world through the perfect unity of plot and pictorial appearance. (p. 220)

ENDNOTES

[1]These observations and those to follow have been presented elsewhere (Kubey, 1989e).

[2]With regard to many of the classic dichotomies in television research, we are in general agreement with Reeves, Thorson, and Schleuder (1986):

> Television as a psychological stimulus is too complex; it is viewed in too many different situations, for too many different reasons, in combination with too many

other activities to ever represent a stimulus located precisely in one category and never in the other. (p. 273)

[3]We are referring here to phenomena apart from news and politics that are the areas most typically studied by agenda setting researchers. See McCombs and Weaver (1985) for a discussion of gratifications and traditional agenda-setting research.

Television and the Structuring of Experience

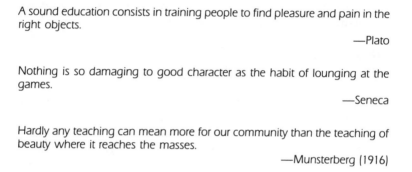

A sound education consists in training people to find pleasure and pain in the right objects.

—Plato

Nothing is so damaging to good character as the habit of lounging at the games.

—Seneca

Hardly any teaching can mean more for our community than the teaching of beauty where it reaches the masses.

—Munsterberg (1916)

Much remains to be said about the implications of this study and the role television plays in the quality of everyday life, individual development, and the future and health of human societies. Does television help people live more rewarding and meaningful lives? Is television viewing different from other forms of leisure? Is it just as well that people continue to use television as they are doing now or could changes in the audience make a difference in how television is used and experienced, or in how it is created? Why is television programming the way it is, and could it be changed? These are a few of the questions that will be pursued in the pages ahead.

ORDER AND COMPLEXITY REVISITED

At the very beginning of this book we pointed out that human attention was limited, and that attention was required to bring order to experience. Experience is not naturally ordered, and, without a focus for attention that provides patterns for thoughts, experience rarely remains in an ordered state for very long.

Television and Routine Reality Maintenance

As we suggested in the first chapter, food and sleep are not enough to maintain psychological order. Certain types of information are also necessary. To help restore assurance in the world as we know it, "reality-maintenance" work is regularly needed (Berger & Luckmann, 1967). *Emergency* reality maintenance is called for when events suddenly threaten our most basic goals. A war, the loss of a job, the inevitable death of loved ones or the approach of one's own, will often put ordered reality into question. At such times, more than ever, messages are needed to confirm the value of the goals by which we live.[1]

But routine reality maintenance is just as crucial for daily mental well-being. We typically engage in such maintenance unconsciously by falling into the routines of social living. Upon awaking we tell our spouse, "A gloomy day outside again," and when he or she absent-mindedly agrees we get a small confirmation that the world is indeed as we believe it to be. Then we glance at the paper,[2] listen to the radio, have breakfast, and so on—at each step compiling further messages that reassure us of the order in the world. Without such reassurance it would be difficult to make plans for our personal goals, and disorder might enter consciousness in the form of a disabling anxiety.

For Gregory Bateson (1972), as for Berger and Luckmann, much of the information we seek out and produce for ourselves is aimed at creating redundancy that will help maintain a reliable sense that things are as they seem. So, although we often seek novelty and complexity, reassuring redundancy is also necessary to maintain consciousness in an organized state.[3] (Klapp, 1986, called this "good"—or functional—redundancy and included rules, codes, customs, and traditions among the redundant phenomena that help provide order and meaning to experience.)

Berger and Luckmann also posited that it is ordinary conversation that is the primary mechanism of routine reality maintenance. People keep their subjective universes in recognizable shape by constantly talking about them. When we exchange words about our work or the weather, yesterday's football games or television shows, useful information in the sense of increasing knowledge is rarely exchanged. Yet the information is often valuable because it helps connect and integrate us with our fellow human beings while confirming what we already know, but might begin to doubt unless confirmed. Redundancy reminds us of the order in the universe—of what is "real," what is worth paying attention to, working for, and living for.

For many of us, television now performs some of the function that conversation once played in maintaining everyday order. Whether it is because modern life is increasingly privatized, offering fewer opportunities to have friendly or meaningful chats, or because it is easier or seems more enjoyable to watch television than to hold a conversation,[4] most people in our culture now spend 2 to 4 hours daily in contact with televised information, the bulk of which can be thought of as redundant, particularly in its repetitive use of well accepted genres, "frames," and scenarios (Gamson, 1988; Gitlin, 1980; Tuchman, 1974).

Indeed, the majority of television viewers interviewed by the Corporation for Public Broadcasting (1978) said that they preferred commercial television over public television because in watching commercial TV they were more likely to see familiar actors and episodes of programs they had viewed previously. In fact, many viewers are disappointed and even outraged if their expectations are not met by the programs they regularly watch. The CBS comedy "Rhoda" began to lose its audience when an unconventional plot element was added: Rhoda's new marriage was not working and she and her TV husband separated. CBS also received thousands of angry letters and telephone calls after a favorite leading character in the comedy "M*A*S*H" was killed on his way home from the war. In both instances, the comedies in question were taken to task for breaking with the tradition of amusement and escape, by conflicting with viewers' expectations and thus producing psychic entropy. In this sense, television may not only perform some of the reality-maintenance functions of conversation, but also those of a much repeated fairy tale; it is familiar and predictable.

As television comedy writer and producer Stu Silverman told Kubey (1989d), "Television reassures us, it's 'nice,' it doesn't offend or challenge an audience. It's designed to do the opposite of art, to reassure rather than excite. That often is what people want." Bob Shanks, a successful television producer and writer has drawn similar conclusions:

> Television is used mostly as a stroking distraction from the truth of an indifferent and silent universe and the harsh realities just out of sight and sound of the box. Television is a massage, a "there, there," a need, an addiction, a psychic fortress—a friend. (see Fowles, 1982, pp. 46–47)

Steven Bochco (1983), creator of "Hill Street Blues" and "L.A. Law" has concluded that many viewers wish to be left "in a very pleasant state of semiconsciousness" (p. 160) before going to bed, and Aaron Spelling, the creator of more fanciful programs such "Fantasy Island" and "Charlie's Angels," has observed that workers "come home and use the TV set as a paintbrush to paint over the horrors of the day, to forget what real life is" (see Fowles, 1982, p. 43). Television critic William Henry (1983), in examining his own viewing motivations would concur: "I run to television for solace. In times of personal turmoil it provides familiarity, emotional connections, and the promise of resolution" (p. 48).

The "days of the week" and the "hours of the day," are also among the most powerful social conventions that help structure experience and maintain reality.[5] Activities such as sleeping, eating, working, leisure, and religious observance take place at particular times and intervals based exclusively, or in large part, on what day of the week and what hour of the day it is, thereby providing order and regularity as well as giving direction to what we believe we should be doing and experiencing at any given time.

Regarding television, specific programs are also available at certain times of the day and on particular days of the week and, especially in the United States, these programs are neatly packaged into familiar and regular "time slots" of 30 minutes, 60 minutes, and so on. Indeed, the timing of viewing depends to a great extent on the day of the week, the time of day, and the scheduling of work and meals.

Because the scheduling of different kinds of television programs is dependent on these same social conventions, television viewing itself reinforces the already existing time structure that society has devised for itself and thereby helps further communicate a sense of regularity and orderliness. Indeed, it might be disorienting if one suddenly found children's cartoons on all of the major networks late one night or "The Wide World of Sports" airing on a weekday morning. In fact, since the early 1950s the TV industry has titled a good many of its entertainment and news programs by what time of day they were broadcast, in part, as a reminder to viewers and to help increase ratings ("The Noon News," "The Eleven O'Clock News," and so on). (Among NBC's longest running programs have been "Tonight" and "Today," and more recently, "Tomorrow," "Late Night," and "Later.")

Many viewers, particularly those with less structure in their lives such as retired persons and the unemployed, use television to give shape to the day and to demarcate time (Davis, 1973; Kubey, 1980; Schalinske, 1968). A quote from one of Steiner's (1963) older respondents provides evidence of how television can help provide structure and psychological order, particularly for someone who has lost many of his previous social roles:

> I'm an old man and the TV brings people and music and talk into my life. Maybe without TV I would be ready to die; but this TV gives me life. It gives me what to look forward to—that tomorrow if I live, I'll watch this and that program.

Our colleague Marten deVries (personal communication, June 9, 1989) has reported that in an ESM study of drug abusers in the Netherlands, 45% of all responses from one recovering heroin addict were instances of television viewing. The subject's feelings during viewing were more relaxed and less sad and angry than normal, and he reported that his thoughts during viewing were more pleasant and less confused. The subject explained that he used television as a self-control mechanism that helped him contain his craving and get his mind "off dope."

But television may also structure experience in ways that are less desirable, and that signal a dependence at variance with the viewer's long-term interests. In one example, another aging man, hospitalized for alcoholism, told Kubey, "I have my drinking under pretty good control. I don't have my first drink of the day until noon when the '$20,000 Pyramid' comes on."

Emphasis on the maintenance functions of television should not imply that the medium does not also produce complex messages. Television can and does provide interesting and thought-provoking information. Some programs are sophisticated and, regardless of content, many viewers derive complex interpretations of what they view. Television can also influence viewers so that their ways of seeing, thinking, and feeling change, and the capacity to order experience is enhanced. Both drama and comedy can help deepen our understanding of ourselves and our culture, while news and educational programs frequently provide information that helps people realize their plans and enriches their store of knowledge.*

Reality Maintenance, Television Content, and the Existing Social Order

But when we speak of the reality-maintenance functions of television, what kind of *reality* does television maintain? Certainly not an absolute reality "out there," but a model of it. Although televised messages can contribute to keeping the individual consciousnesses of viewers in an ordered state, they simultaneously keep attention focused on common societal concerns, thereby contributing to cultural integration (Hirsch, 1977a; Loevinger, 1968). Of course, some critics argue that this integration is likely to benefit the goals of those who own and/or control the communication process more than it benefits the goals of individual

---

*Of course, much television news, especially at the local level, is purposely sensationalized with the primary goal of attracting and holding viewers in order to boost ratings. Critics regularly point out that news programs tend to be a hodgepodge of facts unrelated to any meaningful context; in one jaundiced view, they merely provide information that can be used effectively in a game of Trivial Pursuit (Nystrom, 1984).

viewers. Hence, there are enormous political and ethical implications of television as a medium for shaping consciousness.

But even though most of what appears on the screen exists for commercial reasons, for advertisers to make money by attracting the attention of tens of millions of prospective consumers, television fare must at the same time appeal to many of the goals of the public if it is also to benefit the owners' goals. It must have high enough negentropy and complexity quotients to attract and hold viewer attention, but not so high as to turn them off. As we have shown, most television fare is experienced as mildly pleasant and requiring little mental effort, offering bits of novelty safely packaged in a familiar context. As a result, the information conveyed can be processed in a relaxed manner for several hours each day.

But, again, some critics claim that mass viewing causes a wholesale imitation of TV reality and greater conformity on the part of the public.* And certainly it is the case that television often emphasizes those messages that directly or indirectly will best serve the goals of the people who own or control the medium and who pay for the production of programs.† And as is argued shortly, tens of thousands of hours spent watching television may well help foster an acceptance and attraction for the aims of the commercial world.

Furthermore, although television helps provide psychological order, our research also suggests that the medium may not enrich life as much as one might hope. Like Tantalus, the Lydian king who in Hades was condemned to stand up to his neck in water that always flowed away when he tried to drink it, the modern television viewer is surrounded by

---

*As the Paddy Chayefsky character, Howard Beale, in the movie *Network* put it when he chastized the viewing audience, "You think like the tube, you dress like the tube, you eat like the tube."

†The idea that the mass media serve the interests of the power elite has a long and distinguished history. One of the seminal statements on the topic and the one that underlies many critiques of mass culture is Marx's statement in *The German Ideology* that "the ideas of the ruling class are in every epoch the ruling ideas."

Frankfurt School theorists later held that the mass media tended to lull and assimilate the working class to the ruling elite's interests and thus subverted the revolutionary change forecast by Marx (Horkheimer & Adorno, 1972; Marcuse, 1964). Gramsci (1971) and Hall (1982) were concerned less with the base and class determinants of ideology, focusing instead on the process of hegemony itself (i.e., how dominant ideologies are represented in mass media content and how through the mass media they reproduce themselves in consciousness). Much of George Gerbner and his colleagues' research on "cultivation" effects similarly suggests that heavy viewers tend to share a more narrow, mainstream set of political and social beliefs than light viewers (see Gerbner et al., 1986, for a review). Among many others who have delineated how the mass media serve ruling interests are Gitlin (1980); Herman and Chomsky (1988); Parenti (1986); and Schiller (1973).

interesting stimulation that too often flickers away without slacking his thirst. Or as the former President of MTM, NBC, and current CEO of his own GTG Entertainment Company, Grant Tinker, has said, "I think what is probably the biggest sin of the medium as it exists is that so little sticks to your ribs, that so much effort and technology goes into—what? It's like human elimination. It's just waste" (see Gitlin, 1983, p. 16).*

The irony is that television may benefit most those who least need it. People who are already reasonably happy and in control of their lives will be more inclined to find useful information on television and will be less inclined to become dependent on the medium. Those who are less happy and less able or skilled in creating order in their experience are more likely to become dependent, and yet derive less enjoyment from their viewing.

That those in better emotional condition may be more inclined to use television for serious ends is illustrated in an intriguing study by Zillmann et al. (1980). Subjects in whom a good mood was experimentally induced were more likely to become quickly disenchanted with viewing a game show and gravitated instead to a drama. The authors concluded that these subjects possessed the necessary patience to stick with the drama. In contrast, subjects in whom a bad mood was induced did the opposite—those who first picked the drama deserted it quickly in favor of viewing the game show. Zillmann and Bryant (1985) concluded from this study and similar research that certain programs are selected not because of "particular excitatory and hedonic reactions but primarily because they contain soothing, comforting information" (p. 182).

An examination of one's own use of television may confirm these findings. If you come home anxious and depressed from a particularly frustrating and defeating day at work and you have two movies available on videotape that you very much want to eventually view, are you more likely to pick a light comedy or a very serious, complex drama?

Attraction to comforting, low-complexity easy-to-digest information is one of the prime reasons that television viewing typically supports the viewer's existing set of beliefs, why use of the medium will tend to support the status quo. David Mumford, senior vice president for research at Columbia Pictures Television confirmed that viewers do not want

---

*Edward R. Murrow also took a dim view of much that his industry offered:

And if there are any historians . . . a hundred years from now and there should be preserved the kinescopes for one week of all three networks, they will find recorded, in black-and-white or color, evidence of decadence, escapism and insulation from the realities of the world. . . . If we go on as we are, then history will take its revenge, and retribution will [catch] up with us. (cited in Friendly, 1968, p. 99)

"challenging" programs; they want "leisure-time activity that is absent of discomfort" (cited in Topolnicki, 1989, p. 74).

Dissonance theory (Festinger, 1957), affect-dependent stimulus arrangement theory (Zillmann & Bryant, 1985), cognitive balance theory (Heider, 1946), and our own model of information and experience each predict that people who are unhappy for one reason or another will tend to seek out nonthreatening, confirmatory messages, and will avoid information that challenges their belief system. Of course some people who are unhappy for long periods of time will eventually gravitate to new belief systems to make themselves feel better.

But people who are reasonably happy and who possess greater cognitive complexity are more likely to seek out television programs that contain more complex and challenging information. Even watching the same program, a person more skilled in interpreting information can generally extract more complexity and order. For as Wright and Huston (1981) pointed out:

> Informativeness . . . is a meaningful property only to the viewer who is actively seeking to understand the content at a level of processing beyond superficial enjoyment. To appreciate features for their informativeness, the viewer must be able to encode content, form hypotheses, and develop a context of expectations. (p. 77)

Furthermore, a viewer's expectation about the viewing enterprise plays a role in how the medium is experienced. The research of Salomon and Leigh (1984) confirms that children readily form a "context of expectations" that causes them to approach television with an attitude that precludes actively seeking to understand television content at deeper levels. Still, those children who can order their experiences more actively and who appreciate and seek complexity are more likely to retain greater control and mastery over the information provided by any medium, and therefore will derive more useful information from it.

Viewer expectations are the result of a system of complex reciprocal causality. The nature of television programming is shaped by audience ratings while past viewing experiences and the programs themselves simultaneously help set certain expectations in viewers. These in turn affect how viewers will respond to what is on TV and what will be on in the future. Therefore, both the nature of television form and content, and the nature of television use and experience, are the results of repeated interactions of medium, mind, and the past experiences of both producers and audiences.

This is a good place to debunk the much repeated idea that television is a medium best suited to transmitting emotions, and that it either "cannot" or is not "good" at transmitting ideas. We believe that those who make this claim often confuse what they are accustomed to seeing on television with what television can transmit.

A single example may prove instructive. Every year, for a variety of reasons, many students successfully receive their introductory college lectures in chemistry, biology, and physics via television and/or on videotape. This often happens because lecture halls are overcrowded or as a means of accommodating students' schedules. Regardless of the reason, it is clearly the case that very complex ideas can be readily and inexpensively transmitted via television. We might keep this in mind when considering why television is only occasionally used in this manner. Indeed, it is ironic that the greatest expense in commercial production is involved in taking very simple things—say, a deodorant or a bathroom tissue—and, by employing very costly special effects or a celebrity spokessperson, making these products seem more interesting and more complex than they are.

The answer to why we see what we see on television lies in a combination of how audiences have come to conceive of the medium, what audiences want to watch (or have grown accustomed to watching), and what the people who control and sponsor television believe needs to be created and broadcast in order to maximize profit.

But the medium and the industry can be held only partly accountable if people become dependent on television for escape. Nor is television solely responsible if people have either not obtained, or have lost, the ability to find meaningful goals to direct their consciousness by.

Rather, television content, and how people use and experience the medium, are certainly as much a result of human nature and existing economic and cultural arrangements as their cause. Or as Utley (1948) wrote, "TV appeals to the inherent laziness in all of us" (p. 137). Moreover, if television always presented information requiring substantial effort to interpret and to assimilate, it would fail to provide its therapeutic function, if for no other reason than that people simply lack the inclination and the mental energy to process complex messages all of the time. Thus there is something to be said for the fact that television does not tax the mind—especially if much of life is already challenging, or if one's usual experience alternates between boredom and anxiety.

At one time or another, most of us have come home after a day of dealing with complex problems and dropped in front of the television, appreciatively receiving its attractive, easy-to-receive entertainment. Certainly it can be argued that using television in this manner habitually is no worse, and may indeed be better, than habitually using alcohol or other mood-altering substances.

Although this argument has merit, it is also true that television has become too important a part of daily life for us to ignore what happens during the time it is viewed. Just as a drug that masks pain but does not heal may be of limited value in the long run or may cause addiction, so can viewing encourage a false sense of well-being in some people who might be better off taking active steps to change the conditions of their "real" lives.

If one of the goals of life is to realize one's latent potentialities—the ideal held, among others, by Aristotle, the Christian Tomists, as well as by Marx and most modern psychologists—then the prolonged and indiscriminate viewing of television is likely to present an obstacle in achieving that purpose.

ON ELIMINATING TELEVISION

To stop the analysis at this point would be too easy. Television is an obvious and convenient scapegoat, and it is not unusual for technological innovations, from the steam engine to the mechanical loom, to be blamed for the ills of society. Socrates was critical of writing because he believed it would result in the decay of memory. But were we to abolish television, as Mander (1978) suggested in *Four Arguments for the Elimination of Television*, it is questionable whether things would get better by themselves.

In fact, there is reason to believe that the abolition of television might make things worse—at least in the short run. People depend on habitual routines that organize the day for their well-being—for some it is smoking, for others snacking, or doodling at work—and for most of us the routine includes liberal doses of television. In fact, people begin to fall apart psychologically when they are deprived of sensory input (Heron, 1957) or asked to refrain from going through their habitual routines (Csikszentmihalyi, 1975); they become irritable and anxious and cannot concentrate. Very similar experiences were reported in experiments where people were paid to quit viewing television for a few weeks, or when their only set had broken down and was under repair.

Human behavior and human experience, in other words, are not made up of independent strands; one cannot pull out one habit or activity without altering or unraveling some of the others in the process. Most persons who quit smoking gain weight; few people can start jogging and keep to the same diet and the same routine as before. Nor are leisure patterns independent of work experiences and both are intimately tied to the relations one has with one's family, and with other people.

If television were eliminated, would people flock in great numbers from the glass screen to reading the classics, to learning a new skill or hobby, or even to playing cards and visiting with friends? Actually, many people might, but it takes effort and conviction for an individual, let alone for a family, to establish new patterns or to alter their viewing habits, especially when they are not being forced to change. Probably the most interesting finding in every one of the experiments involving voluntary abstention from TV has been how difficult it is to find a family or an individual willing to stop viewing for a few weeks, even when fairly substantial financial rewards are offered. And frequently, among those who finally do volunteer, many cannot complete even a few days' abstinence.

But there are rewards to reducing viewing. Parents who have suddenly removed the set, although reporting many initial difficulties in adjustment, also report increases in the amount of time devoted to reading and hobbies, as well as joint activities and family communication. Two experimental studies with children have shown that time devoted to reading increased when time with television was reduced (Gadberry, 1980; Wolfe, Mendes, & Factor, 1984).[6]

But sustained success is often difficult to achieve. Eliot Daley (1978), for example, described his family's initial experiences after eliminating television as "sheer hell." After 4 weeks Daley's daughter concluded that her family was better off without TV and told her father that she was pleased that the set had been shelved. But in the fall and with the advent of the football season, the family fell off the television sobriety wagon:

> We had been without TV for over six months now and I felt confident the addiction was fully broken. What I didn't know was how little time it took to reestablish it. About three days. (pp. 147–148)

THE CRISIS OF MEANING

Explanatory models that ignore this systemic nature of behavior and experience do a disservice to our understanding of human activity. They attempt to deal with patterns of behavior independently of each other, not realizing that much of what we do is interconnected, and depends on our goals. And when a person, a group of people, or a society lack clear and compelling goals by which to give direction to their mental energies, then changing a few patterns of behavior and of experience will not necessarily help in a substantial way.

Indeed, there are signs that we are living in a society that is having difficulty imparting valuable meaning to information. Many people seem to have problems directing their energies toward goals that are complex, rewarding, and healthful.

Nowhere is the problem of imparting meaning more evident than in the socialization of the young. Given that a culture is ultimately perpetuated through the socialization of its youth, what goals are being set for youth, and whether young people feel compelled by, or feel comfortable with those goals, become very serious questions.

Discipline in schools, as just one example, has become a nationwide scandal. Because of poor discipline, and the low priority placed on teaching in our culture, a substantial number of schools cannot find enough adequately trained teachers to meet students' needs.

Other indicators that socialization may be less than ideal include dramatic increases in the rates of teenage pregnancy and suicide. The Centers for Disease Control, 1986, reported a 300% increase in suicides for those aged 15–24 over the previous 30 years and the Carnegie Corporation's Council on Adolescent Development, 1989, reported the suicide rate more than doubling for 10- to 14-year-olds between 1980 and 1985.*

The problem of drug and alcohol abuse among children and adolescents is also quite revealing.[7] But whether they be adults or children, people who depend on drugs to give shape to experience, like some of the heavy television viewers in our studies, may be those who encounter difficulty managing their experience when left to themselves.

Mood-altering drugs can also provide a temporary solution to psychological disorder—they generally bring about changes in experience without the person having to invest energy to make it happen. But we cannot escape the fact that the improvement of the self or of one's immediate environment requires the concentration of mental energy. There are few if any short-cuts, and elation without effort is unlikely to lead to personal growth.

Of course, drug and alcohol abuse are only two forms of altering consciousness and experience.[8] For those who follow it mindlessly, Marx's aphorism that religion was "the opiate of the masses" may hold true. Yet most religions do provide an over-arching meaning system for

---

*Admittedly, these are among the worst examples, and there are some statistics that would indicate improvement. Children have received much worse treatment in other historical periods, and yet human societies have continued to evolve. As recently as this century and until child labor laws were enacted, hundreds of thousands of children worked full time in dangerous and inhumane conditions. Between the 4th and 14th centuries many children of all social classes were abandoned to die by their parents (Boswell, 1989). Others were sold into prostitution or slavery. See Phillipe Aries' (1962) *Centuries of Childhood* for an examination of the changing social construction of childhood through history.

ordering events and experiences, which give them a "negentropy quotient" of broader applicability than that of mood-altering drugs.

Other forms of mass entertainment also provide ordered experiences, often with a minimum of concentration. Sporting events, rock concerts, and other spectacles* typically bind attention at a level of complexity that demands little or no new adaptation, and encourages little or no further psychological growth.[9]

For Klapp (1986), in a crisis of meaning such as the one our society would appear to be undergoing, there is little conviction that people can reliably hang onto. He argued that there is a meaning gap that he defined as:

> an inability of people in the same society to agree on larger patterns, purposes, and values even when they share the same factual information, which is piling up at a rate faster than they can agree about purposes and values. . . . (p. 110)

> Traditions are discarded, institutions—even the most hallowed—are weakly legitimated and justify themselves by rhetoric regarded by many as boring or hypocritical. . . . People are continually on the verge of boredom because so much information is irrelevant, meaningless, or trivial—or urgent but they can do nothing about it. (pp. 8–9)†

---

*As with so many other entertainment phenomena, "spectacle" was taken to task long ago by others. Seneca (1965), the ancient Roman stoic, 4? B.C.–65 A.D., wrote, "Nothing is so ruinous to good character as to spend time at any spectacle" (p. 12). More recently, one of Saul Bellow's (1987) characters in *More Die of Heartbreak* warns his uncle, "Naturally you're aware that bad art can finally cripple a man" (p. 261).

†Emile Durkheim was aware of these same phenomena. For him, too wide a range of choices untethered by social regulations, such as rules, norms, and fixed statuses, leads to meaningless consumption and a penchant "for novelties, unfamiliar pleasures, nameless sensations, all of which lose their savor once known. . . . We must bring the extinguished pleasure to life again by means of more energetic stimuli" (1893/1947, p. 252).

Like Durkheim, Klapp (1986) has concluded that modern society is one of little meaning and little meaningful ritual:

> Meanings seem to require natural processes of indigenous communication networks, including the slow growth of languages, beliefs, traditions, "we" feeling, and connections of status—all of which might be called "roots". . . . Mass media take the place of such infrastructure, though not sufficiently. . . . (p. 114)

> Bureaucratic procedures replace ceremonies . . . and genuine, meaningful ritual has deteriorated into . . . commercialized Christmas or the half-time celebrations at football games. . . . We note also the function of shows like musical comedies . . . soap operas, and television evangelism to compensate for an emotional emptiness that is due to the failure of institutions such as the family, and, in part, to the poverty of what ritual . . . there is. The plight of much modern ritual—unless it is put on as entertainment—is to be boring, and to provide no more social and personal continuity than do the shows with which it competes. (p. 77)

It is within this *real* cultural context, not a fanciful utopia, that television must be evaluated. Against this background television would seem to blend in rather well, even though we must keep in mind that commercial television has helped shape the current excesses toward brief and spectacular information dissemination in most every other form of entertainment as well as in newspapers, magazines, and books.

Finding Meaning in Work and Leisure

One benchmark of the success of a culture is how much complex enjoyment it offers in its typical work and leisure roles. As we suggest it seems that few contemporary cultures have been able to actualize the potentialities. In an ironic twist, it seems that both the capitalist and the socialist superpowers perform less successfully in practice where according to their ideologies they should excel, and they seem to do somewhat better in the area that should be the other society's strength.

The Soviet Union, ostensibly built on Marxist principles, has been able to make work resemble a growth experience for only a relatively small minority of privileged technicians, scientists, athletes, and artists. In Eastern bloc countries the attitude toward one's job among many workers is one of unallayed cynicism, despite the heavy official propaganda exalting its nobility. Instead of achieving Marx's implicit abolition of the distinction between work and leisure, some of the socialist economies have helped exacerbate the distinction by failing to make work more satisfying.

Comparatively speaking, in the United States, there is a much greater proportion and a wider selection of jobs that are remunerative and challenging and it would seem that the United States comes closer to Marx's utopia in this respect than does the Soviet Union.*

But what kind of guidance does the culture of the United States provide its citizens for actualizing the potentials inherent in leisure? Although many find satisfaction in work, for many Americans the goal of work is to provide free time (Bell, 1976). In fact our economic, technological, and political arrangements have made such large chunks of free time available that over 30 years ago it was already being suggested that leisure was outstripping work as the central activity of living (Bogart, 1956/1972).

A problem worth posing, then, is to what degree people actually use this time in a manner that is satisfying or for the kind of growth-produc-

---

*Daniel Yankelovich (Harris & Trotter, 1989) claimed that in the middle and late 1980s, increasing numbers of young and better educated American workers have come to believe that work, rather than leisure, will give them the opportunity for self-expression and gratification.

ing involvement that the Greeks had in mind? In socialist countries it has been our observation, as well as that of colleagues who have lived and traveled there, that leisure often seems to be taken more seriously than in the United States (Zuzanek, 1980). It is somewhat sobering to see the extent to which in the Soviet Union and other socialist nations people strive to live by the traditional values of 19th-century bourgeois "Kultur." Art, literature, history, poetry, theater, and amateur science occupy a larger part of the free time of these citizens than they do in the West. Self-improvement through the acquisition of disciplined skill is more frequently seen not only as an opportunity, but a duty of one's leisure time. The corner bookstores may not be well-stocked, but what they do offer has little to do with career and psychological self-improvement. Instead there are proportionately more texts in differential calculus, poetry, classical literature, and literary criticism than there are in the United States.

These cultural trends, as is often the case with cultural trends, may change. For several years now, many youth in the Soviet Union would not be at all reluctant to spend their free time in less demanding pursuits, and embrace instead the more hedonistic lifestyles of Western teenagers. But as we are not blessed with precognitive powers, we must be content with observing what is happening here and now. And as far as leisure is concerned, the current state of affairs in our culture presents a rather ambiguous picture.

At few times in modern history has such a large percentage of the population had so much time to dispose of freely. Nor has there been a period in which so many people had the incredible material resources we now have to do with as we please. It is possible for an American working-class family to own a power boat for summer frolicking, a snowmobile for winter fun, and enough disposable income left over for an annual visit to Disneyland, Las Vegas, or the Grand Canyon.

Yet despite these opportunities that would have been the envy of an emperor of Rome, it remains unclear whether we get the expected benefits. Part of the problem is that in affluent societies such as our own, people are offered a constant oversupply of commodities and entertainment that results in information overload and boredom from satiation, habituation, and desensitization (Klapp, 1986).

Edwin Ettinger, a former Disneyland marketing director, pointed to *leisure* overload in explaining the attraction of Disneyland among Americans already possessing material wealth and enormous amounts of free time:

> It was a kind of mass groping. . . . They felt awkward about all that leisure time thrust onto them and they weren't sure what to really do with it. Sure, they had their two cars, their pool and their golf and all that—the great

American dream. But they were still bored and they weren't sure why. (Cited in Klapp, 1986, p. 148)

There is no simple liner relationship between material means for leisure, and the actual rewards we derive from it; in fact, there may be an inverse relationship. Economists Gary Becker (1976) and Steffan Linder (1970) have each argued that the more money we get for work, the less we can afford to spend time in leisure. Indeed, as we see later, the great expanses of leisure time that wealth can buy present new problems of their own. Nor does more material energy expended (such as electricity or gasoline) in leisure activities necessarily make for more enjoyment in the activity (Graef, Gianninno, Csikszentmihalyi, 1981). This seems to be because the more external energy used, the less mental and physical energy tends to get invested. In fact, in our research people often support the notion that "the best things in life are free." They frequently report that they derive greatest satisfaction from their families and doing things like gardening, woodworking, crocheting—activities that generally require relatively little material energy, but that instead involve skill and effort.

Meaning, Marketing, and Socialization

At this juncture, it is important to explore briefly why our culture has developed as it has, as well as television's role in creating and reflecting that culture. In an ethnically and racially diverse, capitalistic society such as the United States, with fewer well-entrenched and widely agreed upon values than many older and more traditional societies, it is quite understandable that money, achievement, and conspicuous consumption have become important indicators of status and meaning, especially now that most of the media promote materialism. In contrast, in many of the socialist countries being "cultured" and "intellectually informed" are important status indicators and such attainments are used by a broader spectrum of people as a means to "getting ahead" than is the case in the United States (J. Zuzanek, personal communication, August 25, 1989).

Actually, the emphasis on materialism in the United States took a huge leap forward (or backward depending on one's view) in the early 1920s when manufacturers began shifting their marketing orientation from selling their products to other companies to selling their products directly to individuals. The number and proportion of companies marketing to the public grew markedly during the 1920s (J. R. Schement, personal communication, July 24, 1989).

As a result, a new set of institutions arose that began to rival the church, the family, and the school as the primary institutions of socialization empowered to impart to people the values by which they should live. This set of institutions included manufacturers, corporations, marketers, and advertisers and the mass media they sponsored. Thus, a new and powerful voice was regularly heard by the public about how best to live, and among the messages most frequently promulgated was that to be happy, one must own things.

For most of this century, then, the American public has been exhorted by advertisers to buy a thousand different products that we are told we cannot live properly without, lest we smell, look, or feel bad. We are told constantly that we can have "fast, fast" relief from myriad maladies, some of which were created by marketers for the express purpose of selling products.[10]

As marketing grew in the early decades of this century, advertisers inadvertently made an important discovery—new demand could constantly be created because people were never fully satisfied or happy for very long. As a result, we are constantly offered new and improved products that promise a better and happier life.*

Advertising's constant emphasis on material objects and services as providing the keys to happiness has helped foster consumer demand (and discontent), and a considerable degree of restlessness and material mindedness. And while the business community has long conceived of people as consumers, nowadays not a few people behave as if consumption is at the apex of their concerns.[11] It is also well within the realm of possibility that the constant emphasis in advertising on instant relief and on feeling good, or better, is related to many of the current problems with drug abuse.

Perhaps no better proof could be offered of how television has come to absorb a significant proportion of the authority and power that the church, family, and school once held than the fact that television celebrities are now among those people most talked about, admired, and emulated in our culture. Television and its celebrities now compete with church leaders, parents, and teachers for the attention of children and are important sources of information for how one should live. And just as television tells us what to buy and how to look and feel, so too do television celebrities tell us how to manage every other facet of life. These modern day oracles regularly dispense advice on love and mar-

---

*Actually, the idea that new things are good appears to have been part of American thinking long before the rise of advertising. In *Democracy in America*, Tocqueville (1840/ 1945) wrote, "The American lives in a land of wonders; everything around him is in constant movement, and every movement seems an advance. Consequently, in his mind the idea of newness is closely linked with that of improvement."

riage; exercise, personal hygiene, and diet; business and career success; child rearing, and politics. Given the attention that seems to be paid and the number of celebrity advice books, magazines, and videocassettes sold, it would be hard to dispute that celebrity advice is taken seriously by a good many Americans.[12]

Marketing and the Shaping of Television Content

Of course, television program content is closely tied to the goals of manufacturers and marketers because rather than TV programs being sold to viewers, viewer attention is sold to advertisers at a price per 1,000 potential consumers.[13] In fact, the argument is made by some social historians that manufacturers, marketers, and advertisers supported the raising of wages and the shortening of the work week in the early decades of this century in a deliberate attempt to increase consumption of their products (Ewen, 1976). And it is not difficult to make the case that commercial television's dependence on advertising dollars and audience ratings contributes to much TV content of questionable value.*

Even the best-intentioned TV producers, writers, directors, and actors must work under severe time pressures to create new programs each week that both fit within an established genre (police, detective, doctor, lawyer show, or sit-com), and appeal to the most diverse, and hence, the largest audience possible. As a result, violence, sex, stereotype, and imitation are standard commercial television fare, as are hyperbole and glitz in television advertising and promotion.

For those who doubt the negative impact of ratings and competition on the quality of programs, note this telling statement made to TV critic Tom Shales by Phil Donahue, host of one of the longest running and most popular talk shows in the country: "Please do not call me 'intelligent.' Call me 'outrageous.' I'd rather be called 'sleazy' than identified as 'intelligent'." Asked if this wasn't a sad comment on what competition for audiences had wrought, he replied, "Yes it is, but it's also a recognition of the reality of survival on daytime television today" (Tabloid TV, 1989, p. 248).

Intense competition for the attention of prospective consumers also leads producers to try to outdo the competition with each new commer-

---

*Of course, supporters of the medium correctly argue that so much programming would not be made available in the first place were it not for someone standing to profit by creating it. It can also be argued that fierce competition for audiences can enhance program quality. In the middle and late 1980s television writers began to achieve a new and unprecedented control over their work, and as a result not a few programs in that period regularly exhibited considerable wit, nuance, and depth (Koch, 1989; Kubey, 1989b).

cial or promotional ad lest their ad or program be lost in what they themselves call the "clutter" of everything else appearing on the screen.

To summarize for a moment, because consciousness is necessarily formed by exposure to information, media fare helps define what our most important and salient goals should be. Being an intimate part of the consumer society, television tells us that a worthwhile life is measured in terms of how many desirable material objects we get to own, and how many pleasures we get to feel. To achieve such goals complex skills are unnecessary.[14] Even though some people spend a great deal of attention in trying to find bargains, in monitoring prices and sales,[15] in developing culinary taste and fashion sense, in keeping abreast of new models and new gadgets, for the most part consumption does not require much disciplined effort and therefore does not produce psychological growth.

Meaning, Effort, and the Development of the Self

People are encouraged to use their minds in school and on the job. But because study and work are often valued only as a means to the end of consumption, psychological complexity tends to become associated with the part of life that is alienated from the person's goals and with obligatory work instead. We learn that mental effort is hard "work," to be avoided whenever possible.

Because this habit of thought has become so ingrained, people often fail to notice that the supposed pleasures of consumption do not produce such a positive result after all. Conversely, it fails to register that stretching one's abilities, that growing as a result of concentrated effort, can often be more enjoyable and rewarding than the experiences we get from consumption (Csikszentmihalyi & LeFevre, 1989).

Yet despite a lack of enthusiasm for effort and self-discipline, many persons still know, or at least sense, that what they most enjoy doing involves concentration and effort. Ironically, this is often not a reflective knowledge that people think about or express clearly; it tends to be an enacted knowledge that manifests itself in behavioral choices. Indeed, in our studies, the most positive moods and the strongest motivations are very often reported in active leisure activities, particularly hobbies and sports, that require concentration and skill.

For people who have complex jobs, work itself can become nearly addictive because it presents constant challenges that also help one grow in the process. Such persons may complain about not having any free time, about having to take work home, about the constant demands of their occupation, but essentially they would not, or in some cases, could not give up the stimulation provided by the job. Consider David Lodge's

(1988) fictional depiction of the manager of a factory in *Nice Work:* "Nothing depressed him more than the thought of summer holidays: a fortnight of compulsory idleness. . . . Weekends were bad enough. By this point on a Sunday afternoon he was itching to get back to the factory" (p. 176).

Nevertheless, "workaholism" is not an ideal either. When the only meaningful messages are those that relate to occupational and professional goals, dedication to work interferes with a person's ability to attend to other human needs, to the family, and to other people, thereby doing damage to these interpersonal systems. Obsession with work can also lead to compulsive production and senseless consumption. Yet the self undeniably becomes more complex and differentiated through the application of concentrated energy to the challenges of work than to consumption, and what is more, the enjoyment derived from the effort is often higher.

And as with work, the avocations that help give meaning to people's lives require the same investment of complexly structured attention. When people are asked what they enjoy most, and enough time is left for a genuine answer to emerge, we often find that the most enjoyable things involve doing something, and usually something rather complex and demanding. Rarely does watching television get mentioned, or any other passive or consummatory activity. Nor do such answers seem to be the result of social desirability, cultural conditioning, or a desire to impress the questioner. In fact, the first reflex for many people is to say that one most enjoys going on vacations, going to movies or restaurants—the typical "leisure" responses in our culture. But as people think more deeply about their real feelings they will mention enjoyable times with their families, and then there is often a point when their faces light up and they say something like: "Actually, the best times in my life have been . . ." and start talking with great enthusiasm about designing and sewing quilts, rock climbing, playing music, working on a basement lathe, or about other activities that require concentrated skill, that do not separate the individual from the end result of his or her effort, and that provide the kind of exhilaration and highly focused attention of *flow.*

So despite the constant trickle of low-complexity information of which we often partake in free time, we are still able to keep in sight those vivid signposts that show what it is that makes life worth living. Even if words fail to explain it, even without a theory to account for it, most people tacitly know that they never live as fully as when all their resources are harnessed to overcome a demanding challenge. And on reflecting on such occasions, people often say that not only was the experience enjoyable at the time, but that it helped them grow and become more than they had been.

Compared to such optimal experiences, much television watching could be deemed a waste of time. And because time can be thought of as a medium through which we process life, wasting it amounts to wasting life. But must one always put time to good use? Doesn't everyone need a regular respite from concentrated and effortful activities? Should not a person waste a little life, now and then, if that makes the rest of it more tolerable?

These are questions that we leave for the reader to answer. One problem to consider is whether we can necessarily answer them with real freedom or independence. Our culture, like any other culture, has already been structured so as to preempt or limit some of the options, leaving some of us only with the illusion of having made an individual decision.*

A child who is left for hours in front of a television set with nothing else to do, a child who has never been encouraged to independently create information—who does not know how to draw, how to make music, how to pretend, or even how to read—such a child cannot be expected to turn the set off. The child is condemned to develop a viewing habit, the choices determined by the poverty of the environment. What is true of the child may also be true of those adults who, screened by societal deprivations from the surrounding complexity, may be as helpless as the child when they are left with nothing to do.[16]

Sandor Ferenczi (1919/1950) noticed over three generations ago the problems that having nothing to do can cause in some people. He described the anxiety and depression that hit his psychiatric patients on their day of rest and called the phenomenon the "Sunday neurosis." He accounted for it by claiming that free time brings people in closer contact with repressed impulses that are normally held at bay during the more

---

*An extreme version of this view was offered by Theodor Adorno (1975):

The total effect of the culture industry is one of antienlightenment, in which . . . enlightenment, that is the progressive domination of nature, becomes mass deception and is turned into a means for fettering consciousness. It impedes the development of autonomous, independent individuals who judge and decide consciously for themselves. (pp. 18–19)

Adorno's view is characterized by Brantlinger (1983) as follows:

The reified false consciousness of industrialized mass culture has settled like a pall over history, masking the facts of violence and exploitation so completely that the majority of victims (that is, the majority of mankind) move through life like anesthetized zombies, believing themselves to be free individuals (success stories, even) instead of victims. (p. 226)

structured weekdays.[17] Without such a conflict, people would presumably go happily about their business.

This may explain some instances of "Sunday neurosis," but the disturbance can also be caused by consciousness creating conflict within itself because of a lack of organizing focus. No repressed conflict need exist. Rather, when not directed to a purpose, attention begins to proceed more randomly, is less able to produce positive feedback, and psychic entropy therefore ensues.*

Like Ferenczi, we too have noticed in our studies that many contemporary Americans report their lowest moods on Sunday mornings between, roughly, 10 a.m. and 12 p.m. What seems to happen is that after breakfast on Sunday, those who do not attend a religious observance confront the vacuum of unstructured time. By 10 or 11 a.m. they have finished breakfast, they have looked over the Sunday paper, and there is nothing else they have to do. On Saturdays, comparatively more people have regular routines, such as shopping or working in the yard. Sunday is supposed to be the day of rest, but instead some people begin to feel rest*less*. Those who go to church or have some other regular activity planned know what to do, but for those who do not there is no set obligation, no cultural ritual to provide a short-term goal. For an hour or two, entropy reigns; then by about lunchtime or early afternoon, most people succeed in making up their minds. They decide to go to the movies, visit the in-laws, clean the attic, or watch television. What counts is that having found an activity to give them purpose, order is restored in consciousness.

Meaning, Boredom, and Social Class

Although the way one uses television, and leisure time in general, is often related to one's background, it is important to recognize that this is by no means a simple function of income, social class, or education. Wealth is no guarantee that a person will be able to put leisure time to good use. Indeed, great wealth can provide enormous and burdensome expanses of leisure time.

In fact, the ennui of aristocracies is deservedly legendary. By many accounts, weekends in the English country manor were about as exciting

---

*This phenomenon is already present in the youngest of children who presumably have yet to obtain any neurotic complexes or conflicts. An infant of even a few weeks can be readily distracted and made to feel better and stop crying if someone sings or shakes a rattle. In this most elementary example, the child's disorganized state, often borne of tiredness, is temporarily relieved and reordered by the focusing of attention.

as they are in the average Midwest suburb, despite the enormous outlay of resources and manpower to make them otherwise.* Anne Bernays' (1975) descriptions in *Growing Up Rich,* in which life is described as "the same old dreary thing: day after day of marzipan, silk, velvet, Steuben glass, butterballs" convey a similar boredom with a redundant and affluent lifestyle.

Nor is this vacuousness typical only of older, "decadent" ruling classes. It may well be just as endemic to the "jetsetters," the new moneyed elite, whose frenzied lifestyle barely helps disguise its underlying hedonism and redundancy. *Time* magazine, for example, described the wealthy characters in two John Osborne plays as:

> People who have achieved everything except their hearts' desires. They are caught in the joyless round of choosing the top hotel to stay at, the finest restaurant to dine in, the most delectable partner to sleep with. Boredom infects their days and nights, and drink is their anodyne. ("London Stage," 1968, p. 64)

These examples help show how mythical is the notion conveyed in our culture and by our media that money, possessions, or leisure time will bring happiness. Television writer Susan Harris, creator of "The Golden Girls" and "Soap," when asked about her wealth and whether it made her happy, replied:

> God no. It doesn't do anything really except alleviate the worry of money. Money does give you a certain amount of freedom. . . . Beyond that it does nothing for the inner person at all. And that's a very big surprise because you think that when you get there, it's going to be different; you're going to be different and until you get there no one can tell you otherwise. So for a certain amount of time, my life was about attaining certain goals. And when I attained them all and saw that it made no difference, that was the point at which I got a little depressed. What now? And now is where it starts to get interesting. Because you find out, "things" don't do it. Because nothing is permanent. Nothing fills the void. What's nice about having money now is being able to put it to good use, give it away, put it where it's needed. (Kubey, 1989d)

---

*In 1758, Lord Chesterfield compared "living like a gentleman" to "dying of ennui." Lord Byron similarly wrote in *Juan* in 1823: "Society is now one polish'd horde, Formed of two mighty tribes, the *Bores* and *Bored*." The bored and suicidal affluent leisure class depicted in Chekhov's plays serves as still another example. In *Three Sisters,* for example, Baron Lieutenant Tusenbach ridicules "the rotten boredom afflicting our society" and the jaded Colonel Vershinin complains, "It's the same old thing! My wife has attempted suicide again."

So one should not expect from a member of the upper classes, be he or she a Brahmin of Bombay or Boston, any special gift for giving shape to the formless void. Nor is education, if measured in years of schooling and in degrees, necessarily any assurance that a person will make rewarding use of leisure time. Not a few intellectuals are so bored with their field and alienated from learning that they rarely turn to knowledge during free time. But if by education we mean the ability to face any random slice of the world with informed curiosity, then yes, education is what one needs in order to use free time to advantage. But it is a special kind of education, perhaps more widely available in the unschooled past than in the overschooled present.

It may only be an illusion (Gans, 1974; Shils, 1957, 1961), but one wonders if people may have been better prepared to give structure and meaning to free time before industrialization and the rise of technology and mass culture.[18] With the growth to the mass media it does seem that it has become increasingly easy to let attention be structured from the outside. Experiences are gained effortlessly via television and may be pleasant, but how much does one grow psychologically in the process? Indeed, there is a negative relationship between people's level of self-reliance and their dependence on television (Rubin & Rubin, 1982).

The ability to use leisure time effectively depends on inner resources or, as Ferneczi (1919/1950) put it, "on whether man was master of himself" (p. 176). In fact, in recent times it has been suggested that Riesman's (1950/1964) "other-directed man," has become more prevalent, "relying primarily on cues from the outside rather than on a more stable intrapsychic self-concept for guidance" (Gussen, 1967, p. 64).

That television viewing is itself consistently associated with levels of happiness no higher than average also deserves attention in this regard. Obviously, if they possibly could, TV producers would regularly broadcast programs that would make people feel significantly happier than they do normally. They would do so because of the obvious commercial gains that would accrue. That television viewing helps us feel more relaxed than usual but generally does not help us feel substantially happier says something about human nature and what makes for happiness.

Happiness is a more complex state than relaxation. It requires a more elusive set of conditions, and is therefore more difficult to obtain. Others can successfully attract and hold our attention and help us relax, but perhaps only we can provide for ourselves the psychological rewards and meaning that make for happiness.

On Creating One's Own Meaning

Our unflattering references to the current state of society might give the impression that we believe our times to be particularly wicked, and the past blissfully benign. Actually this is not the case. It is all too obvious that every historical period has had its own crisis or has been threatened or riven by disorder.*

In every culture, people have struggled to give meaning to their experiences. But it is precisely through such a struggle that humankind endures. If we stop resisting disorder, if we stop criticizing the trends that destroy complexity and harmony in consciousness, entropy will soon win out.

In this regard it is worth considering a basic paradigm for the ability to give meaning to experience in extreme situations, such as solitary ordeals (Logan, 1985) or the concentration camps described by Victor Frankl (1963), Solzhenitsyn (1976), and others. In a concentration camp (as opposed to an extermination camp) there are many ways to die, but few ways to make survival more probable. For example, in the Gulags, hardened criminals who are prepared to exploit and terrorize fellow victims have an easier time surviving. But many witnesses agree that if one is not a criminal, to keep sane and alive one must be able to fill the deadly monotony with self-generated, self-directed activities that introduce individual goal-directed behavior into what otherwise would be an entirely mechanical routine determined from the outside.[19]

The people who can do this best tend to be of two types. The first kind are often country people, farmers, shepherds, and others accustomed to living in solitude and harsh conditions, who have learned to infuse a personal intentionality even in the most tedious tasks. If they must shovel mud for hours in the rain, they can impose their own secret

---

*In most every period in history there have been those who have thought the world to be heading toward imminent collapse. According to Adams (1949) the French and German newspapers of 1910 regularly presented:

> Some uneasy discussion of supposed social decrepitude; falling off of the birthrate; . . . multiplication of suicides;—increase of insanity or idiocy,—of cancer,—of tuberculosis;—signs of nervous exhaustion,—of enfeebled vitality,—"habits" of alcoholism and drugs, . . .—and so on, without end. (p. 186)

Patrick Brantlinger (1983) has noted that ironically, "the mass media now frequently convey the message of social decline for which, according to the 'bread and circuses' analogy, the mass media themselves are largely to blame" (p. 38).

rhythms on the movements of the shovel until it feels that it is they who are in control of the activity, not the guard with the gun. They know how to sing, how to derive enjoyment from talking, from walking, from feeling with their muscles and with their senses. No matter how oppressive or dehumanizing the external conditions become, some of these people are able to rely on their own attentional habits to give a meaningful order to experience.

The second kind of people who often survive such camps are those trained in a symbolic medium: poets, musicians, mathematicians, philosophers. They carry a portable world of organized information in their heads, and they can withdraw into that world and act within it even under brutal conditions. Equipped only with their minds, they can create rewarding experiences by setting intellectual challenges to which they apply skills developed over years of practiced thinking. The poet might add one new line each day to the store of verse in her memory, and in so doing she preserves a measure of control over her mental equilibrium. The mathematician plays out operations, tries out new rules, makes out new proofs even as he is shoveling the mud. His behavior, his outward countenance may be no different from anyone else's, yet he is able to live in a reality of his own that keeps him active and sane, that actually frees his consciousness from the control of an oppressive and alien system.

Many of those who end up in concentration camps are not as well prepared. They may never have acquired the traditional self-sufficiency skills of the farmer nor the specialized symbolic skills of the literati. These are the typical denizens of mass society, reasonably content as long as they are surrounded by the expected support system of culture—a reasonable job, a home, a family, a television set, a friendly and well-maintained symbolic universe—but lost once they have to make sense of life in the raw. Bereft of a meaningfully ordered experience, confronted by the stark brutality of an order based on the alien goals of the camp, most inmates become helpless pawns of external conditions and to the extent that experience becomes meaningless, such a person might give up the struggle of living altogether.

It might be thought strange to approach the end of a book on television viewing with reflections on survival in concentration camps. Why worry about skills needed only under extreme conditions? Isn't our culture designed to provide everything we need?

In the first place, we should not assume that even the most benign culture's goals are exactly right for everybody, nor all of the time. It is true that the television industry can provide programs to fill everybody's dark night of the soul several times over. In this sense, there is no need to think ever again or to imagine anything fresh, because this can all be done more efficiently for us by the professional packagers of dreams. Still, it is not the same thing, to energize with one's attention another person's dream, and to create it oneself. Therefore, even assuming a culture that has always our best interests at heart, we cannot abdicate the powers of imagination and thought.

We must also recognize the potential fragility and impermanence of even the most snug and comfortable cultural support systems. German society and German culture, after all, were at the forefront of Western civilization just before they became peculiarly untrustworthy guides to civilized action.

There is no substitute for learning to think for oneself, and those who delegate that responsibility to others run the risk of finding themselves adrift when left without reliable external guidelines. From this perspective, the habit of television viewing poses problems. Assuming a benign, stable environment, spending the major part of one's free time doing something that is mildly pleasant and requires relatively little personal or mental investment is not a total loss. But one may well lose opportunities to grow as a human being. And if we admit that no cultural environment can ever be completely benign and entirely stable, then the loss in self-discipline and skills that may be forfeited in the act of watching television can even become threats to survival.

Perhaps it is from such an extreme perspective that the criticism of television makes most sense. The usual approach, which castigates television with great relish while leaving everything else surrounding it intact, is sorely misguided. Those who find fault with the viewing experience must also take seriously the aim of trying to make life as a whole a deeper, more complex, more coherent and enjoyable experience for as many people as possible. Otherwise we set television up as a scapegoat, blaming the most popular form of escape instead of examining why people need to escape, or recognizing that the need for escape is part of the human condition.

Indeed, the need for escape has long shaped television programs, and will surely influence future programming regardless of technological change. It should not come as a surprise that this need is well understood by the creators of television and film. In fact, the provision of escape is often made explicit in promotions for television and movies. Consider this early ad for the motion picture industry found in a *Saturday Evening Post* by Lynd and Lynd (1929/1956):

> Go to a motion picture . . . and let yourself go. . . . Before you know it, you are living the story—laughing, loving, hating, struggling, winning! All the

e excitement you lack in your daily life—in Pictures. They
tely out of yourself into a wonderful new world. . . . Out of
vday existence! If only for an afternoon or an evening—
. . 205)

Even with advances in home television technology such as video re-
corders and cameras, video games, and HDTV, and despite improved
picture quality, greater selectivity, and personal control over "television,"
people will continue to use the medium for escape, distraction, and
relaxation. Television content will go largely unchanged because there
will be continued demand for such experience.

TELEVISION VIEWING AND PERSONAL GROWTH

But how can experience be made deeper and more enjoyable? In terms
of television, the assumption of some observers is that if the industry
provided more complex programs of high quality, the viewing experience would be enhanced. It is quite possible that the television industry
could provide a greater number of complex programs than is currently
the case without losing revenue. Perhaps they would even gain some. We
say this based on the opinions of a number of television producers
(Kubey, 1989d) and because there is a good deal of evidence that when
unusual programs of quality are given a chance by television executives
to withstand early weeks of poor ratings, after a number of months the
shows will be found by regular and loyal viewers (Gitlin, 1983; Kubey,
1989b; Newcomb & Alley, 1983). Among the programs that fit such a
description are "Hill Street Blues," "St. Elsewhere," "60 Minutes," and
"All in the Family." We must add that with some of these programs,
audiences remain relatively small by normal commercial television standards, perhaps *only* 20,000,000 viewers. But because a higher proportion of the viewers are educated and have high incomes, networks are
willing to accept low ratings as advertisers are anxious to reach these
prized audiences, and will pay more per 1,000 viewers.

Furthermore, many of the most critically acclaimed television comedies have also had very large audiences, suggesting that the tastes of the
mass audience are not at complete variance with the tastes of critics and
scholars.

But it has also been observed for many years that when serious cultural fare is offered, whether it be in television or in film, the great majority
of Americans choose light and escapist content (Klein, 1971; Rosten,
1941).[20] The top-rated program in the recent history of PBS, for example, was a serious "Frontline" program on pornography but one with the

sensational, audience-grabbing title, "Death of a Porn Queen." On the evening that one of the commercial networks chose to present a production of "Death of a Salesman" with Dustin Hoffman, standard programming on the other networks received higher ratings.

On Heightening Perception

To improve television programming is certainly one way to confront the problem and there is merit in the call for more democratically controlled media systems (Brantlinger, 1983; Quillian, 1989; Williams, 1974).[21] Certainly the recent diffusion of inexpensive video cameras, VCRs, and satellite dishes has begun to put the means of mass communication into the hands of the less powerful. But the viewing skills of the audience can be improved as well.

Ultimately, a basic sharpening of consciousness is what is needed. In this regard, it may help to consider the insights of the American pragmatic philosopher and psychologist, John Dewey (1915, 1934), who described two antithetical ways of seeing. The first and most common way of processing visual information is what he called "recognition."

An example of recognition follows: You are walking down the street, absorbed in thought, and as your eyes scan the environment many perceptual clusters register in your consciousness. Some of these you recognize as trees; others as buses, cars, houses, people, and so forth. You do not spend much mental energy in processing this information; you do not confront any of these objects as real entities with unique idiosyncrasies. If the particular object happens to fit with current goals—for instance, if you were planning to catch the bus, then you focus further attention on it; otherwise, the object promptly disappears from consciousness. Recognition is indispensable, but it leaves little or no permanent trace in consciousness, and does not contribute to its complexity.

A second way to process visual information is through what Dewey called "perception." In perception, mental energy is invested in information in order to decode it in its various concrete nuances. As we walk down the street a tree suddenly jumps out of its anonymity and we see it as a unique shape covered in a rough bark that now looms in front of our eyes like a continent crisscrossed with an intricate web of valleys, canyons, and ravines. The moving branches encompass convoluted spaces filled with masses of green leaves, each one moving to its own rhythm yet bound to the motion of the rest, each one a distinct shape echoing the shape of innumerable other leaves. And this "tree," now a complex universe of forms, colors, movements, and sounds, might recall from memory into consciousness a variety of past thoughts, dormant emotions, hopes, and goals—a mass of information that can be ordered in new ways as a result of this one act of perception. The tree perceived may lead us to a new thought, a poem, a painting, a botanical observation, a philosophical insight, or a decision to marry the boy or girl next door.

Of course perception does not involve only sight. It can be applied to the work of the other senses as well, when we take the trouble of attending to the information that passes through them. Hearing, taste, kinesthetic sensations, smell, can yield either recognitions, when we simply scan the information so that it can be identified; or they can yield perceptions, when we analyze, reflect on, and synthesize the messages they bring.

Clearly, perception requires a lot more mental energy than does recognition. For this reason, we do not indulge in it most of the time. Yet it is through acts of perception that consciousness grows more complex and creative achievements are attained. What is more to the point perhaps is that life spent in constant recognition becomes boring and meaningless.

Perception, on the other hand, makes life challenging and enjoyable. The British psychoanalyst Winnicott (1951) had this very much in mind in writing that, "It is creative apperception more than anything else that makes the individual feel that life is worth living" (p. 65). As with Winnicott, Raymond Williams (1983) observed that among the most important tasks of education is "to deepen and refine the capacity for significant responses" (p. 62).

A habit of perception, then, is a precondition for the growth of consciousness, and the ability to relate complex information to one's goals—thereby producing psychological order—is often the result of long practice in acts of perception.

Actually, there can be little question but that more perceptive or "mindful" television viewing can be brought about quite quickly by simply asking people to take different perspectives on what they view. Viewers who were instructed by researchers to watch television more "mindfully" performed better on measures of creativity and flexibility after viewing (Langer & Piper, 1988; Piper & Langer, 1986). Television can also stimulate imaginative play in children (Alexander, Ryan, & Munoz, 1984; Reid & Frazer, 1980). But a more difficult question remains: namely, how to bring about more perceptive and imaginative viewing as a regular phenomenon. As we have pointed out, people often seek out television precisely because they want an experience that does not require mindfulness or concentration.

Because recognition is so much easier, and most of the time it is sufficient for getting by, the habit of perception is not always acquired. It requires effort and a certain self-discipline to cultivate, and some people may only develop a small proportion of their perceptual capacities. Even those who do, may engage in perception only on occasion. In fact, perception may also be more difficult to develop in an urban setting* or one as abundant in media diversions as our own.

How do we overcome the inertia of recognition, and learn to see the world in fresh and complex ways? First, it is almost certainly the case that the habit of perception is made easier in part by genetic predispositions. Some children, for example, in the first years of life show a peculiar sensitivity to sound and music. They might love to hear the middle G on which the lawnmower starts, but cringe at the F sharp of the air conditioner. They may beg their parents to listen to tapes and records and fall in love with the first good musical performance they hear. It is from among such children that adult musicians and composers sometimes develop. Other children exhibit exceptional sensitivity to visual patterns early in life. They notice how the lines of cracks between the rows of brick in the neighbor's house differ from those on the walls of their own home. They observe changing shadows and clouds, react violently to colors, and spend unending hours doodling with crayons. Still other children will display an early and unusual interest and aptitude for how things work mechanically.

Virtually all young children display insatiable curiosity. And it is perfectly possible that most children have at least one exceptionally fine-tuned information-processing channel. Howard Gardner (1983) has suggested that there are at least seven main forms of intelligence, each corresponding to a somewhat different area of the central nervous system, and that there are great differences among individuals in the ability to use them. Indeed, it is likely that the number of biological predispositions to interact with the environment along different dimensions is actually much larger, but researchers have not been able to identify these channels as yet.

In any case, the biological endowment a child is born with immediately begins to interact with the sociocultural environment in which he or she must live after birth. Some parents ignore or do not apprehend their children's gifts, and so these may atrophy with time. Others will become so impressed that they will try to take over their children's skills and

---

*Georg Simmel (1950), the early 20th-century sociologist, observed that denizens of the city often shielded themselves against sensation, developing "an incapacity . . . to react to new sensations with the appropriate energy" (p. 414). Deutsch (1961) referred to communication overload as a "disease of cities" and Meier (1962) has also noted the enormous information load carried by modern city dwellers, predicting a crisis in the next half century.

smother them in the process. A few will find ways to expose the children to challenges of the right level of complexity, starting them on a path of growth in which their peculiar bent—as well as the rest of their more normal abilities—has a way of unfolding naturally. Later on, the school, peers, adult models and teachers will either help or hinder the development of the child's ability to process and create information in complex and integrated ways.

In this process of development the truth seems to be that the rich get richer, and the poor get poorer. In other words, those children who are born with a superior sensitivity have a greater chance to learn to use it, and each step forward makes the next more likely to occur. What Erik Erikson (1950) and M. Brewster Smith (1969) have each written in connection with the development of competence applies also to the unfolding of perception. Early in life either a positive or "benign spiral" of growth is established, in which the sense of competence (or perception) builds on earlier achievements and becomes better established and more complex; or what gets set up is a downward spiral in which failure begets more failure.

At times it is possible to break out of even the steepest downward spiral. The 1987 movie, *Stand and Deliver,* tells the true story of how an inspiring and extremely committed teacher was able to take classes of undisciplined, underachieving high school students from poor neighborhoods in East Los Angeles and help them learn enough mathematics to excel on the College Board's Advanced Placement exam in calculus. The story of Helen Keller similarly demonstrates how a dedicated teacher willing to invest enormous amounts of energy in a child unable to process information can bring her back on course. But these events unfortunately do not happen often enough. The very fact that such true stories are made into inspiring movies and plays is testimony to their rarity.

Making Viewing More Rewarding

All of us will pass through life only partly aware and only partly capable of appreciating everything we have seen, heard, or touched. And people for whom the spiral of growth proceeds less positively will be more prone to become dependent on information that is easy to recognize; information that is already labeled and redundant. Some may never have gained or may have lost the skill to shape experience with their own mental energy, and now gravitate to prepackaged experience to fill their life. They may be among those who feel bereft during unstructured time.

What does it take to make television viewing an act that contributes to growth, as against a way of simply killing time? If one applied the general model introduced in chapter 1 and illustrated in chapter 7, the answer would be: "By making the viewing experience more complex, and more integrated with one's goals." But how do we put into practice this abstract injunction?

One approach might be for a person to start with the realistic recognition of the finitude of life, a realization of how much time he or she has to enjoy and experience the world with. The unvoiced question at the back of one's mind might be: "Given that I have at most 5 years' worth of free time left to live, do I want now to sit down and turn the set on?"[22] The answer might be "yes" or "no," depending on what happened earlier in the day, how tired one is, how late it is, and what the choice of programs happens to be. The important thing is that if the answer is "yes," the experience didn't just "happen," but resulted from a goal-directed action.

It could be argued that indiscriminate viewers also get what they want, even if they do not consider each time whether to watch TV or not. Their habit may represent a decision, made years earlier, that television watching is among the best and most enjoyable ways to spend time. However, that may not be the whole story. A long-held habit becomes so ingrained that it borders on addiction. The person may no longer be watching television because of simple want, but because he or she virtually has to. Other alternatives may seem to become progressively more remote. What might have been a choice years earlier is now a necessity.

To retain control over the decision of when to start and when to stop is one of the first steps in making viewing a growth-producing experience. A next step is to exercise choice over which programs are watched. Only about half the U.S. public, for example, reports that they often use a television guide to help them decide what to watch (Bower, 1985).[23]

It is useful also to learn to recognize more clearly when one has become "hooked" by television; when one is viewing beyond the point originally intended. Actually, one of the more difficult abilities to acquire is the ability to readily turn the set off in the middle of a program if and when the show becomes a "waste of time." Viewers might be assisted in this by being made more aware that some of the inertia that accompanies prolonged viewing is reduced shortly after the set is turned off.

Odd as it may sound, some people might be assisted in becoming more discriminate in their viewing and breaking their habit by actually constructing a list of readily available and enjoyable non-TV activities.[24] Such a list could be posted and consulted for alternative activities before automatically turning on the TV. Many people reflexively snap on the set whenever they are bored without giving a moment's consideration to any of the other possible activities that might engage their attention. People often resort to TV because they are under the misconception that there is "nothing else to do," and they might be well served by giving serious consideration to the full range of other available leisure activities.

These simple practices may help some people derive greater rewards from their leisure time and from watching television. But growth requires not only information that fits one's goals, it must also be complex, challenging the person to develop new skills in the effort of decoding it. We have seen, however, that complexity is not only a characteristic of the message, but of the consciousness that interprets it. A tree can provide information of the utmost complexity to the person who can perceive it, whereas *Crime and Punishment* means nothing to the uninterested reader. How can viewing be made more complex?

Part of the responsibility lies with our schools, which must begin to prepare students to understand and analyze both film and television. In this regard, we might recall Plato's claim that "a sound education consists in training people to find pleasure and pain in the right objects." Or as Brightbill (1960) wrote, "The future will belong not only to the educated man but to the man who is educated to use his leisure wisely." Clearly, schools would be well advised to embark on formal instruction in the grammatical and rhetorical forms of film and television in order to help students learn to process media content in more critical and complex ways.

One may scoff at training people to become better television viewers.* But a public well educated in the nuances and methods of the visual media will both demand better quality, and be less readily manipulated by them. Indeed, if most children are going to continue to watch 1,000 hours of television every year of their young lives and 1,000 hours every year for the rest of their lives, it is absurd for them not to receive formal education in the medium. No one thinks twice about instructing children

---

*It is interesting to note Munsterberg's (1916) similar comments to the resistance to film education early in this century:

> Of course, there are those, and they may be legion today, who would deride every plan to make the moving pictures the vehicle of esthetic education. . . . The esthetically commonplace will always triumph over the significant unless systematic efforts are made to reinforce the work of true beauty. The moving picture audience could only by slow steps be brought from the tasteless and vulgar eccentricities of the first period to the best plays of today, and the best plays of today can be nothing but the beginning of the great upward movement which we hope for in the photoplay. . . . The longing for beauty is rudimentary; and yet it means harmony, unity, true satisfaction, and happiness in life. People still have to learn the great difference between true enjoyment and fleeting pleasure, between real beauty and the mere tickling of senses. (pp. 229–230)

in how to read a novel, a poem, or an essay, but in point of fact the amount of time most people will spend reading these forms relative to the amount of time they will spend watching television would boggle the mind.

Methods of teaching about television will obviously vary for different ages. In the past decade many books and curricula intended to develop critical viewing skills in students have been published, and research suggests that such curricula can be effective.[26]

Techniques of mass persuasion and rhetoric need to be taught as do the grammar and syntax of television as well as the elements of plot construction, foreshadowing, character development, and the conventional devices of drama and comedy. Other topics that might be covered in such a curriculum would be general aspects of television production, advertising, and for older students, the economics underpinning television as well as political and organizational phenomena. Students should also be encouraged to think about how television reflects their society and why it reflects certain facets of society in certain ways. Students can be helped to become more aware of their own and others' viewing habits by charting their own, their parents', and their classmates' viewing behavior.

There are also less formal ways to develop a critical stance toward the viewing experience. Parents can help their children to view in more complex ways by comparing the current episode of their favorite show with previous ones, by focusing their attention on aspects of the plot, special effects, characterization, and acting.[27] One can even experiment with turning off the sound to see what can be deduced from the television pictures alone or listen only to the sound and try to guess what the pictures might be. All of this should be done in a very spontaneous, relaxed way, because what counts is not to develop a "right" way of perceiving television, but to learn about the various possible dimensions of perception and evaluation. Children tend to be naturally iconoclastic and they like to make fun of what they see; this irreverence is something to encourage—at least in small doses—because it helps them grow into more savvy media consumers.

In fact, the ideal is to foster differentiated individual criteria of criticism and interpretation, rather than to absorb a culturally sanctioned procedure for decoding visual information. Personally constructed standards cannot fail to be subjectively more complex than learned standards.

These suggestions might sound too weighty. Why take television so seriously? It is only a way of relaxing, a way of taking it easy in a world that is too full already with serious and unpleasant things. Getting all worked up about making television viewing a more complex experience will only spoil the pleasure of this relaxing pastime. Such an attitude, however, is based on the mistaken assumption that mental effort is necessarily unpleasant. As we have argued, perception and growth can be actively enjoyable—rather than passive and relaxing, as television viewing usually is.

So we return again to an earlier conclusion, namely, that the television experience cannot be improved significantly without also improving the rest of life. Even though television takes up the largest part of people's free time, it is not the only dimension of their being that counts. Television viewing cannot become a more harmonious and complex experience unless we find ways to live more harmonious and complex lives.

In this sense, watching television is a crucial slice of existence; like a slide preserving a cross-section of the organism, it allows us to see human behavior and subjective experience manifested in a context of free time. It is a cross-section—or mirror—that reflects the natural bent of the human mind to follow the path of least resistance by turning to information that requires little effort to interpret. It also shows the less than ideal consequences of taking that path. If we learn from what this slice of existence reveals about the human condition we might make the watching of television a better setting for growth. What is more important, we might just succeed in making the rest of life a little more meaningful and enjoyable as well.

ENDNOTES

[1]Kubey and Peluso (1990) have shown that rapid news diffusion following tragic events such as an assassination or the destruction of the space shuttle is partly driven by this same need for reality maintenance.

[2]Stephenson (1967) and Glasser (1982) have claimed that much newspaper reading is ritualistic and serves a reality-maintenance function as much or more than it is driven by a need to obtain new information. Many a sports fan is as likely to read the account of a game he or she has witnessed the day before as the account of a game he or she did not witness.

[3]Or as Sylvan Tomkins (1962) wrote:

Stimuli are extremely attractive to the human organism if they possess both sufficient novelty and sufficient familiarity so that both positive affects are reciprocally activated, interest-excitement by the novel aspects of the stimulus and enjoyment-joy by the recognition of the familiar and the reduction of interest-excitement. (pp. 127–128)

Fiske and Maddi (1961) and Zuckerman (1979), among others, have also explored the alternating affinity for both novelty and familiarity.

[4]It has been claimed that conversation, which is so central to the transmission of ideas and the creation of meaning, has begun to be outpaced by the speed of electronic communications. Franco Ferrarotti (1988) argues that the art of simple conversation is being lost because it is antithetical to the imperatives of mass society and mass media.

Andre Gregory (1983) reported that he and Wallace Shawn became interested in making *My Dinner with Andre,* a full-length film that consists almost entirely of a conversation between the two men, because:

Wally and I were struck by the fact that we found that nobody talked about anything anymore that came from the heart, that was felt. We sensed that most conversation had become automatic. . . . And that there was no real communication going on. As a result we were collectively going into a kind of psychological ice age—becoming so blocked that positive action was becoming impossible. Because in order to have positive action you have to communicate: you have to think and feel. When social intercourse becomes deadly and boring and unlife-enhancing—as it is becoming— then what happens is that humanity starts to become atrophied. (p. 20)

It is also possible that conversation today is no more boring or meaningless than conversation at any other time. In 1732, Berkeley wrote that people "prefer doing anything to the ennui of their own conversation."

[5]E. P. Thompson (1967) focuses on how mechanized production required a new "time sense" that would help discipline workers and separate them from natural forms of time perception.

[6]Marie Winn (1987) has addressed an entire book to helping people reduce their viewing (*Unplugging the Plug-In Drug*) as has Joan Wilkins (1982) in *Breaking the TV Habit.* Jason (1987) and Jason and Rooney-Rebeck (1984) have had some success in reducing the heavy viewing of children via a token economy instituted in the home. The tokens can be used to operate the TV set and are earned by doing chores and other activities.

[7]Some student drug pushers, in another application of pagers, carry beepers to school so that their clients can more easily contact them to arrange a purchase.

[8]Aside from alcohol, tranquilizers are the most heavily used legal drug in the United States with over 5 billion prescribed annually (FDA, 1980).

[9]In *Society of the Spectacle,* DeBord (1977) claimed that spectator sports and television viewing diminish the quality of life and are both the cause and result of increased privatization of the individual in mass society.

Daniel Boorstin (1961) made similar observations about the mass production of imagery: "The making of the illusions which flood our experience has become the business of America. . . . We suffer primarily not from our vices or our weaknesses, but from our illusions" (pp. 5–6). Focusing on television he concluded that,

Television has conquered the nation with blitzkrieg speed and has received unconditional surrender. . . . For television has brought us Too Much Too Soon. . . . We feel our heads swimming with instant experience. (Boorstin, 1975, p. 22)

[10]See "ring around the collar" and "static cling." Marketers in the 1920s and 1930s, in consultation with psychologists, such as the father of American behaviorism, John Watson, developed the first successful campaigns to heighten concern about and sell products designed to eliminate "bad breath" and "B.O." ("body odor").

[11]Young, urban professionals, or "Yuppies" have become the prize segment of the national market because they are said to be both affluent and highly acquisitive. Although we cannot rely solely on the popular media's assessment of such matters, it is interesting to note that in its 1984 cover story on Yuppies, *Newsweek* magazine declared in a bold headline that "They live to buy."

[12]See Richard Schickel's (1985) *Intimate Strangers: The Culture of Celebrity* for an excellent treatment of the phenomenon of celebrity in the United States. Our criticisms of self-absorption and dependence on celebrities for advice are reminiscent of what Riesman,

Glazer, and Denney (1950) called the "other-directed" character in *The Lonely Crowd: A Study of the Changing American Character*. See also Marcuse's (1964) *One Dimensional Man* and Christopher Lasch's (1978) *The Culture of Narcissism: American Life in an Age of Diminishing Expectations.*

[13]Programs are also often targeted to particular agglomerations of people based on what "mix" is expected to compete best against the demographics of the programs on the rival networks. Increasingly, programs, ads, and the products and services advertised are themselves designed with audience and market research, consumer "lifestyles," and "psychographics" in mind.

[14]Tibor Scitovsky (1976) made this same point in *The Joyless Economy.* He blamed much of the joylessness and boredom of modern life on the passive consumption that orients consumers to comfort instead of skill in living. Albert Borgmann (1984) has similarly blamed technology for creating a life dominated by effortless and thoughtless consumption.

[15]Some TV game shows award prizes to the best consumer/contestant—the person who can most accurately guess the price of various products.

Where once people were rewarded for their skills in production, today a premium is placed on one's skill in consumption. Lowenthal (1961) has documented the shift from production to consumption in America by analyzing the content of magazine biographies from the first four decades of this century.

[16]Max Horkheimer (1974), another Frankfurt School theorist, viewed this same potential threat but concluded that it cannot be eliminated either:

> It may indeed be true that when a child acquires its first knowledge of the world not through interaction with his father but through the [TV] screen and its images, not through spontaneous stimuli but through immediate reaction to signs, the end result is intellectual passivity. Yet the absence of a set from his parents' home only leads to the child being looked down on by his companions in school, to feelings of inferiority and worse. The flight into the past is no help to the freedom that is being threatened. (p. 140)

[17]A psychoanalytic explanation of boredom has also been given by Martin Wangh (1975):

> Boredom results from a stalemate between opposing forces in the mind. . . . We discover in the analysis of the complaint of boredom that wish confronts threat. The result is a standoff called boredom. The tension in boredom then is an echo of the pressure for action toward some unconscious aim, and the unpleasure an echo of the threat of pain or punishment. A precarious balance is maintained by partial repression of both longed-for content and feared danger and perhaps also the standstill of time. (pp. 544–545)

[18]Erich Fromm (1955/1976), in speculating about the general mental health of mass society, concluded that:

> Undoubtedly a relatively primitive village in which there are still real feasts, common artistic shared expressions, and no literacy at all—is more advanced culturally and more healthy mentally than our educated, newspaper-reading, radio-listening culture. (p. 348)

Wendell Berry (1977), a farmer and author sounded the same warning as did Fromm when he wrote:

In living in the world by his own will and skill, the stupidest peasant or tribesman is more competent than the most intelligent workers or technicians or intellectuals in a society of specialists. (p. 20)

Berry lamented the dilemma that he believed faces the modern American suggesting that he may be:

The most unhappy citizen in the history of the world. He has not the power to provide himself with anything but money. . . . From morning to night, he does not touch anything that he has produced himself, in which he can take pride. For all his leisure and recreation, he feels bad, he looks bad, he is overweight, his health is poor. His air, water, and food are all known to contain poisons. . . . He suspects that his love life is not as fulfilling as other people's. He wishes that he had been born sooner, or later. He does not know why his children are the way they are. He does not understand what they say. He does not care much and does not know why he does not care. He does not know what his wife wants or what he wants. Certain advertisements and pictures in magazines make him suspect that he is basically unattractive. He feels that all his possessions are under the threat of pillage. He does not know what he would do if he lost his job, if the economy failed, if the utility companies failed, if the police went on strike, if the truckers went on strike, if his wife left him, if his children ran away. . . . And for these anxieties, of course, he consults certified experts, who in turn consult certified experts about *their* anxieties. (pp. 20–21)

Also in this camp is Raymond Aron (1969), who believed that mass culture was ruinous, while "high culture" was enriching:

Without [high] culture and the power to avoid being duped and brutalized by the mass media and mass amusements (the excess leisure of the post-industrial society), society will be as degrading as was the excess labor of the nineteenth century.

Herbert Gans (1974) on the other hand, viewed things quite differently and argued that the mass culture critique leveled by the Frankfurt School and others is historically biased toward a "romantic picture of a happy peasantry creating and enjoying folk culture." According to Gans, the Frankfurt view underemphasizes "that many peasants lived under subhuman conditions, [were] exploited by feudal landlords," and endured "hunger, pestilence, and random violence." During the beginnings of urban industrialization their entertainment included "bearbaiting, visits to the lunatic asylum to taunt the mentally ill, attendance at public executions and widespread drunkenness" (p. 56).

Edward Shils (1957), like Gans, concluded that:

Most of the population (the "mass") now stands in a closer relationship to the center than has been the case either in premodern societies or in the earlier phases of modern society. In previous societies, a substantial proportion, often the majority, were born and forever remained "outsiders." (p. 1)

Shils (1961) believed that much of the criticism of mass culture is the result of simple snobbery: "I think we are not confronting the real problem: why we don't like mass culture. . . . It is repulsive to us. Is it partly because we don't like the working classes and the middle classes?" (pp. 198–199).

[19]Among those who make this observation are Bettelheim (1943); Burney (1952); Charriere (1970); Jackson (1973); and Solzhenitsyn (1976).

[20]Only 25% of the public in Bower's (1985) survey of the United States thought television provided "too many" programs that were designed to provide "escape from everyday life" (p. 75). Put another way, 75% of respondents felt there was either the right amount or too little escapist programming available.

In the late 1980s a rash of so-called "reality-based" shows, dubbed "trash TV" by television critics, broke out in syndication and proved very successful, at least for a time. These programs were typically very inexpensive to produce and highly exploitive. But whether they be the "Morton Downey, Jr., Show," "A Current Affair," "America's Search for Missing Children," or any "professional" wrestling program, their popularity might be best understood as signifying a reaction to the rest of television viewing that, as we have described, is relaxing and mildly enjoyable. These shows, in contrast, often make viewers feel righteous anger or sympathetic sadness. In our view, these programs are popular in large part because they make viewers feel something intensely. For writer Maura Sheehy, "the cornerstone of tabloid psychology" involves "empathy as manipulation."

Actually, the potential for exploiting feelings of empathy was noted long ago by Adam Smith (1759/1971) who suggested that responding with empathy to the suffering of other people permits one to revel in one's own emotional sensitivity. Or as Zillmann and Bryant (1986) wrote: "Sobbing through a tear-jerker is proof to oneself that a valued social skill is abundantly present" (p. 317). Daniel Bell (1976) has also given thought to what such programs may engender in the viewer:

> In the emphasis television . . . places on disasters and human tragedies, it invites not purgation or understanding but sentimentality and pity, emotions that are quickly exhausted, and a pseudo-ritual of a pseudo-participation in the events. (p. 108)

Screenwriter and former reporter, Ben Hecht's 1937 movie *Nothing Sacred,* about a young woman who becomes the toast of New York when the city learns that she is about to die of a rare disease, effectively satirizes journalists' tendencies to exploit human suffering to sell newspapers.

[21]As just one of many examples of the problems associated with dominant commercial control of television, Dye and Zeigler (1989) have concluded from a variety of empirical studies in the United States that, "watching TV does not improve the level of astuteness of the electorate because TV does not cover issues" (p. 165). For them, as for us, television's coverage of issues is severely limited because of the commercial concerns to attract and hold the largest number of viewers.

In capitalist nations, where mass media companies are currently merging into larger and larger corporate entities, greater democratic control of the media would seem to require the reduction of private and monopolistic ownership. Brantlinger suggested that the media in the United States and Western Europe be treated "as public utilities, with missions similar to publicly funded schools and universities" (p. 281). Ross Quillian (1989) has devised an egalitarian media system that he believes should replace what currently exists. In the Communist bloc, centralized bureaucratic control would need to be lifted. Obviously, there has been much movement in this direction in the Soviet Union under Gorbachev and more recently in Eastern Europe as well.

[22]If a person of age 50 has 25 full years left to live and has an average of 5 hours each day available to do with as he or she pleases, then by our calculation he or she has 5 full years of free time available.

[23]Here, education seems to make a difference. Of adults who had received a grade-school education, 29% reported using a television guide "often" while the comparable figure for college-educated respondents was 52% (Bower, 1985).

[24]Engaging in enjoyable leisure activities chosen from such a personally constructed list has proved effective for those suffering from mild depressive episodes (Lewinsohn, 1974).

[25]The orientation of education in the United States in the late 1980s has moved decidedly toward a greater emphasis on preparation for work and to make America "competitive." There is a corresponding and decreasing emphasis on liberal arts training, on physical education, and in the support for extracurricular activities.

[26]See Hefzallah (1987); Lee and Rudman (1982); Masterman (1980); and Ploghoft and Anderson (1981) for curricula or reviews of curricula. For information on the efficacy of critical viewing interventions and curricula, see J. Anderson (1983) and Corder-Bolz (1982) for reviews as well as Abelman and Courtright (1983); Dorr, Graves, and Phelps (1980); Singer, Zuckerman, and Singer (1980). See Greenfield (1984) for a general discussion of media and cognition in children.

Umberto Eco in his essay, "Are We Going Towards a Visual Civilization," concluded that "A democratic civilization will save itself only if it will make the language of the image into a stimulus to critical reflection, not an invitation to hypnosis." However, there are those who take the position that this is a futile enterprise. Zolla (1968), who believed that mass media imagery is inherently problematic and is thus leading to civilization's demise, compares Eco's statement to claiming that "If we find alcohol that makes us sober and temperate, we will be saved from alcoholism" (p. 222).

[27]An excellent compilation of ideas designed to enhance "television literacy" and to encourage critical viewing skills in children can be found in chapter 1 of Barbara Lee and Masha Rudman's (1982) *Mind Over Media.* See also Kubey (1987b, 1989a) for why critical television viewing skills need to be taught in school.

Appendices

APPENDIX A:
RANDOM SIGNALING SCHEDULE

Time Intervals	Monday	Tuesday	Wednesday	Thursday	Friday	Saturday	Sunday
8:00							
			8:25		8:25		8:25
	8:40						
		9:10				9:05	
				9:30			
10:00							
			10:15		10:15		10:10
	10:55			11:05		11:25	
		11:35					
12:00							
		12:25		12:25			
						12:50	
							1:15
	1:30		1:55		1:55		
2:00							
		2:15		2:05		2:15	
					2:40		
	3:10		3:10		3:10		
							3:30
4:00							
			4:20				
	4:35				4:55		4:50
		5:15				5:00	
				5:55			
6:00							
			6:00	6:20			6:10
	6:35				6:45		
		7:05		7:05		7:20	
		7:45					
8:00							
	8:00				8:10		
			8:50				
		9:20				9:25	8:30
	9:30			9:55	9:55		9:50
10:00							

APPENDIX B:
INSTRUCTIONS FOR RESEARCH ASSISTANTS AND SUBJECTS

Introducing Beeper & Materials to Subjects:

1. Hand out materials and "turned off" beepers to subjects.

2. Show subjects how to turn beepers on and stop the beeping by pushing the black button in--not by pushing the button back to the off position.

3. Explain about the beeping: i) beepers will go off during waking hours-- 8am to 10pm --between 6 to 9 times per day, about 50 times in the next 7 days. ii) sometimes the beepers will go off twice in a row within a minute or so, that is because of the 8 towers in the Chicago area. The signal which sets the beepers off may still be in the air

4. IF THE BEEPER DOES NOT SIGNAL FOR A 6 HOUR PERIOD DURING WAKING HOURS CALL THE PERSON WHO IS LISTED IN THE BACK COVER OF THE BEEPER BOOKLET!!

5. Explain the Random Activity Information Sheet. Some points that should be emphasized:

a) One RAIS should be filled out as soon as possible after the beeper signals

b) If more than 20 minutes passes between signal and your filling out an RAIS just put down the time of beeping, where you were, and what you were doing. Don't try to fill out how you were feeling.

c) The first couple times you fill out the RAIS it will take 4 or 5 minutes, but by tomorrow already it should only take 1 to 2 minutes, because you will be more familiar with the wording on the RAIS.

d) Be as complete as possible yet as brief as possible. Give us enough information to know where you were, what you were doing and thinking, and how you felt just before the beeper went off.

e) Try not to let the beeping affect the feelings, etc., that you write down on the RAIS.

f) Always fill out as much of the RAIS as you can each time you are beeped. Fill out as many of the 13 mood pairs as you can apply to each situation.

g) Every situation you are in when the beeper sounds may be slightly different from those before it, so give as immediate and fresh a response as possible. (Don't look back to previous sheets to see how you responded,even if the situation is similar to one before.)

6. Carry the beeper and RAIS booklet with you at all times for the next 7 or 8 days. DO NOT TURN THE BEEPER OFF AT NIGHT or any other time, except if you're attending the opera...

APPENDIX C:
GENERAL QUESTIONNAIRE

SECTION I: GENERAL INFORMATION ABOUT YOURSELF

Please check the correct answers ( ) or write down the correct information for each question below.

Your asnwers to these questions are STRICTLY CONFIDENTIAL; they will not be seen by anyone in this company. Your answers will only be seen by the researchers at the University of Chicago.

1. Are you   ( ) male

               ( ) female

2. Are you   ( ) single

               ( ) married

               ( ) separated

               ( ) divorced

               ( ) widowed

               ( ) other, please

   explain_____

3. How many other people usually live with you in your home (apartment, condominium, or house)?

   _____

4. How old are you?   _____

5. When were you born?   __/__/__
                         mo day yr

6. During an average week in the last month, how many hours did you work, not counting the time you took off for meals?

   _____

7. How long does it take you to get to work in the morning (traveling time)?

   _____

8. Are you   ( ) American Indian

               ( ) Black

               ( ) Oriental

               ( ) Spanish, surnamed American

               ( ) White

               ( ) other, please

   explain_____

9. How much money did you make
    last year from your job?

    ( ) less than $8000

    ( ) $8000 to less than $12,000

    ( ) $12,000 to less than $16,000

    ( ) $16,000 to less than $20,000

    ( ) $20,000 to less than $30,000

    ( ) $30,000 or more

10. How long have you worked for this
    company?

    _____

11. How long have you been in your
    present job for this company?

    ( ) less than 30 days

    ( ) 1 - 3 months

    ( ) 4 - 11 months

    ( ) 1 - 3 years

    ( ) more than 3 years

12. What is the title of your
    present job?

    _____

    _____

13. How much schooling have you
    completed?

    ( ) none

    ( ) some elementary school

    ( ) completed elementary school

    ( ) some high school (1-3 years)

    ( ) graduated from high school

    ( ) some college (1-3 years)

    ( ) graduated from college
        (bachelors degree)

    ( ) some graduate school

    ( ) graduate degree (masters,
        Ph.D., M.D., etc.)

14. Is your income the only source
    of financial support for your
    immediate family?

    ( ) yes   ( ) no

15. How many dependents do you have
    (other people who depend on
    your financial support)?

    _____

SECTION II: INFORMATION ABOUT YOUR JOB

1. Here is a list of things that might be
    important about any job. How important
    is each of the following to you? CIRCLE
    A NUMBER FOR EACH STATEMENT BELOW.

Not very important ... *Somewhat important* ... *Extremely important*

a. The amount of pay you get........................1 2 3 4 5 6 7

b. The quality of the equipment you work with.......1 2 3 4 5 6 7

c. Your chances for getting a promotion............1 2 3 4 5 6 7

d. The physical surroundings on your job............1 2 3 4 5 6 7

e. The chances you have to accomplish something
    worthwhile......................................1 2 3 4 5 6 7

f. The chances you have to learn new things.........1 2 3 4 5 6 7

g. The chances you have to do something that
    makes you feel good about yourself.............1 2 3 4 5 6 7

h. The chances you have to do the things you
    do best..1 2 3 4 5 6 7

i. The chances you have to do a variety of
    different things...............................1 2 3 4 5 6 7

j. The friendliness of the people you work with.....1 2 3 4 5 6 7

k. The way your supervisor treats you..............1 2 3 4 5 6 7

l. The respect you receive from the people you
    work with......................................1 2 3 4 5 6 7

m. Your fringe benefits............................1 2 3 4 5 6 7

n. The chances you have to think about other
    things besides your work.......................1 2 3 4 5 6 7

o. The chances you have to develop your skills
    and abilities..................................1 2 3 4 5 6 7

p. The freedom to talk with people on the job.......1 2 3 4 5 6 7

q. The chances you have to move around during
    your working day...............................1 2 3 4 5 6 7

In the following questions, you are asked to describe your job. For each question circle the number which best describes what your job is like. For example, in the first question, if there is not very much variety in your job, you might circle number 2 . On the other hand, if your job has quite a bit of variety, you might circle number 5 or number 6 .

2. How much variety is there in your job?

1	2	3	4	5	6	7
Very little; I do pretty much the same things over and over, using the same equipment and procedures almost all the time.			Some amount of variety.			Very much; I do many things, using a variety of equipment and procedures.

3. How much does your job involve your producing an entire product or an entire service?

1	2	3	4	5	6	7
My job involves doing only a small part of the entire product or service; it is also worked on by others or by automatic equipment and I may not see or be aware of much of the work which is done on the product or service.			My job involves doing some of the work; while others help as well, my own part is important though.			My job involves making the entire product or service from start to finish; the final outcome of the work is clearly the result of my work.

4. How long does it take to learn the skills (techniques) required to do your job well?

1	2	3	4	5	6	7
Very little time; in a few hours almost anybody can learn all the skills needed to do my job well.			Some time; like a few days or even weeks.			Quite a bit of time; a person must train for a year or more before the skills needed to do my job well can be learned.

5. How much freedom do you have to determine how you do your job?

1	2	3	4	5	6	7
Very little; I have no say about the procedures and equipment used to do my job.			Some freedom; I can make some of the decisions about how the work is done, but many of the decisions are decided for me.			Very much; I have almost complete responsibility for deciding how I will do my job.

6. How often do you find out from your supervisor how well you are doing on your job?

1	2	3	4	5	6	7
Not very often; I may often work for long stretches without my supervisor letting me know how I am doing.			sometimes my supervisor may let me know how I am doing, but sometimes no.			Very often. I get almost constant 'feedback' on my performance from my supervisor.

7. How often do you find out from your co-workers how well you are doing
    on your job?

    1   2   3   4   5   6   7

Not very often; I may
often work for long
stretches without any-
one letting me know
how I am doing.

sometimes people may
let me know how I am
doing; sometimes they
may not.

Very often. I get
almost constant
'feedback' on my
performance from
my supervisor.

8. Do you have an opportunity during the day to talk with your co-workers
    about things other than your work (at times other than breaks)?

    1   2   3   4   5   6   7

No, it's impossible
during the work day to
talk with anyone
(because there is too
much noise or nobody is
near enough to talk to
or I need to concentrate
on what I am doing).

Yes, it's possible
to talk with my co-
workers a few times
during the work day.

Yes. I talk almost
all day long with the
people I work with
about all kinds of
things.

9. How much of your work can be seen in the finished product or service?

    1   2   3   4   5   6   7

None at all; it's hard
to tell what I have
done by looking at the
product or service

Some of my work can
be seen along with
the work of others.

A great amount; my
work is clearly visible,
it makes a noticeable
difference in the final
product or service.

10. Do you have any choice about how long it takes you to do a particular
    job?

    1   2   3   4   5   6   7

No choice; the length
of time for each job
is decided for me.

Sometimes I can decide
how long a job will
take me to do.

Yes; most of the time
I can decide how long
it will take for a
job to be finished.

11. In general, do you do quite high quality work?

    1   2   3   4   5   6   7

No, I generally do not
do very high quality
work.

Sometimes I do very
high quality work and
other times my work
is not very good.

Yes, I generally do
very high quality
work.

12. How many of your skills do you use in your job?

    1   2   3   4   5   6   7

Almost none; the job
I do is very simple
and could be done by
anyone.

Some of my skills.

Most of the skills I
have are required to
perform my job well.

13. As you do your job, can you tell how well you are doing?

1	2	3	4	5	6	7
Not at all; I could work at my job forever without knowing how well I am doing. Somebody must tell me.			Sometimes I can tell how well I'm doing, sometimes I can't.			I can almost always tell how well I'm doing my job.

14. How much challenge is there on your job?

1	2	3	4	5	6	7
There is very little challenge in my job; I don't get a chance to use any special skills and abilities and I never have jobs which require all my abilities to complete them successfully.			Some challenge			There is a great deal of challenge in my job; I get a chance to use my special skills and abilities, and I often have jobs which require all my abilities to complete successfully.

15. Please tell us how satisfied you are with the following aspects of your job. Circle a number for each statement below which tells how satisfied you are.

Very Dissatisfied — Dissatisfied — Slightly Dissatisfied — Neither Satisfied nor Dissatisfied — Slightly Satisfied — Satisfied — Very Satisfied

a. With your pay.....................................1 2 3 4 5 6 7

b. The quality of the equipment you work with.......1 2 3 4 5 6 7

c. Your chances for getting a better job............1 2 3 4 5 6 7

d. The chances you have to accomplish something worthwhile.....................................1 2 3 4 5 6 7

e. The physical surroundings on your job............1 2 3 4 5 6 7

f. The chances you have to learn new things.........1 2 3 4 5 6 7

g. The chances you have to do the things you do best...1 2 3 4 5 6 7

h. The chances you have to do a variety of different things..............................1 2 3 4 5 6 7

i. The chances you have to do something that makes you feel good about yourself as a person.......1 2 3 4 5 6 7

		Very Dissatisfied	Dissatisfied	Slightly Dissatisfied	Neither Satisfied nor Dissatisfied	Slightly Satisfied	Satisfied	Very Satisfied
j.	The friendliness of the people you work with......	1	2	3	4	5	6	7
k.	The way your supervisor treats you................	1	2	3	4	5	6	7
l.	The respect you receive from the people you work with.....................................	1	2	3	4	5	6	7
m.	Your fringe benefits..............................	1	2	3	4	5	6	7
n.	The way you perform your job......................	1	2	3	4	5	6	7
o.	The amount of overtime you work...................	1	2	3	4	5	6	7
p.	The chances you have to take part in making decisions...	1	2	3	4	5	6	7
q.	Your job security.................................	1	2	3	4	5	6	7
r.	The amount of pressure you work under.............	1	2	3	4	5	6	7
s.	The chances you have to develop your skills and abilities....................................	1	2	3	4	5	6	7
t.	The chances you have to think about other things besides your work.......................	1	2	3	4	5	6	7
u.	The freedom to talk with people while on the job...	1	2	3	4	5	6	7
v.	The chances you have to move around during your working day................................	1	2	3	4	5	6	7

16. Describe the way you usually feel when you are working at your job. For example, if you usually feel somewhat friendly but quite tense while you are working at your job, you might mark the following:

	very much	quite much	some what	do not feel either	some what	quite much	very much	
hostile	0	o	.	-	⊙	o	0	friendly
tense	0	⊙	.	-	.	o	0	relaxed

Please circle one answer for each pair of words.

	very much	quite much	some what	do not feel either	some what	quite much	very much	
hostile	0	o	.	-	.	o	0	friendly
alert	0	o	.	-	.	o	0	drowsy
elated	0	o	.	-	.	o	0	depressed
tense	0	o	.	-	.	o	0	relaxed
suspicious	0	o	.	-	.	o	0	trusting
irritable	0	o	.	-	.	o	0	cheerful
strong	0	o	.	-	.	o	0	weak
active	0	o	.	-	.	o	0	passive
lonely	0	o	.	-	.	o	0	sociable
creative	0	o	.	-	.	o	0	dull
resentful	0	o	.	-	.	o	0	satisfied
free	0	o	.	-	.	o	0	constrained
excited	0	o	.	-	.	o	0	bored

17. What is the one thing in your life you enjoy doing most?

_____

Describe the way you usually feel when you are doing what you enjoy most.

	very much	quite much	some what	do not feel either	some what	quite much	very much	
hostile	0	o	.	-	.	o	0	friendly
alert	0	o	.	-	.	o	0	drowsy
elated	0	o	.	-	.	o	0	depressed
tense	0	o	.	-	.	o	0	relaxed
suspicious	0	o	.	-	.	o	0	trusting
irritable	0	o	.	-	.	o	0	cheerful
strong	0	o	.	-	.	o	0	weak
active	0	o	.	-	.	o	0	passive
lonely	0	o	.	-	.	o	0	sociable
creative	0	o	.	-	.	o	0	dull
resentful	0	o	.	-	.	o	0	satisfied
free	0	o	.	-	.	o	0	constrained
excited	0	o	.	-	.	o	0	bored

SECTION III: INFORMATION ABOUT YOUR ATTITUDES

This next section is made up of sentences with which you may agree or disagree. Please indicate how you feel about each item by circling the number that best describes your attitude. To circle number 1 means that you COMPLETELY DISAGREE with the statement, while to circle number 7 means that you COMPLETELY AGREE with the statement.

Look at the following examples:

a. Most women are poor drivers.....................1 ② 3   4   5   6   7

b. Women are better cooks than men.................. 1   2   3 ④ 5   6   7

The first answer means you agree but not completely. The second answer means you disagree completely.

Please read each sentence carefully. Be sure to answer each sentence on the basis of how you feel.

1. I enjoy getting together with my parents often.....1   2   3   4   5   6   7

2. Most of my life is spent doing meaningful things...1   2   3   4   5   6   7

3. Being married and having children means loosing
    your freedom.....................................1   2   3   4   5   6   7

4. Trying to understand myself and others is a
    waste of time...................................1   2   3   4   5   6   7

5. If you have to work, you might as well choose a
    career where you deal with matters of life and
    death, like a policeman, fireman or doctor......1   2   3   4   5   6   7

6. When I try hard I can accomplish much..............1   2   3   4   5   6   7

7. People should work hard at their jobs, because
    hard work benefits our country..................1   2   3   4   5   6   7

8. I am usually enthusiastic about my work...........1   2   3   4   5   6   7

		Strongly Disagree	Disagree	Slightly Disagree	Neither Agree nor Disagree	Slightly Agree	Agree	Strongly Agree

9. No matter how hard I work, I never really seem
    to reach my goals...............................1   2   3   4   5   6   7

10. Life is empty and has no meaning for me............1   2   3   4   5   6   7

11. Ordinary work is interesting and worth doing.......1   2   3   4   5   6   7

12. Most of the time I understand my own actions and
    thoughts..1   2   3   4   5   6   7

13. For me, home and family have meant an awful lot....1   2   3   4   5   6   7

14. The most exciting times in my day are those
    times when I daydream...........................1   2   3   4   5   6   7

15. I was (or am) afraid to marry because I didn't
    (or don't) want to feel tied down...............1   2   3   4   5   6   7

16. What I really like about family life is going on
    trips and vacations.............................1   2   3   4   5   6   7

17. I long for a simpler life than I have now, a
    life in which bodily needs are most important...1   2   3   4   5   6   7

18. The only reason to marry is for convenience and
    security..1   2   3   4   5   6   7

19. If a job is dangerous, it's worth doing............1   2   3   4   5   6   7

20. I work to support myself and family, and that's
    important.......................................1   2   3   4   5   6   7

SECTION IV: INCOMPLETE SENTENCES BLANK--ADULT FORM

Finish the sentences below. Try to write down the first thoughts that come to your mind which finish each sentence. Please try to do them all.

1. I like _____

2. The happiest time _____

3. I regret _____

4. At bedtime _____

5. The best _____

6. What annoys me _____

7. People _____

8. A mother _____

9. In school _____

10. My greatest fear _____

11. I can't _____

12. When I was a child _____

13. I failed _____

14. The future _____

15. I need _____

16. I am best when _____

17. Sometimes _____

18. My job _____

19. The only trouble _____

20. I wish _____

IF YOU HAVE FINISHED THIS QUESTIONNAIRE, PLEASE PUT IT IN THE ENVELOPE, SEAL THE ENVELOPE AND DROP IT IN A MAIL BOX AS SOON AS YOU CAN.

THANK YOU VERY MUCH FOR FILLING OUT THIS QUESTIONNAIRE.

APPENDIX D:
LOCATION CODINGS

Coding for environments (Where the subject was)

Work and/or school

01-own office or work area
02-coworker's office or work area
03-other office
04-supervisor's office
05-cafeteria or eating area
06-lounge or other break area
07-bathroom or locker room
08-in the building (hallway, storeroom)
09-out of the building but on company
        property
10-school
11-

Home

12-kitchen
13-bedroom or other's bedroom
14-dining room
15-living room or family room
16-bathroom
17-basement or laundry room
18-outside of house but on property
19-garage or other

Transportation

20-bicycle
21-walking
22-bus or train
23-car
24-other

Public

25-restaurant, snack bar, club
26-store, shopping center
27-theater or sport arena
28-outdoor recreation facility: park,
        playground, tennis court, etc.
29-indoor recreation facility: WMCA,
        tennis or squash club, etc.
30-museum, library
31-somebody else's house
32-church or temple
33-doctor or dentist office, hospital
34-hairdresser, beauty shop
35-street, street corner
36-other

APPENDIX E:
ACTIVITY CODINGS

Coding for primary and secondary activities

Imagining activities

001-fantasizing
002-daydreaming
003-mental talking to self
004-mental whistling, humming, singing
005-working out problems mentally
006-thinking about the future
007-thinking about the past
008-talking to self
009-talking to pets, plants
010-whistling, humming, singing
011-meditating

Visual and auditory activities

012-staring into space
013-watching nature (trees, flowers...)
014-watching people
015-watching cars, buses, trucks...
016-watching tv
017-watching a movie (not on TV)
018-watching other things
019-reading the paper
020-reading a magazine
021-reading a book
022-listening to the radio
023-listening to records, tapes
024-listening to other people talking
025-listening to other sounds
026-listening to noises

Oral activities

027-eating a meal
028-eating a snack
029-taking a drink
030-smoking
031-chewing tobacco
032-chewing gum
033-taking medicine
034-sucking on fingers
035-biting finger nails
036-chewing on objects

Physical activities

037-walking
038-pacing
039-running
040-exercising
041-playing a game alone
042-driving a motorized vehicle
043-riding in a motorized vehicle

044-peddling a bicycle
045-doing art work
046-playing a musical instrument
047-cooking
048-washing dishes
049-cleaning at home
050-doing laundry
051-sewing
052-repairing something
053-breaking something
054-having an accident
055-writing a letter
056-writing a paper
057-writing other things
058-doing bookkeeping, bill paying
059-keeping other written records
060-doodling
061-going shopping for food alone
062-going shopping for other things alone
063-going to a gallery or concert alone
064-rubbing or stroking body or clothing
065-scratching ones body
066-picking at body or clothing
067-rubbing, stroking, scratching animal
068-rubbing, stroking, scratching other things
069-picking at things
070-fiddling with objects
071-grooming self
072-grooming pets or plants
073-rocking or swivelling a chair or stool
074-tapping fingers or feet
075-wiggling legs, arms...
076-sleeping, napping

Social activities

077-talking or joking with peers
078-talking or joking with adults
079-arguing with peers
080-arguing with adults
081-going to a party
082-entertaining guests at home
083-going to a sports event
084-playing a game or sport
085-going to a concert
086-participating in a drama or concert
087-going to a gallery
088-shopping for food
089-other shopping or browsing
090-going to a club, organization meeting
091-attending a religious service
092-taking care of a child
093-being examined by a doctor or dentist
094-talking with a therapist
095-kissing or petting another person
096-being rubbed or massaged

097-having sexual intercourse

Work or school activities

098-driving a vehicle to or from work/school
099-driving a vehicle on the job
100-riding in a vehicle to or from work
101-riding in a vehicle on the job
102-walking to or from work
103-thinking about some decision
104-thinking about some problem
105-thinking how to solve a problem
106-doing research or studying a problem
107-talking about a decision with someone
108-talking about a problem with someone
109-working on a problem on paper
110-listening to instructions
111-listening to other work related issues
112-listening to a lecture
113-listening to a report
114-listening to a class discussion
115-participating in a class discussion
116-talking with a supervisor or teacher
117-discussing school or work with peers
118-correcting classwork or test materials
119-purchasing something for work
120-studying for a class
121-studying for a test
122-writing a paper or report
123-making diagrams, charts, figures...
124-doing bookkeeping, record keeping
125-doing other paper work
126-talking on the phone
127-using a dictaphone or tape recorder
128-typing paper, letter, report...
129-typing forms or other things
130-working a duplicating, copy machine
131-operating other light machines
132-operating heavy machines (lathe, press...)
133-working at a computer terminal
134-doing assembly work
135-doing electronic testing
136-doing other work related testing
137-fixing equipment
138-stacking, shelving things
139-moving things from one place to another
140-preparing to teach or present something
141-teaching or presenting
142-seeling something to a person(s)
143-selling something over the phone
144-writing up an order form
145-operating a cash register
146-examining people
147-examining pets or plants
148-operating on people
149-operating on pets or plants
150
151-operating a telephone switchboard
152-talking on an intercom
200-thinking about or talking about the study

APPENDIX F:
COMPARISONS OF MEAN ACTIVATION
RESPONSES[a] BY DEMOGRAPHICS

Demographic Variables	n	All Acts Minus TV	Television	Working at Work	Meals
Race					
Black	17	4.8	4.7	5.0	4.9
White	79	4.8	4.3	4.9	4.8
t value		.1	1.4	.6	.2
Education					
H.S. or less	45	4.9	4.4	5.1	4.9
Some college	58	4.8	4.4	4.9	4.8
t value		.9	.4	1.4	.6
Sex					
Male	38	4.8	4.3	4.9	4.8
Female	66	4.8	4.5	5.0	4.9
t value		−.6	−1.2	−.4	−.6
Income					
Under $12,000	68	4.7	4.4	4.8	4.8
Above $12,000	35	4.9	4.4	5.2	4.9
t value		−1.6	−.2	−2.4***	−.7
Marital Status					
Single	31	4.6	4.5	4.7	4.6
Married	56	4.9	4.4	5.1	4.9
t value		−2.2**	.5	−2.4***	−1.3

[a]Means were generated from individual means in each activity and were compared by *t* tests. For each activity, *n*s differed slightly due to the need to use only those subjects who had at least one primary report of TV, working, or meals.

*$p < .10$; **$p < .05$; ***$p < .025$; two-tailed.

APPENDIX G:
COMPARISONS OF MEAN AFFECT RESPONSES[a] BY DEMOGRAPHICS

Demographic Variables	n	All Acts Minus TV	Television	Working at Work	Meals
Race					
Black	17	4.8	4.9	5.0	4.8
White	79	5.0	4.9	4.9	5.3
t value		−1.6	−.2	.3	−1.3
Education					
H.S. or less	45	5.1	5.0	5.1	5.3
Some college	58	4.9	4.8	4.8	5.2
t value		1.3	.9	1.7*	.5
Sex					
Male	38	4.8	4.9	4.7	5.1
Female	66	5.1	4.9	5.0	5.3
t value		−1.6*	−.2	−2.4**	−.7
Income					
Under $12,000	68	5.0	4.9	4.9	5.2
Above $12,000	35	5.0	5.0	4.9	5.2
t value		.1	−.5	−.1	.0
Marital Status					
Single	31	4.8	4.9	4.7	4.7
Married	56	5.0	4.9	4.9	5.4
t value		−1.0	−.2	−1.2	−2.7***

[a]Means were generated from individual means in each activity and were compared by t tests. For each activity, ns differed slightly due to the need to use only those subjects who had at least one primary report of TV, working, or meals.

*$p < .10$; **$p < .025$; ***$p < .01$; two-tailed.

References

Abelman, R., & Courtright, J. (1983). Television literacy: Amplifying the cognitive level effects of television's prosocial fare through curriculum intervention. *Journal of Research and Development in Education, 17,* 45–57.

Adams, H. (1949). *The degradation of the democratic dogma.* New York: Peter Smith.

Adorno, T. W. (1957). Television and the patterns of mass culture. In B. Rosenberg & D. Manning (Eds.), *Mass culture: The popular arts in America* (pp. 474–488). Glencoe, IL: The Free Press.

Adorno, T. W. (1975). The culture industry reconsidered. *New German Critique, 6,* 13–19.

Alexander, A., Ryan, M., & Munoz, P. (1984). Creating a learning context: Investigations on the interactions of siblings during television viewing. *Critical Studies in Mass Communication, 1,* 345–364.

Allen, C. (1965). Photographing the TV audience. *Journal of Advertising Research, 5,* 2–8.

Allen, R. (1983). On reading soaps: A semiotic primer. In E. A. Kaplan (Ed.), *Regarding television: Critical approaches* (pp. 97–107). New York: University Publications of America.

Allport, G. (1953). The trend in motivational theory. *American Journal of Orthopsychiatry, 23,* 107–19.

Altmann, J. (1980). *The ecology of motherhood and infancy in the savannah baboon.* Cambridge, MA: Harvard University Press.

Altmann, S. A. (1984, January 17). Interview. *Chicago Maroon,* p. 6.

Anderson, D. R. (1983). *Home television viewing by preschool children and their families.* Paper presented at the Society for Research in Child Development, Detroit, MI.

Anderson, D. R., Alwitt, L. F., Lorch E. P., & Levin, S. T. (1979). Watching children watch television. In G. Hale & M. Lewis (Eds.), *Attention and the development of cognitive skills* (pp. 331–361). New York: Plenum.

Anderson, D. R., & Collins, P. (1988). *The impact on children's education: Television's influence on cognitive development.* Washington, DC: U.S. Department of Education.

Anderson, D. R., & Lorch, E. P. (1983). Looking at television: Action or reaction? In J. Bryant & D. R. Anderson (Eds.), *Children's understanding of television: Research on attention and comprehension* (pp. 1–33). New York: Academic Press.

Anderson, D. R., Lorch, E. P., Field, D. E., & Sanders, J. (1981). The effects of TV program comprehensibility on preschool children's visual attention to television. *Child Development, 52,* 151–7.

Anderson, J. (1980). *An agenda for the social sciences and the study of mass communication.* Paper presented at the Speech Communication Association, New York.

Anderson, J. (1983). Television literacy and the critical viewer. In J. Bryant & D. Anderson (Eds.), *Children's understanding of television: Research on attention and comprehension* (pp. 297–330). New York: Academic Press.

Andrew, J. D. (1976). *The major film theories: An introduction.* New York: Oxford University Press.

Ang, I. (1985). *Watching "Dallas": Soap opera and the melodramatic imagination.* London: Methuen.

Appel, V., Weinstein, S., & Weinstein, C. (1979). Brain activity and recall of TV advertising. *Journal of Advertising Research, 19,* 7–15.

Arendt, H. (1958). *The human condition.* Chicago: The University of Chicago Press.

Aries, P. (1962). *Centuries of childhood: A social history of family life.* New York: Vintage.

Arnheim, R. (1935). A forecast of television. *Intercine.* (Republished in *Film as art.* Berkeley: University of California Press, 1969.)

Arnheim, R. (1971). *Entropy and art: An essay on disorder and order.* Berkeley, CA: University of California Press.

Aron, R. (1969). *Les desillusions du progres* [The illusion of progress]. Paris: Calmann-Levy.

Arons, L. (1960). *Advertising and the dynamics of mass media.* New York: Television Bureau of Advertising, Inc.

Ashby, W. R. (1956). *An introduction to cybernetics.* London: Chapman & Hall.

Attneave, F. (1954). Some informational aspects of visual perception. *Psychological Review, 61,* 183–193.

Ball-Rokeach, S. J. (1985). The origins of individual media-system dependency—A sociological framework. *Communication Research, 12,* 485–510.

Bateson, G. (1972). *Steps to an ecology of mind.* New York: Ballantine.

Bauer, R. A., & Bauer, A. H. (1960). America, "mass society" and mass media. *Journal of Social Issues, 16,* 3–66.

Bechtel, R., Achelpohl, C., & Akers, R. (1972). Correlates between observed behavior and questionnaire response on television viewing. In E. Rubinstein, G. Comstock, & J. Murray (Eds.), *Television and social behavior, Vol. 4: Television in day-to-day life: Patterns of use* (pp. 274–344). Washington, DC: U.S. Government Printing Office.

Becker, G. (1976). *The economic approach to human behavior.* Chicago: University of Chicago Press.

Bell, D. (1976). *The cultural contradictions of capitalism.* New York: Basic Books.

Bellow, S. (1987). *More die of heartbreak.* New York: William Morrow.

Belson, W. (1967). *The impact of television.* London: Cheshire.

Beniger, J. R. (1986). *The control revolution: Technological and economic origins of the information society.* Cambridge, MA: Harvard University Press.

Bennett, C. H., & Landauer, R. (1985). The fundamental physical limits of computation. *Scientific American, 253,* 1.

Berelson, B., & Steiner, G. (1964). Mass communications. In B. Berelson & G. Steiner (Eds.), *Human behavior* (pp. 527–555). New York: Harcourt, Brace, & World.

Berger, C. R. (1980). Self-consciousness and the adequacy of theory in relationship development. *Western Journal of Speech Communication, 44,* 93–96.

Berger, P. L., & Luckmann, T. (1967). *The social construction of reality.* Garden City, NY: Doubleday Anchor.

Berkowitz, L., & Rogers, K. H. (1986). A priming effect analysis of media influence. In J. Bryant & D. Zillmann (Eds.), *Perspectives on media effects* (pp. 57–71). Hillsdale, NJ: Lawrence Erlbaum Associates.

Berlyne, D. E. (1958). The influence of complexity and novelty in visual figures on orienting responses. *Journal of Experimental Psychology, 44,* 289–296.

Berlyne, D. E. (1960). *Conflict, arousal, and curiosity.* New York: McGraw-Hill.

Berlyne, D. E. (1971). *Aesthetics and psychobiology.* New York: Appleton-Century-Crofts.

Bernard, H. R., Killworth, P., Kronenfeld, D., & Sailer, L. (1984). On the validity of retrospective data: The problem of informant accuracy. *Annual Review of Anthropology, 13,* 495–517.

Bernays, A. (1975). *Growing up rich.* Boston: Little, Brown.

Berry, W. (1977). *The unsettling of America.* New York: Avon.

Bettelheim, B. (1943). Individual and mass behavior in extreme situations. *Journal of Abnormal and Social Psychology, 38,* 417–452.

Bettelheim, B. (1976). *The uses of enchantment: The meaning and importance of fairy tales.* New York: Knopf.

Bettelheim, B. (1985, October). A child's garden of fantasy. *Channels,* 54–56.

Bieri, J. (1955). Cognitive complexity-simplicity and predictive behavior. *Journal of Abnormal and Social Psychology, 51,* 263–268.

Biggers, T. (1983, November). *An emotion based theory of television program viewing behavior.* Paper presented at the Speech Communication Association, Washington, DC.

Birkhoff, G. (1933). *Aesthetic measure.* Cambridge, MA: Harvard University Press.

Blumler, J. G. (1979). The role of theory in uses and gratifications studies. *Communication Research, 6,* 9–36.

Blumler, J., Gurevitch, M., & Katz, E. (1985). Reaching out: A future for gratifications research. In K. E. Rosengren, L. A. Wenner, & P. Palmgreen (Eds.), *Media gratifications research: Current perspectives* (pp. 255–273). Beverly Hills: Sage.

Bochco, S. (1983, October). Interview. *Playboy,* pp. 157–164.

Bogart, L. (1965). The mass media and the blue collar worker. In A. Shostak & W. Gomberg (Eds.), *Blue-collar world: Studies of the American worker* (pp. 416–428). Englewood Cliffs, NJ: Prentice-Hall.

Bogart, L. (1972). *The age of television.* New York: Ungar. (Originally published 1956)

Boorstin, D. (1961). *The image: A guide to pseudo-events in America.* New York: Atheneum.

Boorstin, D. (1975). *Democracy and its discontents: Reflections on everyday America.* New York: Vintage.

Booth, W. (1982). The company we keep: Self-making in imaginative art, old and new. *Daedelus, 111,* 33–59.

Borgmann, A. (1984). *Technology and the character of contemporary life: A philosophical inquiry.* Chicago, IL: University of Chicago Press.

Boswell, J. (1989). *The kindness of strangers: The abandonment of children in Western Europe from late antiquity to the Renaissance.* New York: Pantheon.

Bower, R. T. (1973). *Television and the public.* New York: Holt, Rinehart, & Winston.

Bower, R. T. (1985). *The changing television audience in America.* New York: Columbia University Press.

Boyer, L. B. (1955). Christmas neurosis. *Journal of the American Psychoanalytic Association, 3,* 467–488.

Bradburn, N. M. (1969). *The structure of psychological well-being.* Chicago: Aldine.

Bramson, L. (1961). *The political context of sociology.* Princeton: Princeton University Press.

Brantlinger, P. (1983). *Bread and circuses: Theories of mass culture as social decay.* Ithaca, NY: Cornell University Press.

Braverman, H. (1974). *Labor and monopoly capital: The degradation of work in the twentieth century.* New York: Monthly Review Press.

Brightbill, C. K. (1960). *The challenge of leisure.* Englewood Cliffs, NJ: Prentice-Hall.

Broadbent, D. E. (1958). *Perception and communication.* New York: Pergamon Press.

Brodbeck, A., & Jones, D. (1963). Television viewing and the norm-violating practice and perspective of adolescents: A synchronized depth and scope program of policy research. In L. Arons & M. May (Eds.), *Television and human behavior: Tomorrow's research in mass communication* (pp. 98–135). New York: Appleton-Century-Croft.

Brody, G. H., Stoneman, Z., & Sanders, A. (1980). Effects of television viewing on family interactions: An observational study. *Family Relations, 29,* 216–220.

Bronfenbrenner, U. (1973). Television and the family. In A. Clayre (Ed.), *The impact of broadcasting* (p. 20). London: Compton Russell.

Brown, J., Campbell, K., & Fisher, L. (1986). American adolescents and music videos: Why do they watch? *Gazette, 37,* 19–32.

Bryant, J., & Anderson, D. (Eds.). (1983). *Children's understanding of television. Research on attention and comprehension.* New York: Academic Press.

Bryant, J., & Zillmann, D. (1984). Using television to alleviate boredom and stress: Selective exposure as a function of induced excitational states. *Journal of Broadcasting and Electronic Media, 28,* 1–20.

Bryant, J., Zillmann, D., & Brown, D. (1983). Entertainment features in children's educational television: Effects on attention and information acquisition. In J. Bryant & D. R. Anderson (Eds.), *Children's understanding of television. Research on attention and comprehension* (pp. 221–240). New York: Academic Press.

Bryce, J. W. (1987). Family time and television use. In T. R. Lindlof (Ed.), *Natural audiences: Qualitative research of media uses and effects* (pp. 121–138). Norwood, NJ: Ablex.

Burney, C. (1952). *Solitary confinement.* London: Macmillan.

Calvert, S., & Gersh, T. (1985, May). *Developmental differences in children's television comprehension: Effects of content cues and auditory formal production features.* Paper presented at the Annual Meeting of the International Communication Association, Honolulu, HI.

Cantor, M., & Cantor, J. (1986). American television in the international marketplace. *Communication Research, 13,* 509–520.

Cantor, J., & Reilly, S. (1982). Adolescents' fright reactions to television and films. *Journal of Communication, 32,* 87–99.

Carey, J., & Kreiling, A. (1974). Popular culture and uses and gratifications: Notes toward an accommodation. In J. Blumler & E. Katz (Eds.), *The uses of mass communications: Current perspectives on gratifications research* (pp. 225–248). Beverly Hills: Sage.

Carli, M., Fave, A. D., & Massimini, F. (1988). The quality of experience in the flow channels: Comparison of Italian and U.S. students. In M. Csikszentmihalyi & I. S. Csikszentmihalyi (Eds.), *Optimal experience: Psychological studies of flow in consciousness* (pp. 60–81). Cambridge, UK: Cambridge University Press.

Carnegie Council on Adolescent Development. (1989). *Turning points: Preparing American youth for the 21st century.* Washington, DC: Author.

Carpenter, E. (1972). *Oh, what a blow that phantom gave me!* New York: Holt.

Carter, R. F., Pyska, R. H., & Guerraro, J. L. (1969). Dissonance and exposure to aversive information. *Journalism Quarterly, 46,* 37–42.

Carver, C. S., & Scheier, M. F. (1981). *Attention and self-regulation.* New York: Springer-Verlag.

Cattell, J. P. (1955). The holiday syndrome. *Psychoanalytic Review, 42,* 39–43.

Cazenueve, J. (1974). Television as a functional alternative to traditional sources of need satisfaction. In J. Blumler & E. Katz (Eds.), *The uses of mass communications: Current perspectives on gratifications research* (pp. 213–223). Beverly Hills: Sage.

Centers for Disease Control. (1986). *Youth suicide surveillance. Summary: 1970–1980.* Atlanta, GA: U.S. Department of Health and Human Services.

Charlesworth, J. C. (1964). A comprehensive plan for the wise use of leisure. In J. C. Charlesworth (Ed.), *Leisure in America: Blessing or curse* (pp. 30–46). Philadelphia: American Academy of Political Social Science.

Charriere, H. (1970). *Papillon.* New York: Morrow.

Christ, W. G., & Biggers, T. (1983, November). *An exploratory investigation into the relationship between television program preference and emotion-eliciting qualities—A new theoretical approach.* Paper presented to the Speech Communication Association, Washington, DC.

Christ, W. G., & Medoff, N. (1984). Affective state and the selective exposure to and use of television. *Journal of Broadcasting and Electronic Media, 28,* 51–63.

Cline, V. C., Croft, R. G., & Courrier, S. (1973). Desensitization of children to televised violence. *Journal of Personality and Social Psychology, 27,* 360–365.

Coffin, T. (1955). Television's impact on society. *American Psychologist, 10,* 6.

Collett, P. (1986). *Video-recording the viewers in their natural habitat.* Paper presented at ESOMAR seminar on Developments in media research, Helsinki.

Collins, A. M., & Quillian, M. R. (1969). Retrieval time from semantic memory. *Journal of Verbal Learning and Verbal Behavior, 8,* 240–247.

Comisky, P., & Bryant, J. (1982). Factors involved in generating suspense. *Human Communication Research, 9,* 49–58.

Comstock, G., Chaffee, S., Katzman, N., McCombs, M., & Roberts, D. (1978). *Television and human behavior.* New York: Columbia University Press.

Condry, J. (1989). *The psychology of television.* Hillsdale, NJ: Lawrence Erlbaum Associates.

Conrad, P. (1982). *Television: The medium and its manners.* Boston: Routledge & Kegan-Paul.

Cooley, C. H. (1897). The process of social change. *Political Science Quarterly, 12,* 73–81.

Cooley, C. H. (1902). *Human nature and the social order.* New York: Charles Scribner's Sons.

Cooley, C. H. (1926). *Personal journal* (Vol. 23, 24).

Corder-Bolz, C. (1982). Television literacy and critical viewing skills. In D. Pearl, L. Bouthlilet, & J. Lazar (Eds.), *Television and behavior: Ten years of scientific progress and implications for the eighties* (Vol. 2, pp. 91–102). Rockville, MD: U.S. Department of Health and Human Services.

Corporation for Public Broadcasting. (1978). *A qualitative study: The effect of television on peoples' lives.* Washington, DC: Author.

Crockett, W. H. (1965). Cognitive complexity and impression formation. In B. A. Maher (Ed.), *Progress in experimental personality research* (Vol. 2). New York: Academic Press.

Cronbach, L., & Meehl, P. (1955). Construct validity in psychological tests. *Psychological Bulletin, 52,* 285–302.

Csikszentmihalyi, M. (1975). *Beyond boredom and anxiety: The experience of play in work and games.* San Francisco: Jossey-Bass.

Csikszentmihalyi, M. (1978). Attention and the wholistic approach to behavior. In K. S. Pope & J. S. Singer (Eds.), *The stream of consciousness* (pp. 335–358). New York: Plenum.

Csikszentmihalyi, M. (1979). *The value of leisure: Towards a systematic analysis of leisure activities.* Waterloo, Ontario: Otium Publications.

Csikszentmihalyi, M. (1982). Towards a psychology of optimal experience. In L. Wheeler (Ed.), *Review of personality and social psychology* (pp. 13–36). Beverly Hills, CA: Sage.

Csikszentmihalyi, M., & Graef, R. (1980). The experience of freedom in daily life. *American Journal of Community Psychology, 8,* 401–414.

Csikszentmihalyi, M., & Kubey, R. W. (1981). Television and the rest of life: A systematic comparison of subjective experience. *Public Opinion Quarterly, 45,* 317–328.

Csikszentmihalyi, M., & LeFevre, J. (1989). Optimal experience in work and leisure. *Journal of Personality & Social Psychology, 56,* 815–822.

Csikszentmihalyi, M., & Larson, R. (1984). *Being adolescent.* New York: Basic Books.

Csikszentmihalyi, M., & Larson, R. (1987). Validity and reliability of the Experience-Sampling Method. *Journal of Nervous and Mental Disease, 175,* 526–536.

Daley, E. A. (1978). *Father feelings.* New York: William Morrow.

Danowski, J. (1975, November). *Informational aging: Interpersonal and mass communication patterns in a retirement community.* Paper presented to the Gerontological Society, Louisville, KY.

Davis, R. H. (1973). Television's value and potentials for the older viewer. *Perspective on Aging, 2,* 2–5.

Davis, R. H. (1975). Television communication and the elderly. In D. Woodruff & J. Birren (Eds.), *Aging: Scientific perspectives and social issues* (pp. 217–249). New York: Van Nostrand.

Davis, R. H., & Kubey, R. W. (1982). Getting old on and with television. In D. Pearl, L. Bouthilet, & J. Lazar (Eds.), *Television and behavior: Ten years of scientific progress and implications for the eighties* (Vol. 2, pp. 201–208). Washington, DC: U.S. Government Printing Office.

DeBord, G. (1977). *Society of the spectacle.* Detroit: Red & Black.

De Charms, R., & Muir, M. S. (1978). Motivation: Social approaches. *Annual Review of Psychology, 29,* 91–113.

de Grazia, S. (1962). *Of time, work, and leisure.* Garden City, NY: Doubleday.

Deiter, P. J., & Heeter, C. S. (1989, March). *MTV viewing and adolescents' beliefs about violence, sex and sexual violence.* Paper presented to the Association for Women in Psychology, Providence, RI.

Delia, J. G., O'Keefe, B. J., & O'Keefe, D. J. (1982). The constructivist approach to communication. In F. Dance (Ed.), *Human communication theory* (pp. 147–191). New York: Harper & Row.

Deutsch, K. W. (1961). On social communication and the metropolis. *Daedalus, 90,* 99–110.

Dewey, J. (1915). *Democracy and education.* New York: MacMillan.

Dewey, J. (1934). *Art as experience.* New York: Putnam.

Dimmick, J., McCain, T., & Bolton, W. (1979). Media use and the life span: Notes on theory and method. *American Behavioral Scientist, 23,* 7–31.

Dominick, J. R. (1984). Videogames, television violence, and aggression in teenagers. *Journal of Communication, 34,* 136–147.

Donohew, L., Sypher, H. E., & Higgins, E. T. (Eds.). (1988). *Communication, social cognition, and affect.* Hillsdale, NJ: Lawrence Erlbaum Associates.

Dorr, A. (1980). When I was a child I thought as a child. In S. Withey & R. Abeles (Eds.), *Television and social behavior: Beyond violence and children* (pp. 191–230). Hillsdale, NJ: Lawrence Erlbaum Associates.

Dorr, A. (1986). *Television and children: A special medium for a special audience.* Beverly Hills: Sage.

Dorr, A., Graves, S. B., & Phelps, E. (1980). Television literacy for young children. *Journal of Communication, 30,* 71–83.

Douglas, M., & Isherwood, B. (1980). *The world of goods: Towards an anthropology of consumption.* New York: Penguin.

Dumazedier, J. (1967). *Toward a society of leisure.* London: Collier.

Dumazedier, J. (1974). *Sociology of leisure.* Amsterdam: Elsevier.

Durkheim, E. (1947). *The division of labor in society.* Glencoe, IL: The Free Press. (Originally published 1893)

Dye, T. R., & Zeigler, H. (1989). *American politics in the media age.* Pacific Grove, CA: Brooks/Cole.

Eco, U. (1979). *Role of the reader: Explorations in the semiotics of texts.* Bloomington, IN: Indiana University Press.

Edgar, P. (1977). Families without television. *Journal of Communication, 27,* 73–77.

Ellingwood, C. (1969). *Age development of verbal expression of feeling in psychotherapy interviews and TAT protocols.* Unpublished doctoral dissertation, University of Chicago, Chicago, IL.

Ellison, H. (1969). *The glass teat.* New York: Ace.

Emerson, R. W. (1837). *The American scholar.* Address to the Phi Beta Kappa Society, Cambridge, MA.

Emery, F., & Emery M. (1976). *A choice of futures.* Leiden, The Netherlands: Martin Nijhoff.

Erikson, E. (1950). *Childhood and society.* New York: Norton.

Ewen, S. (1976). *Captains of consciousness: Advertising and the social roots of the consumer culture.* New York: McGraw-Hill.

Faber, R. J., Brown, J. D., & McLeod, J. M. (1979). Coming of age in the global village: Television and adolescence. In E. Wartella (Ed.), *Children communicating: Media and development of thought, speech, and understanding* (pp. 215–249). Beverly Hills: Sage.

FDA. (1980). *Report on prescription drugs.* Washington, DC: U.S. Government Printing Office.

Ferneczi, S. (1950). Sunday neuroses. In S. Ferenczi (Ed.), *Further contributions to the theory and technique of psychoanalysis* (pp. 174–177). London: Hogarth Press. (Originally published 1919)

Ferrarotti, F. (1988). *The end of conversation: The impact of mass media on modern society.* Westport, CT: Greenwood Press.

Feshbach, S. (1976). The role of fantasy in the response to television. *Journal of Social Issues, 32,* 71–85.

Feshbach, S., & Singer, R. D. (1971). *Television and aggression: An experimental field study.* San Francisco: Jossey-Bass.

Festinger, L. (1957). *A theory of cognitive dissonance.* Evanston, IL: Row, Peterson.

Finn, S., & Roberts, D. (1984). Source, destination, and entropy: Reassessing the role of information theory in communication research. *Communication Research, 11,* 453–476.

Firth, R. (1929). *Primitive economics of the New Zealand Maori.* New York: Dutton.

Fiske, D. W., & Maddi, S. R. (Eds.). (1961). *Functions of varied experience.* Homewood, IL: Dorsey.

Fiske, J. (1986). Television: Polysemy and popularity. *Critical Studies in Mass Communication, 3,* 391–408.

Fiske, J., & Hartley, J. (1978). *Reading television.* London: Methuen.

Foley, J. M. (1968). *A functional analysis of television viewing.* Unpublished doctoral dissertation, University of Iowa, Iowa City, IA.

Foss, K., & Alexander, A. (1987, May). *Trashing the tube: Explaining television addiction and abstention.* Paper presented at the meeting of the International Communication Association, Montreal, Canada.

Fowles, J. (1982). *Television viewers versus media snobs.* New York: Stein & Day.

Frank, R., & Greenberg, M. (1980). *The public's use of television: Who watches and why.* Beverly Hills: Sage.

Frankl, V. (1963). *Man's search for meaning.* New York: Washington Square.

Freedman, J. L., & Sears, D. O. (1965). Selective exposure. In L. Berkowitz (Ed.), *Advances in experimental social psychology* (Vol. 2, pp. 57–97). New York: Academic Press.

Freeman, M. (1982). *The dialectic of immediate experience and reflection in adolescence.* Unpublished manuscript, University of Chicago, Chicago, IL.

Freud, S. (1946). *Mourning and melancholia* (Collected papers, Vol. 4). London: Hogarth Press.

Freud, S. (1960). *Jokes and their relation to the unconscious.* New York: Norton. (Originally published 1905)

Freud, S. (1961). *Civilization and its discontents.* New York: Norton. (Originally published 1929)

Freud, S. (1965). *The intrepretation of dreams.* New York: Avon Books. (Originally published 1900)

Friedson, E. (1953). The relation of the social situation of contact to the media in mass communication. *Public Opinion Quarterly, 17,* 230–38.

Friendly, F. (1968). *Due to circumstances beyond our control.* New York: Vintage.

Fromm, Erich (1976). *The sane society.* New York: Holt, Rinehart & Winston. (Originally published 1955)

Fry, D., Fry, V. H., & Alexander, A. (1988, May). *The relative importance of primary and secondary contexts in the constitution of textual meaning.* Paper presented at the meeting of the International Communication Association, New Orleans, LA.

Furu, T. (1971). *The function of television for children and adolescents.* Tokyo: Sophia University Press.

Gadberry, S. (1980). Effects of restricting first graders' TV viewing on leisure time use, IQ change, and cognitive style. *Journal of Applied Developmental Psychology, 1,* 45–47.

Gamson, W. A. (1988). The 1987 distinguished lecture: A constructionist approach to mass media and public opinion. *Symbolic Interaction, 11,* 161–174.

Gans, H. (1974). *Popular culture and high culture: An analysis and evaluation of taste.* New York: Basic Books.

Gans, H. (1980). The audience for television—and in television research. In S. Withey & R. Abeles (Eds.), *Television and social behavior: Beyond violence and children* (pp. 55–81). Hillsdale, NJ: Lawrence Erlbaum Associates.

Gardner, H. (1983). *Frames of mind: The theory of multiple intelligences.* New York: Basic Books.

Garner, W. R. (1962). *Uncertainty and structure as psychological concepts.* New York: Wiley.

Gerbner, G., & Gross, L. (1976). Living with television: The violence profile. *Journal of Communication, 26,* 173–179.

Gerbner, G. L., Gross, L., Morgan, M., & Signorielli, N. (1980). The mainstreaming of America: Violence profile no. 11. *Journal of Communication, 28,* 10–29.

Gerbner, G., Gross, L., Morgan, M., & Signorielli, N. (1986). Living with television: The dynamics of the cultivation process. In J. Bryant & D. Zillmann (Eds.), *Perspectives on media effects* (pp. 18–40). Hillsdale, NJ: Lawrence Erlbaum Associates.

Gitlin, T. (1972). Sixteen notes on television and the movement. In G. White & C. Newman (Eds.), *Literature in revolution.* New York: Holt, Rinehart, & Winston.

Gitlin, T. (1980). *The whole world is watching: The mass media in the making and unmaking of the new left.* Berkeley: University of California Press.

Gitlin, T. (1983). *Inside prime time.* New York: Pantheon.

Gitlin, T. (Ed.). (1986). *Watching television.* New York: Pantheon.

Glasser, T. L. (1982). Play, pleasure and the value of newsreading. *Communication Quarterly, 30,* 101–107.

Glick, I., & Levy, S. (1962). *Living with television.* Chicago: Aldine.

Glynn, E. (1956). Television and the American character: A psychiatrist looks at television. In W. Elliot (Ed.), *Television's impact on American culture* (pp. 177–182). East Lansing, MI: Michigan State University Press.

Goethals, G. (1981). *The TV ritual: Worship at the video altar.* Boston: Beacon Press.

Goldings, H. H. (1954). On the avowal and projection of happiness. *Journal of Personality, 23,* 30–47.

Goldsen, R. (1977, September). Changing channels: How TV shapes American minds. *Human Behavior,* 63–67.

Goodhardt, G., Ehrenberg, A., & Collins, M. (1975). *The television audience: Patterns of viewing.* Westmead, England: Saxon House.

Goodman, W. (1989, April 2). On television. *New York Times,* p. H31.

Gottheil, E., & Stone, G. (1968). Factor analytic study of orality and anality. *Journal of Nervous and Mental Diseases, 146,* 1–17.

Graef, R. (1979). *Behavioral consistency: An analysis of the person by situation interaction through repeated measures.* Unpublished doctoral dissertation, University of Chicago, Chicago, IL.

Graef, R., Gianninno, S., & Csikszentmihalyi, M. (1981). In J. D. Claxton, C. D. Anderson, J. R. Brent Ritchie, & G. McDougall (Eds.), *Consumer and energy consumption: International perspectives on research and policy options* (pp. 47–55). New York: Praeger.

Graham, K. R., Rudnick, A., & Battista, M. (1983, October). *Effect of televised messages as a function of hypnotic suggestibility.* Paper presented at the Society of Clinical and Experimental Hypnosis, Cambridge, MA.

Gramsci, A. (1971). *Selections from the prison notebooks.* London: Lawrence and Wishart.

Greenberg, B. S. (1974). Gratifications of television viewing and their correlates for British children. In J. Blumler & E. Katz (Eds.), *The uses of mass communications: Current perspectives on gratifications research* (pp. 71–92). Beverly Hills: Sage.

Greenfield, P. M. (1984). *Mind and media: The effects of television, video games, and computers.* Cambridge, MA: Harvard University Press.

Gregory, A. (1983, February 7). Artists and their inspiration. *Christian Science Monitor,* p. 20.

Grinstein, A. (1955). Vacations—A psychoanalytic study. *International Journal of Psychoanalysis, 36,* 177–186.

Group for the Advancement of Psychiatry. (1958, August). *The psychiatrist's interest in leisure-time activities* (Rep. #39). New York: Author.

Gunter, B. G., & Gunter, N. C. (1980). Leisure styles: a conceptual framework for modern leisure. *Sociological Quarterly, 21,* 361–74.

Gussen, J. (1967). The psychodynamics of leisure. In P. A. Martin (Ed.), *Leisure and mental health: A psychiatric viewpoint* (pp. 51–69). Washington, DC: American Psychiatric Association.

Gutman, J. (1973). Self-concepts and television viewing among women. *Public Opinion Quarterly, 37,* 388–397.

Haberman, C. (1989, May 15). Florence's art makes some go to pieces. *New York Times,* p. A3.

Hall, S. (1980). Encoding/decoding. In S. Hall, D. Hobson, A. Lowe, & P. Willis (Eds.), *Culture, media, language* (pp. 128–138). London: Hutchinson.

Hall, S. (1982). The rediscovery of ideology: Return of the repressed in media studies. In M. Gurevitch, T. Bennet, J. Curran, & J. Woollacott (Eds.), *Culture, society, and the media* (pp. 56–90). London: Methuen.

Hamilton, J. A. (1981). Attention, personality, and the self-regulation of mood: Absorbing interest and boredom. *Progress in Experimental Personality Research, 10,* 281–315.

Harré, R., & Secord, P. F. (1972). *The explanation of social behavior.* Oxford: Basil Blackwell.

Harris, T. G., & Trotter, R. J. (1989, March). Work smarter, not harder. *Psychology Today,* 33.

Hartmann, H. (1958). *Ego psychology and the problem of adaptation* (D. Rapaport, Trans.). New York: International Universities Press.

Hasher, L., & Zacks, R. T. (1979). Automatic and effortful processes in memory. *Journal of experimental psychology, 108,* 356–88.

Hawkins, R. P., & Pingree, S. (1986). Activity in the effects of television on children. In J. Bryant & D. Zillmann (Eds.), *Perspectives on media effects* (pp. 233–250). Hillsdale, NJ: Lawrence Erlbaum Associates.

Hazard, W. (1967). Anxiety and preference for television fantasy. *Journalism Quarterly, 44,* 461–469.

Hefzallah, I. M. (1987). *Critical viewing of television: A book for parents and teachers.* New York: University Press of America.

Heider, F. (1946). Attitudes and cognitive organization. *Journal of Psychology, 21,* 107–12.

Hendry, L. B., & Patrick, H. (1977). Adolescents and television. *Journal of youth and adolescence, 6*, 325–336.

Henry, W. A. (1983, January/February). Column. *Channels*, pp. 48–50.

Herman, E., & Chomsky, N. (1988). *Manufacturing consent: The political economy of the mass media*. New York: Pantheon.

Heron, W. (1957, January). The pathology of boredom. *Scientific American, 196*, 52–56.

Hess, B. (1974). Stereotypes of the aged. *Journal of Communication, 24*, 76–85.

Heyduk, R. G. (1975). Rated preference for musical compositions as it relates to complexity and exposure frequency. *Perception and Psychophysics, 17*, 84–91.

Hilgard, E. (1980). The trilogy of mind: Cognition, affectation, and conation. *Journal of the History of the Behavioral Sciences, 16*, 107–117.

Himmelweit, H., Oppenheim, A., & Vince, P. (1958). *Television and the child*. London: Oxford University Press.

Himmelweit, H., & Swift, B. (1976). Continuities and discontinuities in media usage and taste: A longitudinal study. *Journal of Social Issues, 32*, 133–156.

Himmelweit, H., Swift, B., & Jaeger, M. (1980). The audience as critic: A conceptual analysis of television entertainment. In P. Tannenbaum (Ed.), *The entertainment functions of television* (pp. 67–106). Hillsdale, NJ: Lawrence Erlbaum Associates.

Hirsch, P. (1977a). Public policy toward television: Mass media and education in American society. *School Review, 85*, 481–512.

Hirsch, P. (1977b). Social science approaches to popular culture: A review and critique. *Journal of Popular Culture, 11*, 401–413.

Hirsch, P. (1980a). *A research agenda for approaching the study of television*. Paper commissioned for the Aspen Institute Conference on Proposals for a Center for the Study of Television, Aspen, CO.

Hirsch, P. (1980b). An organizational perspective on television (Aided and abetted by models from economics, marketing, and the humanities). In S. Withey & R. Abeles (Eds.), *Television and social behavior: Beyond violence and children* (pp. 83–102). Hillsdale, NJ: Lawrence Erlbaum Associates.

Hirsch, P. M., & Panelas, T. (1980). *Television watching is harmless: New study finds no ill effects*. Unpublished manuscript, University of Chicago, Chicago, IL.

Hirsch, P., & Panelas, T. (1981, May). *Who watches how much television (or none at all?): Profiles and changes since 1975*. Paper presented to the American Association of Public Opinion Research, Buck Hill Falls, PA.

Hoover, M. (1983). *Individual differences in the relation of heart rate to self-reports*. Unpublished doctoral dissertation, University of Chicago, Chicago, IL.

Horkheimer, M. (1974). *Critique of instrumental reason*. New York: Seabury.

Horkheimer, M., & Adorno, T. W. (1972). The culture industry: Enlightenment as mass deception. In M. Horkheimer & T. Adorno (Eds.), *The dialectics of enlightenment* (pp. 120–167). New York: Seabury Press.

Hormuth, S. E. (in press). *The self-concept and change: An ecological approach*. Cambridge, UK: Cambridge University Press.

Hormuth, S. E. (1986). The sampling of experiences *in situ*. *Journal of Personality, 54*, 262–293.

Hovland, C. I. (1959). Reconciling conflicting results derived from experimental and survey studies of attitude change. *American Psychologist, 14*, 8–17.

Howe, I. (1957). Note on mass culture. In B. Rosenberg & D. M. White (Eds.), *Mass culture: The popular arts in America* (pp. 496–503). Glencoe, IL: The Free Press.

Howie, G. (Ed.). (1969). *St. Augustine: On education*. South Bend, IN: Gateway Editions.

Husson, W., & Krull, J. (1983). *Theoretical implications of nonstationarity in children's attention to television*. Paper presented at the International Communication Association, Dallas, TX.

Hutchins, R. (1970). From a news article, January 2, 1954. *International thesaurus of quotations.* New York: Crowell.

Innis, H. A. (1964). *The bias of communication.* Toronto: University of Toronto Press.

Innis, H. A. (1972). *Empire and communication.* Toronto: University of Toronto Press.

Jackson, G. (1973). *Surviving the long night.* New York: Vanguard.

James, W. (1890). *Principles of psychology* (Vol. 1). New York: Holt.

Jason, L. A. (1987). Reducing children's excessive television viewing and assessing secondary changes. *Journal of Clinical Child Psychology, 16,* 245–250.

Jason, L. A., & Rooney-Rebeck, P. (1984). Reducing excessive television viewing. *Child and Family Behavior Therapy, 6,* 61–69.

Jasper, H. H. (1930). The measurement of depression-elation and its relation to a measure of extraversion-introversion. *Journal of Abnormal and Social Psychology, 25,* 307–18.

Johnstone, J. W. C. (1961). *Social structure and patterns of mass media consumption.* Unpublished doctoral dissertation, University of Chicago, Chicago, IL.

Johnstone, J. (1974). Social integration and mass media use among adolescents. In J. Blumler & E. Katz (Eds.), *The uses of mass communications: Current perspectives on gratifications research* (pp. 35–47). Beverly Hills: Sage.

Kahneman, D. (1973). *Attention and effort.* Englewood Cliffs, NJ: Prentice-Hall.

Kaplan, M. (1975). *Leisure: Theory and policy.* New York: Wiley.

Katz, E. (1987). Communications research since Lazarsfeld. *Public Opinion Quarterly, 51,* 25–45.

Katz, E., Blumler, J., & Gurevitch, M. (1974). Utilization of mass communication by the individual. In J. Blumler & E. Katz (Eds.). *The uses of mass communications: Current perspectives on gratifications research* (pp. 19–32). Beverly Hills, CA: Sage.

Katz, E., & Foulkes, D. (1962). On the use of the mass media as "escape": Clarification of a concept. *Public Opinion Quarterly, 26,* 377–383.

Katz, E., & Gurevitch, M. (1976). *The secularization of leisure: Culture and communication in Israel.* Cambridge, MA: Harvard University Press.

Katz, E., & Lazarsfeld, P. F. (1955). *Personal influence.* Glencoe, IL: The Free Press.

Kelly, H., & Gardner, H. (Eds.). (1981). *Viewing children through television.* San Francisco: Jossey-Bass.

Kelly, J. R. (1982). *Leisure.* Englewood Cliffs, NJ: Prentice-Hall.

Klapp, O. E. (1986). *Overload and boredom: Essays on the quality of life in the information society.* Westport, CT: Greenwood Press.

Klapper, J. T. (1960). *The effects of mass communications.* Glencoe, IL: The Free Press.

Klein, P. (1971, January 25). The men who run TV aren't stupid. *New York,* pp. 20–29.

Kline, F. (1971). Media time budgeting as a function of demographics and life style. *Journalism Quarterly, 48,* 211–221.

Klinger, E. (1971). *Structure and functions of fantasy.* New York: Wiley.

Klinger, E., Gregoire, K., & Barta, S. (1973). Physiological correlates of mental activity: Eye movements, alpha, and heart rate during suppression, concentration, search, and choice. *Psychophysiology, 10,* 471–477.

Koch, N. (1989, May). TV's new ruling class. *Channels, 9,* pp. 30–35.

Kohak, E. (1978). *Idea and experience.* Chicago: University of Chicago Press.

Kotsch, W., Gerbing, D., & Schwartz, L. (1982). The construct validation of the differential emotions scale as adapted for children and adolescents. In C. Izard (Ed.), *Measuring emotions in infants and children.* New York: Cambridge University Press.

Kripke, D., & Sonnenschein, D. (1978). A biologic rhythm in waking fantasy. In K. Pope & J. Singer (Eds.), *The stream of consciousness.* New York: Plenum.

Kris, E. (1952). *Psychoanalytic explorations in art.* New York: International Universities Press.

Krugman, H. E. (1971). Brain wave measures of media involvement. *Journal of Advertising Research, 11*, 3–9.

Krugman, H. E. (1977). Memory with recall, exposure without perception. *Journal of Advertising Research, 17*, 7–12.

Krugman, H. E. (1980). Point of view: sustained viewing of television. *Journal of Advertising Research, 20*, 65–68.

Krull, R., & Husson, W. (1979). Children's attention: The case of TV viewing. In E. Wartella (Ed.), *Children communicating: Media and development of thought, speech, understanding* (pp. 83–114). Beverly Hills: Sage.

Kubey, R. W. (1979). Radiation and decline of Scholastic Aptitude Scores. *Psychological Reports, 45*, p. 862.

Kubey, R. W. (1980). Television and aging: Past, present, and future. *Gerontologist, 20*, 16–35.

Kubey, R. W. (1984). *Leisure, television, and subjective experience*. Unpublished doctoral dissertation. University of Chicago, Chicago, IL.

Kubey, R. W. (1986). Television use in everyday life: Coping with unstructured time. *Journal of Communication, 36*, 108–123.

Kubey, R. W. (1987a, May). *Advances in the Experience Sampling Method: The second decade of research*. Paper presented to the American Association for Public Opinion Research, Hershey, PA.

Kubey, R. W. (1987b). Testimony before the Subcommittee on Antitrust, Monopolies and Business Rights of the Committee on the Judiciary, United States Senate, on a Television Violence Antitrust Exemption, June 25. (Serial No. J-100-27). Washington, DC: U.S. Government Printing Office.

Kubey, R. W. (1988, October 23). The aging of Aquarius. *Chicago Tribune Magazine*, pp. 11–21.

Kubey, R. W. (1989a, May). *Children's use and experience of leisure time and television: Using television to promote psychological growth*. Paper presented to the Children's Television Workshop, New York, NY.

Kubey, R. W. (1989b, May). *Writing for television: The conflict between art and commerce*. Paper presented to the International Communication Association, San Francisco, CA.

Kubey, R. W. (1989c). *Television and the quality of family life*. Manuscript submitted for publication.

Kubey, R. W. (1989d). *Creating television*. Manuscript submitted for publication.

Kubey, R. W. (1989e). *A critical review of the uses and gratifications approach*. Manuscript submitted for publication.

Kubey, R. W., & Barnett, A. L. (1989). Esthetic preference for rectangles of vertical and horizontal orientation. *Bulletin of the Psychonomic Society, 27*, 239–240.

Kubey, R. W., & Csikszentmihalyi, M. (in press). Television as escape: Subjective experience before an evening of heavy viewing. *Communication Reports*.

Kubey, R. W., & Larson, R. (1990). The use and experience of the new video media among children and young adolescents. *Communication Research, 17*.

Kubey, R. W., & Peluso, T. (1990). Emotional response as a cause of interpersonal news diffusion: The case of the space shuttle tragedy. *Journal of Braodcasting and Electronic Media, 34*.

LaBerge, D. (1975). Acquisition of automatic processing in perceptual and associative learning. In P. M. A. Rabbit (Ed.), *Attention and performance* (pp. 50–64). London: Academic Press.

LaBerge, D., & Samuels, S. J. (1974). Toward a theory of automatic information processing in reading. *Cognitive Psychology, 6*, 293–323.

Lachrenbruch, D. (1989, June 5). HDTV. *TV Guide*, p. 19.

Langer, E., & Piper, A. (1988). Television from a mindful/mindless perspective. In S. Oskamp (Ed.), *Television as a social issue* (pp. 247–260). Newbury Park, CA: Sage.

Larson, R. (1979). *The significance of solitude in adolescents' lives.* Unpublished doctoral dissertation, University of Chicago, Chicago, IL.

Larson, R., & Csikszentmihalyi, M. (1983). The experience sampling method. In H. Reis, (Ed.), *New directions for naturalistic methods in the behavioral sciences* (pp. 41–56). San Francisco: Jossey-Bass.

Larson, R., Csikszentmihalyi, M., & Graef, R. (1980). Mood variability and the psychosocial adjustment of adolescents. *Journal of Youth and Adolescence, 9,* 469–490.

Larson, R., & Delespaul, P. (in press). Analyzing Experience Sampling data: A guidebook for the perplexed. In M. deVries (Ed.), *The experience of psychopathology.* Cambridge, UK: Cambridge University Press.

Larson, R., & Kleiber, D. (in press). Free time activities as factors of adolescent adjustment. In P. Tolan & B. Cohler (Eds.), *Handbook of clinical research and practice with adolescents.* New York: Wiley.

Larson, R., & Kubey, R. (1983). Television and music: Contrasting media in adolescent life. *Youth and Society, 15,* 13–31.

Larson, R., & Kubey, R. (1989). *Passive spillover after television viewing in adolescents.* Manuscript submitted for publication.

Larson, R., Kubey, R., & Colletti, J. (1990). Changing channels: Early adolescent media choices and shifting investments in family and friends. *Journal of Youth and Adolescence, 18*(1).

Lasch, C. (1978). *The culture of narcissism: American life in an age of diminishing expectations.* New York: Norton.

Lasswell, H. D. (1927). *Propaganda techniques in the world war.* New York: Knopf.

Lazarsfeld, P. F., Berelson, B., & Gaudet, H. (1944). *The people's choice.* New York: Duell, Sloan, & Pearce.

Lazarus, R. S. (1966). *Psychological stress and the coping process.* New York: McGraw-Hill.

Le Bon, G. (1896). *The crowd: A study of the popular mind.* London: Ernest Benn.

Lee, B., & Rudman, M. K. (1982). *Mind over media.* New York: Seaview Books.

Le Goff, J. (1980). *Time, work and culture in the middle ages.* Chicago: The University of Chicago Press.

Lemish, D. (1987). Viewers in diapers: The early development of television viewing. In T. R. Lindlof (Ed.), *Natural audiences: Qualitative research of media uses and effects* (p. 33–57). Norwood, NJ: Ablex.

Le Play, P. G. F. (1879). *Les auvriers europeens* [The European worker]. Paris: Alfred Mame et Fils.

Lepper, M. R., & Greene D. (1978). *The hidden cost of reward.* Hillsdale, NJ: Lawrence Erlbaum Associates.

Le Roy Ladurie, E. (1979). *Montaillou.* New York: Vintage.

Levy, M. R., & Windahl, S. (1984). Audience activity and gratifications: A conceptual clarification and explorations. *Communication Research, 11,* 51–78.

Levy, M. R., & Windahl, S. (1985). The concept of audience activity. In K. E. Rosengren, L. A. Wenner, & P. Palmgreen (Eds.), *Media gratifications research: Current perspectives* (pp. 109–122). Beverly Hills: Sage.

Lewinsohn, P. M. (1974). Behavioral approach to depression. In R. J. Friedman & M. M. Katz (Eds.), *The psychology of depression: Contemporary theory and research* (pp. 157–185). New York: Wiley.

Liebert, R. M., & Schwartzberg, N. S. (1977). Effects of mass media. *Annual Review of Psychology, 28,* 141–173.

Linder, S. B. (1970). *The harried leisure class.* New York: Columbia University Press.

Lindlof, T. R. (1982). A fantasy construct of television viewing. *Communication Research, 9,* 67–112.

Lindlof, T. R. (1987). *Natural audiences: Qualitative research of media uses and effects.* Norwood, NJ: Ablex.

Linz, D., Donnerstein, E., & Penrod, S. (1984). The effects of multiple exposures to filmed violence against women. *Journal of Communication, 34,* 130–147.

Lodge, D. (1988). *Nice work.* London: Penguin.

Loevinger, L. (1968). The ambiguous mirror: The reflective-projective theory of broadcasting and mass communication. *Journal of Broadcasting, 12,* 97–116.

Logan, R. D. (1985). The flow experience in solitary ordeals. *Journal of humanistic psychology, 25*(4), 79–89.

London stage: Fossils and ferment. (1968, August 9). *Time,* p. 64.

LoScuito, L. (1972). A national inventory of television viewing behavior. In E. Rubinstein, G. Comstock, & J. Murray (Eds.), *Television and social behavior, Vol. 4: Television in day-to-day life: Patterns of use* (pp. 33–86). Washington, DC: U.S. Government Printing Office.

Lowenthal, L. (1961). The triumph of mass idols. In L. Lowenthal (Ed.), *Literature, popular culture, and society* (pp. 109–136). Englewood Cliffs, NJ: Prentice-Hall.

Lowenthal, L., & Fiske, M. (1957). The debate over art and popular culture in eighteenth century England. In M. Komarovsky (Ed.), *Common frontiers of the social sciences* (pp. 33–96). Glencoe, IL: The Free Press.

Lowery, S. A., & De Fleur, M. L. (1988). *Milestones in mass communication research.* White Plains, NY: Longman.

Loye, D., Gorney, R., & Steele, G. (1977). An experimental field study. *Journal of Communication, 27,* 206–216.

Lull, J. (1980). Family communication patterns and the social uses of television. *Communication Research, 7,* 319–334.

Lull, J. (1985). On the communicative properties of music. *Communication Research, 12,* 363–372.

Lull, J. (1987). Audience texts and contexts. *Critical Studies in Mass Communication, 4,* 318–322.

Lyle, J. (1972). Television in daily life: Patterns of use. In E. Rubinstein, G. Comstock, & J. Murray (Eds.), *Television and social behavior, Vol. 4: Television in day-to-day life: Patterns of use* (pp. 1–32). Washington, DC: U.S. Government Printing Office.

Lyle, J., & Hoffman, H. R. (1972). Children's use of television and other media. In E. Rubinstein, G. Comstock, & J. Murray (Eds.), *Television and social behavior, Vol. 4: Television in day-to-day life: Patterns of use* (pp. 129–256). Washington, DC: U.S. Government Printing Office.

Lynd, R. S., & Lynd, H. M. (1956). *Middletown: A study in contemporary American Culture.* New York: Harcourt, Brace & World. (Originally published 1929)

Lynn, R. (1966). *Attention, arousal and the orientation reaction.* London: Pergamon Press.

Maccoby, E. (1951). Television: Its impact on school children. *Public Opinion Quarterly, 15,* 421–444.

Maccoby, E. (1954). Why do children watch television? *Public Opinion Quarterly, 18,* 239–244.

Maddi, S. R., Kobasa, S., & Hoover, M. (1979). An alienation test. *Journal of Humanistic Psychology, 19,* 73–76.

Malik, S. (1981). *Psychological modernity: A comparative study of some African and American graduate students in the midwest.* Unpublished doctoral dissertation, University of Chicago, Chicago, IL.

Mander, J. (1978). *Four arguments for the elimination of television*. New York: Morrow Quill.

Mandler, G. (1975). The search for emotion. In L. Levi (Ed.), *Parameters measurement*. New York: Revon.

Marc, D. (1984). *Demographic vistas: Television in American culture*. Philadelphia: University of Pennsylvania Press.

Marc, D. (1989). *Comic visions: Television comedy and American culture*. London: Unwin Hyman.

Marcuse, H. (1964). *One dimensional man*. Boston: Beacon.

Marx, K. (1972). Economic and political manuscripts of 1844. In R. C. Tucker (Ed.), *The Marx–Engels reader* (pp. 66–125). New York: Norton.

Maslow, A. H. (1954). *Motivation and personality*. New York: Harper & Row.

Maslow, A. H. (1967). Self-actualization and beyond. In J. F. T. Bugental (Ed.), *Challenges of humanistic psychology*. New York: McGraw-Hill.

Massimini, F., & Carli, M. (1986). The systematic assessment of flow in daily experience. In M. Csikszentmihalyi & I. Csikszentmihalyi (Eds.), *Optimal experience* (pp. 266–287). Cambridge: Cambridge University Press.

Mast, G., & Cohen, M. (1979). *Film theory and criticism: Introductory readings* (2nd ed.). New York: Oxford University Press.

Masterman, L. (1980). *Television and teaching*. London: MacMillan Press LTD.

Masters, J. C., Ford, M. E., & Arend, R. A. (1983). Children's strategies for controlling affective responses to aversive social experience. *Motivation and Emotion, 7*, 103–116.

Mayers, P. (1978). *Flow in adolescence and its relations to school performance*. Unpublished doctoral dissertation, University of Chicago, Chicago, IL.

Mayron, L. W., Mayron, E. L., Ott, J. N., & Nations, R. (1976). Light, radiation, and academic achievement: Second-year data. *Academic Therapy, 11*, 397–407.

McCombs, M. E., & Weaver, D. H. (1985). Toward a merger of gratifications and agenda-setting research. In K. E. Rosengren, L. A. Wenner, & P. Palmgreen (Eds.), *Media gratifications research: Current perspectives* (pp. 95–108). Beverly Hills: Sage.

McGaan, L. A. (1983, May). *Alienation: A concept for communication research*. Paper presented at the International Communication Association, Dallas, TX.

McGhee, P. (1980). Towards the integration of entertainment and educational functions: The role of humor. In P. Tannenbaum (Ed.), *The entertainment functions of television* (pp. 183–208). Hillsdale, NJ: Lawrence Erlbaum Associates.

McIlwraith, R. D., & Schallow, J. R. (1983). Adult fantasy life and patterns of media use. *Journal of Communication, 33*, 78–91.

McIlwraith, R. D., & Josephson, W. L. (1985). Movies, books, music, and adult fantasy life. *Journal of Communication, 35*, 167–179.

McLeod, J., & Reeves, B. (1980). On the nature of mass media effects. In S. Withey & R. Abeles (Eds.), *Television and social behavior: Beyond violence and children* (pp. 17–54). Hillsdale, NJ: Lawrence Erlbaum Associates.

McLeod, J., Ward, S., & Tancill, K. (1965). Alienation and the uses of mass media. *Public Opinion Quarterly, 29*, 583–594.

McLuhan, M. (1964). *Understanding media*. New York: Signet.

McQuail, D. (1985). Gratifications research and media theory: Many models or one? In K. E. Rosengren, L. A. Wenner, & P. Palmgreen (Eds.), *Media gratifications research: Current perspectives* (pp. 149–167). Beverly Hills: Sage.

McQuail, D., Blumler, J. G., & Brown, J. R. (1972). The television audience: A revised perspective. In D. McQuail (Ed.), *Sociology of mass communications* (pp. 135–165). Harmondsworth, England: Penguin.

McQuail, D., & Gurevitch, M. (1974). Explaining audience behavior: Three approaches considered. In J. Blumler & E. Katz (Eds.), *The uses of mass communications: Current perspectives on gratifications research* (pp. 287–301). Beverly Hills: Sage.

Meier, R. L. (1962). *Communications theory of urban growth.* Cambridge, MA: Joint Center for Urban Studies of MIT and Harvard University, MIT Press.

Mendelsohn, H. (1966). *Mass entertainment.* New Haven, CT: Connecticut College and University Press.

Mendelsohn, H., & Spetnagel, H. (1980). Entertainment as a sociological enterprise. In P. Tannenbaum (Ed.), *The entertainment functions of television* (pp. 13–29). Hillsdale, NJ: Lawrence Erlbaum Associates.

Meyersohn, R. B. (1965). *Leisure and television: A study in compatability.* Unpublished doctoral dissertation, Columbia University, New York.

Meyersohn, R. B. (1969). The sociology of leisure in the United States: Introduction and bibliography, 1945–1965. *Journal of Leisure Research, 1,* 53–68.

Meyersohn, R. (1978). The sociology of popular culture: Looking backwards and forwards. *Communication Research, 5,* 330–338.

Meyrowitz, J. (1985). *No sense of place: The impact of electronic media on social behavior.* New York: Oxford.

Milgram, S., & Shotland, R. L. (1973). *Television and antisocial behavior: Field experiments.* New York: Academic Press.

Miller, G. A. (1967). *A psychology of communication.* New York: Basic Books.

Miller, G. T. (1971). *Energetics, kinetics, and life.* Belmont, CA: Wadsworth.

Miller, J. (1989). Comment. *Journal of Communication, 39,* 5–6.

Mischel, W. (1973). Toward a cognitive social learning reconceptualization of personality. *Psychology Review, 80,* 252–283.

Mischel, W. (1981). A cognitive-social learning approach to assessment. In T. Merluzzi, C. Glass, & M. Genest (Eds.), *Cognitive assessment.* New York: Guilford Press.

Mokros, H., Merrick, W. A., Poznanski, E. (1987, September). *The experience sampling method as a way to assess mood variation in depressed children and adolescents.* Paper presented to the Consortium for Research in Child and Adolescent Affective Disorders, Massachusetts General Hospital, Boston, MA.

Montaigne, M. E. de (1927). *The essays of Montaigne* (Vols. 1 & 2). London: Oxford University Press.

Montani, A., & Pietranera, G. (1946). First contribution to the psycho-analysis and aesthetics of motion-picture. *The Psychoanalytic Review, 33,* 177–196.

Morgan, M. (1983, March). *How are the heavy viewers?* Paper presented at the International Conference on Culture and Communication, Temple University, Philadelphia, PA.

Mulholland, T. (1973). Objective EEG methods for studying covert shifts of visual attention. In F. J. McGuigan & R. A. Schoonauer (Eds.), *The psychophysiology of thinking* (pp. 109–151). New York: Academic Press.

Mulholland, T. (1974). Training visual attention. *Academic Therapy, 10,* 5–17.

Munsterberg, H. (1916). *The photoplay: A psychological study.* New York: D. Appleton.

Murray, J. P. (1980). *Television and youth.* Boys Town, NE: The Boys Town Center for the Study of Youth and Development.

Murray, J. P., & Kippax, S. (1978). Children's social behavior in three towns with differing television experience. *Journal of Communication, 28,* 19–21.

Murray, J. P., & Kippax, S. (1979). From the early window to the late night show: International trends in the study of television's impact on children and adults. In L. Berkowitz (Ed.), *Advances in experimental and social psychology* (Vol. 12, pp. 253–320). New York: Academic Press.

Narkewicz, R. M., & Gravens, S. N. (1966). When children complain of fatigue. *Child and Family, 5,* 32–36.

National Institute of Mental Health. (1982). *Television and behavior: Ten years of scientific progress and implications for the eighties* (Vol. 1). Rockville, MD: U.S. Department of Health and Human Services.

Neisser, U. (1976). *Cognition and reality.* San Francisco: Freeman.

Neulinger, J. (1974). *The psychology of leisure.* Springfield, IL: Charles C. Thomas.

Neulinger, J. (1981). *To leisure: An introduction.* Boston: Allyn & Bacon.

Neuman, W. R. (1982). Television and American culture: The mass medium and the pluralist audience. *Public Opinion Quarterly, 46,* 471–487.

Neuman, W. R., & de Sola Pool, I. (1986). The flow of communications into the home. In S. J. Ball-Rokeach & M. G. Cantor (Eds.), *Media, audience, and social structure* (pp. 71–86). Newbury Park, CA: Sage.

Newcomb, H. (1974). *TV: The most popular art.* Garden City, NY: Doubleday.

Newcomb, H. (1979). *Television: The critical view.* New York: Oxford University Press.

Newcomb, H. (1984). On the dialogic aspects of mass communication. *Critical Studies in Mass Communication, 1,* 34–50.

Newcomb, H., & Alley, R. S. (1983). *The producer's medium: Conversations with the creators of American TV.* New York: Oxford University Press.

Nielsen, A. C. (1982). *Nielsen estimates: National audience demographic reports.* Northbrook, IL: Author.

Nielsen, A. C. (1989). *Nielsen report on television.* Northbrook, IL: Author.

Nietzke, A. (1978, June). Getting it on with "Gunsmoke." *Human Behavior,* 63–67.

Nisbett, R. E., & Wilson, T. D. (1977). Telling more than we can know: Verbal reports on mental processes. *Psychological Review, 84,* 231–259.

Nordlund, J. (1978). Media interaction. *Communications Research, 5,* 150–175.

Norman, D. A. (1976). *Memory and attention.* New York: Wiley.

Nystrom, C. (1984, May). *Epistemology in the brave new world.* Paper presented to the International Communication Association, San Francisco, CA.

Osgood, C. E., Suci, G. J., & Tannenbaum, P. H. (1957). *The measurement of meaning.* Urbana, IL: University of Illinois Press.

Ott, J. N. (1973). *Health and light: The effects of natural and artificial light on man and other living things.* New York: Pocket Books.

Palmer, P. (1986). *The lively audience: A study of children around the TV set.* Boston, MA: Allen & Unwin.

Parenti, M. (1986). *Inventing reality: The politics of the mass media.* New York: St. Martin's Press.

Park, R. (1927). Community organization and the romantic temper. *Social Forces, 3,* 675.

Parsons, T. (1951). *The social system.* Glencoe, IL: The Free Press.

Pascal, B. (1941). *Pensees.* New York: The Modern Library. (Originally published 1900)

Pavlov, I. P. (1927). *Conditioned reflexes.* Oxford: Clarendon.

Pearlin, L. (1959). Social and personal stress and escape television viewing. *Public Opinion Quarterly, 23,* 255–259.

Pearson, P. H. (1971). Differential relationships of four forms of novelty experiencing. *Journal of Consulting and Clinical Psychology, 37,* 23–30.

Peper, E., & Mulholland, T. (1971). Occipital alpha and accommodative vergence, pursuit, tracking, and fast eye movements. *Psychophysiology, 5,* 556–575.

Piaget, J. (1977). *The development of thought: Equilibration of cognitive structures.* New York: Viking. (Originally published 1975)

Piper, A., & Langer, E. (1986). *Mindful televiewing.* Unpublished manuscript, Harvard University, Cambridge, MA.

Ploghoft, M. E., & Anderson, J. A. (1981). *Education for the television age.* Springfield, IL: Charles C. Thomas.

Postman, N. (1986). *Amusing ourselves to death: Public discourse in the age of show business.* New York: Viking.

Quillian, R. (1969). The teachable language comprehender. *Communications of the ACM, 12,* 459–476.

Quillian, R. (1989). *Better than mercenary democracy.* Manuscript submitted for review.

Radway, J. A. (1984). *Reading the romance: Women, patriarchy, and popular literature.* Chapel Hill, NC: University of North Carolina Press.

Reeves, B., & Thorson, E. (1986). Watching television: Experiments on the viewing process. *Communication Research, 13,* 343–361.

Reeves, B., Thorson, E., Rothschild, M., McDonald, D., Hirsch, J., & Goldstein, R. (1986). Attention to television: Intrastimulus effects of movement and scene change on alpha variation over time. *International Journal of Neuroscience, 27,* 241–255.

Reeves, B., Thorson, E., & Schleuder, J. (1986). Attention to television: Psychological theories and chronometric measures. In J. Bryant & D. Zillmann (Eds.), *Perspectives on media effects* (pp. 251–279). Hillsdale, NJ: Lawrence Erlbaum Associates.

Reid, L., & Frazer, C. (1980). Children's use of television commercials to initiate social interaction in family viewing situations. *Journal of Broadcasting, 24,* 149–158.

Rice, M. L., Huston, A. C., & Wright, J. C. (1982). The forms of television: Effects on children's attention, comprehension, and social behavior. In D. Pearl, L. Bouthlilet, & J. Lazar (Eds.), *Television and behavior: Ten years of scientific progress and implications for the eighties* (Vol. 2, pp. 29–38). Rockville, MD: U.S. Department of Health and Human Services.

Riesman, D. (1954). The themes of work and play in the structure of Freud's thought. In D. Riesman (Ed.), *Individualism reconsidered.* New York: Cambridge University Press.

Riesman, D., Glazer, N., & Denney, R. (1950). *The lonely crowd: A study of the changing American character.* New Haven, CT: Yale University Press.

Rifkin, J. (1980). *Entropy: A new world view.* New York: Viking.

Riley, J., Cantwell, R., & Ruttiger, K. (1949). Some observations on the social effects of television. *Public Opinion Quarterly, 13,* 223–224.

Rimmer, T. (1986). Visual form complexity and TV news. *Communication Research, 13,* 221–238.

Ritchie, D. (1986). Shannon and Weaver: Unravelling the paradox of information. *Communication Research, 13,* 278–298.

Robinson, J. P. (1969). Television and leisure time: Yesterday, today, and (maybe) tomorrow. *Public Opinion Quarterly, 33,* 210–222.

Robinson, J. P. (1972a). Television's impact on everyday life: Some cross-national evidence. In E. Rubinstein, G. Comstock, & J. Murray (Eds.), *Television and social behavior, Vol. 4: Television in day-to-day life: Patterns of use* (pp. 410–431). Washington, DC: U.S. Government Printing Office.

Robinson, J. P. (1972b). Toward defining the functions of television. In E. Rubinstein, G. Comstock, & J. Murray (Eds.), *Television and social behavior, Vol. 4: Television in day-to-day life: Patterns of use* (pp. 568–603). Washington, DC: U.S. Government Printing Office.

Robinson, J. P. (1977). *How Americans use time: A social-psychological analysis of everyday behavior.* New York: Praeger.

Robinson, J. P. (1981). Television and leisure time: A new scenario. *Journal of Communication, 31,* 120–130.

Robinson, J. (1989, April). Time for work. *American Demographics,* p. 68.

Robinson, J., & Converse, P. (1967). *Basic tables of time-budget data for the United States.* Ann Arbor, MI: Survey Research Center.

Robinson, J. P., & Converse, P. (1972). The impact of television on mass media usage. In

A. Szalai (Ed.), *The use of time: Daily activities of urban and suburban populations in twelve countries* (pp. 197–212). Paris: Mouton.

Robinson, J. P., Converse, P., & Szalai, A. (1972). Everyday life in twelve countries. In A. Szalai (Ed.), *The use of time: Daily activities of urban and suburban populations in twelve countries* (pp. 114–133). Paris: Mouton.

Rochberg-Halton, E. (1979). *Cultural signs and urban adaptation.* Unpublished doctoral dissertation, University of Chicago, Chicago, IL.

Roe, K. (1983). *Mass media and adolescent schooling: Conflict or co-existence?* Stockholm: Almqvist & Wiksell International.

Rogers, E. M. (1983, October). *The diffusion of home computers in silicon valley.* Paper presented at the Association for Consumer Research, Chicago, IL.

Rosenberg, M. (1978). *Television and its viewers.* Radio broadcast of conversations at Chicago, University of Chicago, Chicago, IL.

Rosenblatt, P., & Cunningham, M. (1976). Television watching and family tensions. *Journal of Marriage and the Family, 31,* 105–111.

Rosenbleuth, A., Wiener, N., & Bigelow, J. (1943). Behavior, purpose, and teleology. *Philosophy of Science, 10,* 18–24.

Rosengren, K. E., Wenner, L. A., & Palmgreen, P. (Eds.). (1985). *Media gratifications research: Current perspectives.* Beverly Hills, CA: Sage.

Rosengren, K., & Windahl, S. (1972). Mass media consumption as a functional alternative. In D. McQuail (Ed.), *Sociology of mass communications* (pp. 166–194). Harmondsworth: Penguin.

Rosten, L. C. (1941). *Hollywood: The movie colony.* New York: Harcourt, Brace.

Roszak, T. (1968). The summa popologica of Marshall McLuhan. In R. Rosenthal (Ed.), *McLuhan: Pro and con* (pp. 257–269). Baltimore: Penguin.

Rothschild, M., Thorson, E., Reeves, B., Hirsch, J., & Goldstein, R. (1986). EEG activity and the processing of television commercials. *Communication Research, 13,* 182–220.

Ruben, B. D. (1972). General systems theory: An approach to human communication. In R. W. Budd & B. D. Ruben (Eds.), *Approaches to human communication* (pp. 120–144). Rochelle Park, NJ: Spartan Books.

Rubin, A. (1984). Ritualized and instrumental television viewing. *Journal of Communication, 34,* 67–77.

Rubin, A. M. (1986). Uses, gratifications, and media effects research. In J. Bryant & D. Zillmann (Eds.), *Perspectives on media effects* (pp. 281–301). Hillsdale, NJ: Lawrence Erlbaum Associates.

Rubin, A., & Perse, E. (1987). Audience activity and television news gratifications. *Communication Research, 14,* 58–84.

Rubin, A. M., & Rubin, R. B. (1982). Contextual age and television use. *Human Communication Research, 8,* 228–244.

Rubin, A., & Windahl, S. (1986). The uses and dependency model of mass communication. *Critical Studies in Mass Communication, 3,* 184–199.

Ryan, B. H. (1974, June 9). Would you free your children from the monster? *Denver Post.*

Ryle, G. (1949). *The concept of mind.* New York: Barnes & Noble.

Sahlins, M. (1972). *Stone age economics.* Chicago: Aldine Press.

Salomon, G. (1979). *Interaction of media, cognition, and learning.* San Francisco: Jossey-Bass.

Salomon, G. (1981). Introducing AIME: The assessment of children's mental involvement with television. In H. Gardner & H. Kelly (Eds.), *Children and the worlds of television* (pp. 223–246). San Francisco: Jossey-Bass.

Salomon, G. (1983). Television watching and mental effort: A social psychological view. In J. Bryant & D. R. Anderson (Eds.), *Children's understanding of television. Research on attention and comprehension* (pp. 181–198). New York: Academic Press.

Salomon, G. (1984). Television is "easy" and print is "tough": The differential investment of mental effort in learning as a function of perceptions and attributions. *Journal of Educational Psychology, 76,* 647–658.

Salomon, G., & Leigh, T. (1984). Predispositions about learning from print and television. *Journal of Communication, 34,* 119–135.

Samuelson, R. J. (1989, May 15). Rediscovering the rat race. *Newsweek,* p. 57.

Sarbin, T. R. (1977). Contextualism: A world view for modern psychology. In J. K. Cole & A. W. Landfield (Eds.), *Nebraska Symposium on Motivation* (Vol. 24). Lincoln: University of Nebraska Press.

Schalinske, T. (1968). *The role of television in the life of the aged person.* Unpublished doctoral dissertation, Ohio State University, Columbus, OH.

Scheuch, E. K. (1972). The time-budget interview. In A. Szalai (Ed.), *The use of time* (pp. 69–87). The Hague: Mouton.

Schickel, R. (1985). *Intimate strangers: The culture of celebrity.* New York: Doubleday.

Schiller, H. (1973). *The mind-managers.* Boston: Beacon Press.

Schramm, W. (1973). *Men, messages, and media: A look at human communication.* New York: Harper & Row.

Schramm, W., Lyle, J., & Parker, E. B. (1961). *Television in the lives of our children.* Stanford, CA: Stanford University Press.

Schudson, M. (1987). The new validation of popular culture: Sense and sentimentality in academia. *Critical Studies in Mass Communication, 4,* 51–68.

Schwartz, T. (1973). *The responsive chord.* Garden City, NY: Anchor Press/Doubleday.

Schwartz, N. J. (1969). *Entropy, negentropy, and the psyche: An inquiry into the structure of psychic energy.* Manuscript available from John Cotton Dona Library, Newark, NJ.

Scitovsky, T. (1976). *The joyless economy.* New York: Oxford University Press.

Seneca. (1965). *Ad Lucilium Epistulae Morales* [Letters from a Stoic]. Oxford: Clarendon.

Seyrek, S. K., Corah, N. L., & Pace, L. F. (1984). Comparison of three distraction techniques in reducing stress in dental patients. *Journal of American Dental Association, 108,* 327–329.

Shanks, B. (1977). *The cool fire.* New York: Random House.

Shannon, C., & Weaver, W. (1949). *The mathematical theory of communication.* Urbana: University of Illinois Press.

Sherman, B. L., & Dominick, J. R. (1986). Violence and sex in music videos: TV and rock 'n' roll. *Journal of Communication, 36,* 79–93.

Shils, E. (1957). Daydreams and nightdreams: Reflections on the criticism of mass culture. *Sewanee Review, 65,* 587–608.

Shils, E. (1961). Mass society and its culture. In N. Jacobs (Ed.), *Culture for the millions* (pp. 1–27). Princeton, NJ: Van Norstrand.

Shils, E. A., & Janowitz, M. (1948). Cohesion and disintegration in the Wehrmacht in World War II. *Public Opinion Quarterly, 2,* 280–315.

Simmel, G. (1950). *The sociology of Georg Simmel.* Glencoe, IL: The Free Press.

Simon, H. (1978). Rationality as a process and as a product of thought. *American economic review, 68,* 1–16.

Singer, D. G., Zuckerman, D. M., & Singer, J. L. (1980). Teaching elementary school children television viewing skills: An evaluation. *Journal of Communication, 30,* 84–93.

Singer, J. (1980). The power and limitations of television: A cognitive-affective analysis. In P. Tannenbaum (Ed.), *The entertainment functions of television* (pp. 31–65). Hillsdale, NJ: Lawrence Erlbaum Associates.

Singer, J. L., & Singer, D. G. (1979, March). Come back, Mister Rogers, come back. *Psychology Today,* pp. 56–60.

Singer, J. L., & Singer, D. G. (1983). Implications of childhood television viewing for cognition, imagination, and emotion. In J. Bryant & D. R. Anderson (Eds.), *Children's understanding of television: Research on attention and comprehension* (pp. 269–296). New York: Academic Press.

Singer, J. L., Singer, D. G., & Rapaczynsk, W. (1984). Family patterns and television viewing as predictors of children's beliefs and aggression. *Journal of Communication, 34,* 73–89.

Skinner, B. F. (1969). *Contingencies of reinforcement: A theoretical analysis.* New York: Appleton-Century-Crofts.

Smith, A. (1971). *The theory of moral sentiments.* New York: Garland. (Originally published 1759)

Smith, A. (1980). *An inquiry into the wealth of nations.* London: Methuen. (Originally published 1776)

Smith, M. B. (1969). *Social psychology and human values.* Chicago, IL: Aldine.

Smith, R. (1986). Television addiction. In J. Bryant & D. Zillmann (Eds.), *Perspectives on media effects* (pp. 109–128). Hillsdale, NJ: Lawrence Erlbaum Associates.

Solzhenitsyn, A. (1976). *The Gulag Archipelago.* New York: Harper & Row.

Sparks, G. G. (1986). Developmental differences in children's reports of fear induced by the mass media. *Child Study Journal, 16,* 55–66.

Steiner, G. (1963). *The people look at television.* New York: Alfred A. Knopf.

Stephenson, W. (1967). *The play theory of mass communication.* Chicago: University of Chicago Press.

Streufert, S., & Streufert, S. C. (1978). Cognitive complexity: A review of theory, measurement, and research. In S. Streufert & S. C. Streufert (Eds.), *Behavior in the complex environment* (pp. 87–130). New York: Wiley.

Swank, C. (1979). Media uses and gratifications: Need salience and source dependence in a sample of the elderly. *American Behavioral Scientist, 23,* 95–117.

Szalai, A. (Ed.). (1972). *The use of time: Daily activities of urban and suburban populations in twelve countries.* The Hague: Mouton.

Tabloid TV. (1989, Spring). *Skeptical Inquirer, 13,* p. 248.

Tannenbaum, P. (1980). Entertainment as a vicarious emotional experience. In P. Tannenbaum (Ed.), *The entertainment functions of television* (pp. 107–131). Hillsdale, NJ: Lawrence Erlbaum Associates.

Tannenbaum, P. (1985). "Play it again, Sam": Repeated exposure to television programs. In D. Zillmann & J. Bryant (Eds.), *Selective exposure to communication* (pp. 225–241). Hillsdale, NJ: Lawrence Erlbaum Associates.

Tart, C. (1972). *Altered states of consciousness.* New York: Doubleday.

Television Audience Assessment, Inc. (1981). *Audience attitudes and alternative program ratings.* Cambridge, MA: Author.

Thompson, E. P. (1967). Time, work-discipline, and industrial capitalism. *Past and Present, 38,* 56–97.

Thorndike, E. L. (1932). *The fundamentals of learning.* New York: Columbia University, Teachers College, Bureau of Publications.

Thorson, E., Reeves, B., & Schleuder, J. (1985). Message complexity and attention to television. *Communication Research, 12,* 427–454.

Tichi, C. (1989). Television and recent American fiction. *American Literary History, 1,* 114–130.

Tocqueville, A. (1945). *Democracy in America.* New York: Knopf. (Originally published 1840)

Tomkins, S. (1962). *Affect, imagery, and consciousness* (Vol. I & II). New York: Springer.

Topolnicki, D. (1989, June). Do marketers control what we see? *Psychology Today,* pp. 73–74.

Tuchman, G. (1974). *The TV establishment: Programming for power and profit.* Englewood Cliffs, NJ: Prentice-Hall.

United Nations. (1981). *Population estimates.* New York: Author.

Utley, C. (1948). How illiterate can television make us? *Commonweal, 49,* 137–138.

Venkatesh, A., & Vitalari, N. (1987). A post-adoption analysis of computing in the home. *Journal of economic psychology, 8,* 161–180.

Villani, K. (1975). Personality/life style and television viewing behavior. *Journal of Marketing Research, 12,* 432–439.

Wakshlag, J., Tims, A., Fitzmaurice, M., Hancock, D., & McCarthy, K. (1986). *Viewing selections after work-induced stress.* Bloomington, IN: Indiana University, Department of Telecommunications.

Walker, E. L. (1973). Complexity and preference theory. In D. Berlyne & K. B. Madsen (Eds.), *Pleasure, reward, preference* (pp. 65–97). New York: Academic Press.

Walker, J. (1980). Changes in EEG rhythms during television viewing: Preliminary comparisons with reading and other tasks. *Perceptual and Motor Skills, 51,* 255–262.

Wallace, A. F. C. (1978). *Rockdale.* New York: Knopf.

Wangh, M. (1975). Boredom in psychoanalytic perspective. *Social Research, 42,* 538–550.

Warner, W. L., & Henry, W. E. (1948). The radio day time serial: A symbolic analysis. *Genetic Psychology Monograph, 37,* 3–71.

Warshow, R. (1964). *The immediate experience.* New York: Atheneum.

Wartella, E., & Ettema, J. S. (1974). Cognitive developmental study of children's attention to television commercials. *Communication Research, 1,* 69–88.

Wartella, E., (Ed.). (1979). *Children communicating: Media and development of thought, speech, and understanding.* Beverly Hills: Sage.

Washburne, J. N. (1941). Factors related to the social adjustment of college girls. *Journal of Social Psychology, 13,* 281–89.

Watt, J., & Krull, R. (1974). An information theory measure for television programming. *Communication Research, 1,* 44–68.

Watt, J., & Welch, A. (1983). Effects of static and dynamic complexity on children's attention and recall of television instruction. In J. Bryant & D. R. Anderson (Eds.), *Children's understanding of television. Research on attention and comprehension* (pp. 69–102). New York: Academic Press.

Weber, M. (1958). *The protestant ethic and the spirit of capitalism.* New York: Scribner. (Originally published 1904)

Webster, J. G., & Wakshlag, J. J. (1983). A theory of television program choice. *Communication Research, 10,* 430–446.

Webster, J. G., & Wakshlag, J. (1985). Measuring exposure to television. In D. Zillmann & J. Bryant (Eds.), *Selective exposure to communication* (pp. 35–62). Hillsdale, NJ: Lawrence Erlbaum Associates.

Weigel, R. (1976). American television and conventionality. *Journal of Psychology, 94,* 253–255.

Weinstein, S., Appel, V., & Weinstein, C. (1980). Brain-activity responses to magazine and television advertising. *Journal of Advertising Research, 20,* 57–63.

Weiss, W. (1969). The effects of the mass media of communication. In G. Lindzey & E. Aronson (Eds.), *Handbook of social psychology* (Vol. 5, pp. 77–195). Reading, MA: Addison-Wesley.

Wessman, A., & Ricks, D. (1966). *Mood and personality.* New York: Holt, Rinehart, & Winston.

Wiebe, G. (1969). Two psychological factors in media audience behavior. *Public Opinion Quarterly, 33,* 523–536.

Wiener, N. (1961). *Cybernetics or control and communication in the animal and the machine.* New York: MIT Press.

Wilensky, H. L. (1964). Mass society and mass culture: Interdependence or independence. *American Sociological Review, 29,* 173–197.

Wilkins, J. A. (1982). *Breaking the TV habit.* New York: Charles Scribner's Sons.

Williams, R. (1974). *Television: Technology and cultural form.* New York: Schocken.

Williams, R. (1983). *The year 2000.* New York: Pantheon Books.

Wilson, B. J., Hoffner, C., & Cantor, J. (1987). Children's perceptions of the effectiveness of techniques to reduce fear from mass media. *Journal of Applied Developmental Psychology, 8,* 39–52.

Wilson, E. O. (1975). *Sociobiology: The new synthesis.* Cambridge, MA: Harvard University Press.

Wimsatt, W. K., & Brooks, C. (1957). *Literary criticism.* New York: Random House.

Windahl, S. (1981). Uses and gratifications at the crossroads. In G. C. Wilhoit & H. deBock (Eds.), *Mass communication review yearbook* (Vol. 2, pp. 174–185). Beverly Hills: Sage.

Winick, C. (1988). The functions of television: Life without the big box. In S. Oskamp (Ed.), *Television as a social issue* (pp. 217–237). Newbury Park: Sage.

Winn, M. (1977). *The plug-in drug.* New York: Viking.

Winn, M. (1987). *Unplugging the plug-in drug: Help your children kick the TV habit.* New York: Viking.

Winnicott, D. W. (1951). *Collected papers.* New York: Basic Books.

Withey, S. (1980). An aerial view of television and social behavior. In S. Withey & R. Abeles (Eds.), *Television and social behavior: Beyond violence and children* (pp. 291–301). Hillsdale, NJ: Lawrence Erlbaum Associates.

Wittfogel, K. (1957). *Oriental despotism.* New Haven, CT: Yale University Press.

Wober, J. M. (1986). The lens of television and the prism of personality. In J. Bryant & D. Zillmann (Eds.), *Perspectives on media effects* (pp. 210–231). Hillsdale, NJ: Lawrence Erlbaum Associates.

Wolfe, D., Mendes, M., & Factor, D. (1984). A parent-administered program to reduce children's television viewing. *Journal of Applied Behavior Analysis, 17,* 267–272.

Wolfenstein, M., & Leites, N. (1950). *Movies: A psychological study.* Glencoe, IL: The Free Press.

Wolman, R., Lewis, W., & King, M. (1971). The development of the language of emotions: Conditions of emotional arousal. *Child Development, 42,* 1288–1293.

Wren-Lewis, J. (1983). The encoding/decoding model: Criticisms and redevelopments for research on decoding. *Media, Culture and Society, 5,* 197–198.

Wright, J. C., & Huston, A. C. (1981). The forms of television: Nature and development of television literacy in children. In H. Gardner & H. Kelly (Eds.), *Children and the worlds of television* (pp. 73–88). San Francisco: Jossey-Bass.

Wright, R. (1988). *Three scientists and their gods: Looking for meaning in an age of information.* New York: Times Books.

Yarmey, D. (1979). *The psychology of eyewitness testimony.* New York: Free Press.

Zillmann, D. (1971). Excitation transfer in communication-mediated aggressive behavior. *Journal of Experimental Social Psychology, 7,* 419–434.

Zillmann, D. (1978). Attribution and misattribution of excitatory reactions. In J. H. Harvey, W. J., Ickles, & R. F. Kidd (Eds.), *New directions in attribution research* (Vol. 2, pp. 335–368). Hillsdale, NJ: Lawrence Erlbaum Associates.

Zillmann, D. (1979). *Hostility and aggression.* Hillsdale, NJ: Lawrence Erlbaum Associates.

Zillmann, D. (1980). Anatomy of suspense. In P. Tannenbaum (Ed.), *The entertainment functions of television* (pp. 133–163). Hillsdale, NJ: Lawrence Erlbaum Associates.

Zillmann, D. (1982). Television viewing and arousal. In D. Pearl, L. Bouthilet, & L. Lazar (Eds.), *Television and behavior: Ten years of scientific progress and implications for the eighties* (Vol. 2, pp. 53–67). Rockville, MD: National Institute of Mental Health.

Zillmann, D. (1985). The experimental exploration of gratifications from media entertainment. In K. E. Rosengren, L. A. Wenner, & P. Palmgreen (Eds.), *Media gratifications research: Current perspectives* (pp. 225–239). Beverly Hills: Sage.

Zillmann, D., & Bryant, J. (1981). *Uses and effects of humor in educational television.* Paper presented at the Conference on Experimental Research in TV Instruction, St. John's, Newfoundland, Canada.

Zillmann, D., & Bryant, J. (1985). Affect, mood, and emotion as determinants of selective exposure. In D. Zillmann & J. Bryant (Eds.), *Selective exposure to communication* (pp. 157–190). Hillsdale, NJ: Lawrence Erlbaum Associates.

Zillmann, D., & Bryant, J. (1986). Exploring the entertainment experience. In J. Bryant & D. Zillmann (Eds.), *Perspectives on media effects* (pp. 303–324). Hillsdale, NJ: Lawrence Erlbaum Associates.

Zillmann, D., Hezel, R. T., & Medoff, N. J. (1980). The effect of affective states on selective exposure to televised entertainment fare. *Journal of Applied Social Psychology, 10,* 323–339.

Zillmann, D., & Wakshlag, J. (1986). Fear of victimization and the appeal of crime drama. In D. Zillmann & J. Bryant (Eds.), *Selective exposure to communication* (pp. 141–156). Hillsdale, NJ: Lawrence Erlbaum Associates.

Zolla, E. (1968). *The eclipse of the intellectual.* New York: Funk & Wagnalls.

Zuckerman, M. (1975). *Manual and research report for the sensation seeking scale (SSS).* Newark, DE: University of Delaware.

Zuckerman, M. (1979). *Sensation seeking: Beyond the optimal level of arousal.* Hillsdale, NJ: Lawrence Erlbaum Associates.

Zuckerman, M. (1988). Behavior and biology: Research on sensation seeking and reactions to the media. In L. Donohew, H. E. Sypher, & E. T. Higgins (Eds.), *Communication, social cognition, and affect* (pp. 173–194). Hillsdale, NJ: Lawrence Erlbaum Associates.

Zuzanek, J. (1980). *Work and leisure in the Soviet Union: A time budget analysis.* New York: Praeger.

Author Index

Subject Index